THE THEATER O

THE THEATER OF ESSENCE

AND OTHER ESSAYS

JAN KOTT

With an Introduction by Martin Esslin

NORTHWESTERN UNIVERSITY PRESS   /   EVANSTON   ·   1984

Northwestern University Press, Evanston, Illinois 60201

Library of Congress Catalog Card Number 84-61440
ISBN 0-8101-0664-7

The following persons rendered invaluable assistance to this collection. For translations from the Polish: Krystyna Bittenek ("After Grotowski: The End of the Impossible Theater"); Bogdana Carpenter ("Witkiewicz, or The Dialectic of Anachronism," Parts 1 and 3); Joanna Clark ("The Author of Comedy, or *The Inspector General*" and "Noh, or About Signs"); Joanna Clark and James P. McCandlish ("Witkiewicz, or The Dialectic of Anachronism," Parts 2, 4, and 5); E. J. Czerwiński ("Why Should I Take Part in the Sacred Dance?"); Klara Główczewska ("Ibsen Read Anew"); Michael Kandel ("Tadeusz Borowski: A European Education"); Michael Kott ("Ionesco, or A Pregnant Death" and "A Cage in Search of a Bird"); Ludwik Krzyżanowski ("On Gombrowicz," Part 1); Daniela Międzyrzecka ("Shakespeare's Riddle"); Deniz Şengel and Michael Kott ("The Theater of Essence: Kantor and Brook" and "The Serpent's Sting"); Bolesław Taborski ("Bunraku and Kabuki, or About Imitation"); and Lillian Vallee ("On Gombrowicz," Part 2, "The Icon of the Absurd," "The Seriousness of Theater," and additions to some other essays). Eileen Fischer and James P. McCandlish edited the final version of "Ibsen Read Anew." My special and warm thanks are due to Jonathan Brent, who not only carefully edited the whole book but also with his impossible stubbornness asked me infinite times to make corrections and additions.

The essays collected in *The Theater of Essence* were revised and often expanded from the following original publications and are used here with permission: "Noh, or About Signs" from *Arion*; "Tadeusz Borowski: A European Education" from Introduction to *This Way for the Gas, Ladies and Gentlemen* (New York: Penguin, 1976); "The Icon of the Absurd" from *The Discontinuous Universe* (New York and London: Basic Books, 1972); "Why Should I Take Part in the Sacred Dance?" from *Drama Review*; "Ionesco, or A Pregnant Death" from *The Dream and the Play: Ionesco's Theatrical Quest* (Malibu: Undena, 1982); "Witkiewicz, or The Dialectic of Anachronism," Parts 1 and 3, from *Encounter* and Introduction to *The Madman and the Nun* (Seattle: Univ. of Washington Press, 1968); "On Gombrowicz," Part 1, from Introduction to *The Marriage* (New York: Grove Press, 1969); "The Serpent's Sting" from *Formations*; "Shakespeare's Riddle" from *The New York Times Book Review*; "A Cage in Search of a Bird" from *Partisan Review*; "Bunraku and Kabuki, or About Imitation" from *Salmagundi*; "Ibsen Read Anew," "On Gombrowicz," Part 2, and "The Theater of Essence: Kantor and Brook" from *Theater* [Yale]; "The Author of Comedy, or *The Inspector General*," "Witkiewicz, or The Dialectic of Anachronism," Parts 2, 4, and 5, and "After Grotowski: The End of the Impossible Theater" from *Theatre Quarterly*.

CONTENTS

THE THEATER OF ESSENCE

INTRODUCTION

Martin Esslin

It does not often happen that a critic is acknowledged, by a great creative personality, to have exercised a major influence on one of his finest works.

Jan Kott is such a critic: Peter Brook has spoken of the deep impression Kott's essay "King Lear or Endgame" made on him and of the way it shaped his conception of the play when he directed it for the Royal Shakespeare Company in 1962, in a production which has come to be regarded as a major turning point in the theater of our time.

When the Royal Shakespeare Company took that producton to Eastern Europe in 1964, its impact in Prague, Budapest, Bucharest, Warsaw, Leningrad, and Moscow was even more electrifying than it had been in Britain and elsewhere in the West. It is generally regarded as the starting point of a new approach to directing the classics in the countries of the Soviet Empire.

This is a curious illustration of how, even in a divided world, artistic and cultural crosscurrents operate across Iron Curtains, minefields, watchtowers and Berlin walls: for Kott's essay had been written in Eastern Europe. It formed part of his book *Shakespeare Our Contemporary* which, apart from being a collection of essays on Shakespeare, was an ingenious and daring attempt at a critique of Soviet Marxism-Leninism-Stalinism in "Aesopian language." Kott's essay on Lear formed part of a book that had made a truly sensational impact both in the Eastern and, when it appeared first in French and then in English, in the Western world. For here Kott had succeeded in embodying his critique of the Stalinist brand of dictatorship in a form that could only with difficulty be banned as politically subversive in the totalitarian East: after all, Shakespeare is a revered classic, he has written history plays—so it is only legitimate to analyze his attitude to history, even if it contradicts the Marxist concept of historical change; and in his great tragedies Shakespeare has drawn a profound portrait of human nature, however different that may be from the orthodox Soviet "Marxist" image of the nature of mankind. Thus for an Eastern reader, accustomed as he is to read between the lines, Kott's essays on Shakespeare came as an electrifying flash of insight. To Western readers they gave a moving account of how it felt to have lived through events even more horrifying and tragic than those depicted by Shakespeare. This is how *Shakespeare Our Contemporary* struck, among many Western readers, Peter Brook; and that is how a reading of Shakespeare by a man of the twentieth century who had passed through its horrors in the underground of wartime Poland, in the shadow of the smoking chimneystacks of Auschwitz and Maidanek, had come as a revelation to a Western director. And that Western director's vision, in turn, initiated a revolution in the East European theater.

Only a personality like Jan Kott could have become the focal point of such a remarkable process of cross-fertilization. For Kott is more than merely an outstanding theater critic, a fine scholar of drama.

He is also, among many other things, a representative of a tradition that has played a major part in the history of European literature and which, alas, seems to be on the point of near-extinction: the tradition of the literary essay, as erudite as the best scholarship, as urbane as the most cultured conversation, as deeply felt and finely wrought as poetry; a genre of writing emanating from an outstanding human type, the "homme de lettres"—whose lineage goes back to Francis Bacon and Montaigne—writers who, while able to deal with a wide range of subjects with deep insight and originality of thought, were also able to present them in a readable form.

Such essayists fulfill an essential function: they concentrate and reflect the spirit of the times across the ever-more-rigid boundaries of specialization; they stimulate the dialectical process between the leading ideas of their time; they provoke contradiction as well as agreement; and often are the truly creative thinkers whose contributions set in motion new lines of speculation and research by the specialists of various disciplines. That is how Lessing originated the rise of the great German classical drama; Brandes inspired Ibsen; Kott influenced Peter Brook and other contemporary directors.

Writers like these exercise such influence not only by the depth of their thought and the originality of their insights, but also by their ability to communicate widely and well. They are masters of the light touch, the delicately wrought *bon mot*, the revealing anecdote, and above all, they are most adept in projecting their own personality: their thought, however profound, innovative, and revolutionary, can always be seen as the distillation of a human individuality. They succeed in showing not only what they were thinking, but also how their thought mirrors the personality in which it had its roots. Here truly "the style is the man" and the man is mirrored in his thought.

The frightening increase of compartmentalization in the educational system of our times threatens this species of literary animal with extinction. As long as a solid core of classical and literary learning, an equal grounding in the sciences and the humanities, remained at the basis of education, it was possible to develop into a "Renaissance man," an individual with the widest possible range of interests, with an erudition that could be far-ranging without becoming shallow. For such an individual it was not necessary to know the details of every branch of learning, it was sufficient for him or her to be aware of the scope, the methods, and basic concepts of a wide range of disciplines, and—what is even more necessary, and more difficult—to keep abreast of major changes in their methodology, their theoretical paradigms. It may be more than a coincidence that some of the last representatives of this species of "homme de lettres" hail from Central Europe, where the educational system resisted the pressure toward specialization longer than in Western Europe and America.

Jan Kott, as a Pole, is an outstanding representative of this vanishing type of the universally educated "homme de lettres." Able to read the principal European languages, he is as interested in philosophy, linguistics, anthropology, politics, and the natural sciences as he is in his own chosen field—literature and the theater.

But, as a Central European and a Pole, Kott also comes from a tradition in which the intellectual, the man of wide and universal education, has a social importance far greater than that of his counterpart in the English-speaking world: in a country like Poland, always threatened in its independence and autonomy, the intellectual, the man of letters and learning, functions as the natural guardian of its culture, which is the core and substance of its perpetually endangered national identity.

This, in turn, places the Central European intellectual and "homme de lettres" into the very center of his nation's political life. Jan Kott, for one, played an active part in Poland's wartime underground. Like so many young intellectuals of his generation who reached their maturity in the years when the Nazi threat loomed over the whole of Europe, he had been drawn into the orbit of Marxist-Leninist thought and Communist party politics. It is a measure of his integrity as a man and as a thinker that, having emerged from the war on the winning side and with access to all the fruits of victory, in the light of his concrete experience of the postwar developments in a country that was undergoing not a revolution but a brutal foreign neocolonial domination, he gradually thought his way through the theoretical problems of Marxism. Kott emerged from this rethinking (as did contemporaries and fellow-Poles like Czesław Miłosz and Leszek Kołakowski) with a chastened neo-humanistic outlook. He lived up to the consequences of this ideological growth and exchanged his privileged status in his own country for the hazards of emigration into a new cultural sphere where, though guaranteed a comfortable academic life, he lost not only the language of which he was a master (and had henceforth to rely on translation) but also, and above all, his position as a leading figure in his own country where every utterance from him had been a major event.

A Central European man of letters with a wide-ranging, universalist erudition and a politically aware individual who has been through the most intense and dangerous ordeals in the very center of the holocaust of our times, Jan Kott is truly representative of the nation that more than any other today has become the crucible in which the ideas and problems of the age are being tested: Poland. Politically, culturally, and spiritually the Polish experience in the twentieth century has been—as more than once before in the history of Europe—the testing ground and battlefield of ideologies, religions, philosophies. On Polish soil and on the living bodies of Polish men, women, and children, these abstract conflicts have been translated into gruesome suffering and martyrdom. And out of this torment and pain has emerged, astonishingly after so much bloodletting, the most vital and brilliant intellectual and artistic landscape of the post-World War II era.

The essays in this volume give a lively picture of the nature and range of contemporary Polish intellectual and artistic life: with its openness towards the East as well as the West, towards the most traditional as well as the most up-to-date (not to say the most fashionable) tenets of art and philosophy, its mixture of the abstract with the concrete, the speculations of metaphysicians and structuralists and the theatrical experimentation of innovative directors and designers.

Owing to its deplorable ignorance of foreign languages and its consequent provincialism, the intellectual and academic community of the English-speaking world has a frighteningly narrow outlook: anything that is not in English or French seems remote (translations of haphazardly selected material come belatedly and are often inaccurate and misleading); even German work is but dimly perceived in a semi-limbo. For this reason, the infusion into this intellectual climate of men like Kott and other outstanding East and Central European intellectuals, who have been driven into exile by the rulers of the even more insular and provincial Soviet Empire, has opened up much-needed windows. There are few scholars and critics active today in the Western world to whom access to Witkiewicz is as open as to Artaud, to Gombrowicz as to Proust, to whom Shakespeare and Słowacki, Gogol and Kafka, Ionesco and Goethe, Grotowski and the puppets of Bunraku are equally familiar.

This collection of essays and papers, written over a decade is more than a mere miscellany of casual and unconnected observations. It is something like the self-portrait of an intellectual milieu, the product of the intellectual atmosphere of those countries of Central Europe where an awareness of what is going on in the major cultural spheres of the world is a matter of necessity, where the products of the French, English, or American avante-garde, as well as of the official and unofficial culture of the Soviet Empire, are absorbed and evaluated long before they become more widely known in their countries of origin.

Such a collection is also the self-portrait of a personality: as an essayist in the tradition of Montaigne and Hazlitt, Jan Kott draws a fascinating likeness of himself: a man of ebullient wit and great warmth; always eager to absorb the new; a great traveler, immensely responsive to fresh images and landscapes; an insatiable reader, always overflowing with enthusiasm and gratitude towards thinkers and artists to whom he owes excitement, stimulation, and the profound pleasure of a deep emotional or intellectual experience.

For those who have had the pleasure to have met Jan Kott in person, these essays preserve the quality and flavor of his conversation, his brilliance as a raconteur with an inexhaustible store of anecdote and reference, his puckish yet self-deprecating tone of voice, whether in French or in his own inimitable brand of English, which he calls "Kottish" (but which has become increasingly easy to understand over the years). Kott's ability to be enthralled and exhilarated by new ideas, new insights, and new discoveries about ancient texts has the freshness and magic of eternal youthfulness. He is not the critic as fault-finder and carper, but the critic as enhancer of his readers' understanding and enjoyment of artistic experiences and intellectual insights. He may have some of the shortcomings that flow from this attitude—a premature readiness perhaps to be seduced by the new and seemingly original, a tendency to accept it before it has been tested by time—but these are far outweighed by the immense benefits such an attitude brings in its ability to stimulate debate, widen horizons, and break through the boundaries of narrow, blinkered compartmentalization.

Hence a volume like the present fulfills a multitude of important functions: it makes some brilliant individual accounts of topics and personalities hardly ever discussed in the English-speaking world accessible and widely available; it opens up links between areas of thought and scholarship that tend to remain narrowly divided by the compartmentalization of specialized disciplines; and, above all, it distills a self-portrait of a personality of unique authority, wit, and charm which has left its imprint on the thought and art of our time in East and West.

SHAKESPEARE'S
RIDDLE

The Hilton Hotel was filled with Shakespeareans. There were nearly a thousand of them at their second world convention in Washington in April 1976. In the large lobby young hostesses were handing out tags with the name, degree, and institution of the participants so everyone would recognize one another. In the arcades surrounding the lobby Shakespearean publications were being exhibited. Among them were the new Shakespeare concordances containing all of the 22,000 words of his vocabulary computerized and placed in context. There were also ads for the new, improved Shakespeare reference works for which the inexhaustible computers will have gathered and sorted the Shakespearean stage directions and, separately, all of the punctuation marks down to the last comma, as well as counted the frequency and possible relations of exclamation points to question marks. Shakespearology feeds not only on Shakespeare, but also on itself. There are over two thousand Shakespeare professorships in the United States alone, and nearly a thousand in the rest of the world. And every year there are nearly three hundred new doctoral dissertations on Shakespeare: there is a new one every day of every year excluding Jewish and Christian holidays, Saturdays and Sundays.

The previous Shakespeare convention, the first worldwide one, took place in Vancouver in 1971. It was rather a pleasant surprise, not yet terrifying, that there were so many Shakespeare scholars in the world. Vancouver is closer to Kyoto than to Stratford, and after the American delegation, the most numerous representation was Japanese. The participants stayed in little houses with strange

Indian names amid the rose gardens of British Columbia. The congress at Vancouver was illuminated by the sad smile of Grigori Kozintsev, the Russian stage director (I saw him there for the last time; he was to die two years later). Walking in the gardens one night, we spoke of Vsevolod Meyerhold. Kozintsev was one of the few pupils and friends of Meyerhold's who managed to survive all the purges. "That time with Meyerhold," he said, "these were the only years of happiness, maybe two years, maybe three, and afterwards everything was despair." To this congress Kozintsev brought his *King Lear*, whose action takes place on the Russian steppes.

Washington is beautiful in the spring, white and pink in the blooming cherry trees. But the fragrance of the cherry orchards did not reach the Hilton. The congress took place with the iron rigidity of all American conventions (in the same Hilton, a few weeks earlier, a convention of the Daughters of the American Revolution had been held, and a few days later a meeting of Quakers from all over the world). During these five days, which were divided into plenary meetings, sections, subsections, and seminars, the convention participants would stop only to drink up their coffees like travelers at a station afraid to miss their train and run off with briefcases stuffed with piles of lecture papers in the direction of one of the six conference halls where the Shakespeare scholars unceasingly and simultaneously lectured to their colleagues about Shakespeare. Back and forth about Shakespeare, from traditional text analysis to the latest hermeneutic news. There were seminars on the existentialist interpretation of Shakespeare and on the Marxist Shakespeare. During the last seminar, staffed mainly by scholars from East Germany, I had a momentary impression that time had stopped and that, as fifteen years before, I heard the same voice repeating over and over again: "Shakespeare was progressive and was not progressive. . . ."

There were also formal receptions; we were taken to the State Department in twenty buses. And private parties. One was given by a distinguished Washington lady at her ranch overlooking the Potomac. It was Shakespeare's birthday. Meat was roasted on grills, and towards the end of the evening every one of us received a souvenir: a large cowboy hat—the lady was from Texas.

But the high point of the congress, the day before its closing, was a lecture by Jorge Luis Borges. He had come especially to address the convention. The largest hall of the Hilton was filled to capacity an hour before the lecture was to begin. Only the first four rows of chairs stood empty. They were being watched by school children so that no uninvited guest would sit in them. But finally, when no official guests showed up, the children took the seats themselves.

Two men helped Borges to the podium. They walked across the stage very slowly, holding his arms. For a moment it looked as if they were walking a wooden figure. They finally positioned him in front of the microphone. Everyone in the hall stood up; the ovation lasted many minutes. Borges did not move. Finally the clapping stopped. Borges started moving his lips. Only a vague humming noise was heard from the speakers. From this monotonous humming one could distinguish only with greatest pains a single word which kept returning like a repeated cry from a faraway ship, drowned out by the sea: "Shakespeare, Shakespeare, Shakespeare. . . ."

The microphone was placed too high. But no one in the room had the courage to walk up and lower the microphone in front of the old blind writer. Borges spoke for an hour, and for an hour only this one repeated word—Shakespeare—would reach the listeners. During this hour no one got up or left the room. After Borges finished, everyone got up and it seemed that this final ovation would never end.

Borges's lecture was entitled: "The Riddle of Shakespeare." Like the Orator in Eugène Ionesco's *The Chairs*, he was called upon to solve the riddle. And like the Orator in *The Chairs*, who could produce only incomprehensible sounds from his throat, Borges solved the riddle: "Shakespeare, Shakespeare, Shakespeare. . . ."

THE AUTHOR

OF COMEDY,

OR

THE INSPECTOR

GENERAL

1 In no other great comedy is there as much talk about eating as in Gogol's *The Inspector General*. This is natural, since everything begins near the stall where they sell hot pies. That is where Dobchinsky and Bobchinsky run to each other eager to exchange "the nasty news" which the Mayor has received in a letter, from "an absolutely reliable source." Soon they go to the nearby inn for a mid-morning snack of freshly arrived salmon. And it is over the salmon that they first recognize the government inspector in Khlestakov, a thin young man recently arrived from Petersburg. "And my Lord, what an observant fellow—he took in everything. He noticed that Dobchinsky and I were eating salmon . . . . He looked right into our plates, too. Why, I was simply scared stiff."

Khlestakov and his servant Osip are very hungry. Osip, stretched out on his master's bed, his top-boots on, in an attic room of the local inn, talks about nothing but food. "Devil take me; I am so hungry that there is a continual rumbling in my stomach as though the whole regiment were beginning to blow their trumpets." He ends his monologue with a pitiful moan: "Oh Lord, my God, if only

I had some cabbage soup, good or bad! I think I could gobble up the world." Like Caliban, whose second line in *The Tempest* is "I must eat my dinner," Khlestakov above all wants his dinner. "Why, go down to the dining room . . . tell them . . . to send up something for my dinner." After sending Osip off he has fantasies about food. "It's awful how hungry I am! I thought that if I'd just take a walk my appetite would go; but no, damned if it would." They finally bring him dinner, but what a dinner! "Only two courses?"

KHLESTAKOV: And why is there no gravy?

WAITER: There just isn't any.

KHLESTAKOV: And why isn't there? I saw with my own eyes when I was passing through the kitchen that there were a great many things being prepared. And in the dining room this morning I saw two chubby little men gulping down salmon and lots of other things.

So we are back to the salmon. Later the same evening the Mayor takes Khlestakov to a truly splendid dinner with truly excellent fish. Next morning we have an exact account of what they ate.

KHLESTAKOV: What do you call the fish we had?

DIRECTOR
OF CHARITIES: Labardan, sir.

KHLESTAKOV: Very tasty. Where was it we dined? At the hospital, wasn't it?

Labardan! In the very sound of this Russian word there is magnificence and luxury. In his famous essay on Gogol's "The Overcoat" (1919), Boris Eichenbaum gave the name of "vocal gesture" to the use of words with especially rich intonations. When Artemy Filippovich, the Director of Charities, answers Khlestakov's question, he leans close to him as if he wanted to whisper a secret in his ear. A moment later Khlestakov repeats to himself (Gogol writes "with pathos") that lush word which is in itself like an enormous fish: *labardan!* The cruel comedy of this scene lies in the fact that the lavish treat for Khlestakov was served in the hospital. "I remember, I remember. There were a lot of cots standing empty there. Have all the patients recovered?" The Director of Charities has an unforgettable reply: "They recover like . . . like flies."

We have known the hospital from the first scene of the play: ". . . as far as the treatment goes, we don't go in for fancy medicines— the more chances you give nature the better. Our patients are all simple folk: if any of them is going to get well, he'll get well." The rule is that all patients get oatmeal for breakfast, yet "the stinking odour of cabbage hangs in every corridor; better keep your nose shut!" In this materialistic Gogolian world, filled with flavors and smells, where the nose is the most important organ, and class differences and distinctions are reflected in emptied bowls, plates, and platters, as in a coarse farce, Khlestakov has been taken to dinner, but his servant Osip is still hungry.

> OSIP: Well, now, what have you got in the way of plain fare?
> MISHKA: Cabbage soup, buckwheat groats, and hot pie.
> OSIP: Bring on your soup, your groats, and hot pie. It doesn't matter—we'll eat anything.

Like Plautus's slaves, Molière's servants, and Sancho Panza, Osip knows well enough that tomorrow one has to eat as well. When the shopkeepers come to Khlestakov to complain about the Mayor's crookedness and bring him the traditional bread, salt, and sugar on a silver tray, Osip eagerly takes the bread and salt and sugar, then the basket with wine, and finally the silver tray. For him, the value of bread and salt has no symbolic meaning, since both can be eaten. He even takes a piece of string. Anything can prove useful.

In *The Elementary Structures of Kinship* (1949) Lévi-Strauss describes the rigid rules governing the distribution of meat among Eskimo hunters, the tribes of Burma and East Africa. To the reader "inclined to appraise them in the perspective of our traditional culture, which likes to contrast the pathos of unhappy love and the comedy of the full stomach," he gives a very characteristic warning: "In the great majority of human societies, the two problems are set on the same plane, since, with love as with food, nature presents man with the same risk. The lot of the satiated man is just as liable to excite emotion, and is just as much an excuse for lyrical expression, as the lot of the loved man. Moreover, primitive experience asserts the continuity between organic sensations and spiritual experience. Food is completely riddled with signs and dangers." In Gogol food is also riddled with rank and place.

In Khlestakov's ramblings, as well as in the Mayor's greedy imagination, Petersburg is a gastronomical paradise. To dream about power is to dream about food. One watermelon on his table, brags Khlestakov, costs seven hundred rubles! "Why, they say," the Mayor confesses to his wife, "you can get two particular kinds of fish there, so tasty that they make your mouth water at the first bite—sea-eels and smelts." Even for poor Dobchinsky, fashionable life in the capital begins with delicious soups: "Marya Antonovna! I have the honor of congratulating you! You'll be ever so happy: you'll wear a dress of gold and eat all sorts of exquisite soups; you'll have a most amusing time."

A stroke of Gogol's genius appears in a letter that the Mayor fleetingly scribbled to his wife on a restaurant bill in the inn: "I write you in haste, dearest, to inform you that my situation was a most lamentable one; but placing my trust in the mercy of God, 2 salted cucumbers extra, and half a portion of caviar, 1 ruble, 25 kopecks."

Nothing is unusual in the letter and in the bill. But read together, one on top of the other as in a strange palimpsest, letter and bill are suddenly ludicrous. This reading however, is not only ludicrous, it is also revealing: letter/bill exposes the hidden structure of *The Inspector General* in which divine mercy may cost more than a half-portion of caviar. ". . . placing my trust in the mercy of God . . . it seems that everything will come out right . . . don't bother preparing anything extra, we are going to have a bite at the Department of Public Charities, with its Director. But as for wine, order as much as possible . . . ."

This apparent incongruity contains the whole topography and economy of this country town (from which if you were to gallop even at top speed for three years in any direction you wouldn't come to any other country). There are barely concealed links between the mercy of God, fear and power, between pickles in a restaurant and labardan in a hospital, between wine on the Mayor's table and in a merchant's cellar. "Tell the shopkeeper Abdulin to send his best, for otherwise I will turn his whole wine cellar upside down myself." This gastronomical collage, probably the first surrealistic collage, reveals the circulation of goods: the merchant Abdulin must always ante up for God's mercy.

2 Gogol's grandfather, Vassily Transky, used to write popular farces which in their coarse humor, their gallery of traditional characters, and crude realism seem to be borrowed directly from the Ukrainian *vertep*. *Vertep*, like the Russian *Petrushka*, was a folk puppet-theater. Its main puppet was Petrushka, a humpbacked fellow with a long crooked nose, a close cousin of Pulcinella and a remote one of Punch. He lied, cheated the rich, would often get badly whipped, yet he always had the last word. Other puppets represented the devil, an orthodox priest, a merchant, a jealous husband, a suitor, an unfaithful wife, a vagrant soldier, a greedy policeman. The *vertep* tradition also inspired Gogol's father, an author of one-act farces which were played and sung by serfs in the house of his rich neighbor. Among them was *Bog-Lamb*, the story of a village simpleton who is made to believe that his lamb is in fact an officer's dog—and must thus be returned. The title of another was *Tricky Wife Tricked by a Soldier*.

No nineteenth-century comedy, except the superb *Ubu Roi* by Alfred Jarry, is as close in its theatrical manner to popular farce and the puppet theater as Gogol's *The Inspector General*. The Mayor in a panic puts a hat box instead of a hat on his head. Dobchinsky, leaning against the attic door to overhear the conversation between Khlestakov and the Mayor, falls into the room: the hinges could not sustain his weight. The mother finds Khlestakov kneeling in front of her daughter, and a moment later the daughter discovers him in the same situation with her mother. In the next scene the Inspector from the capital, like Molière's Don Juan, simultaneously seduces two women. This oldest kind of humor, the "clockwork" repetitions of overdrawn situations, the indignity of object, the mechanical gestures and puppetlike grimaces, which Henri Bergson analyzed so brilliantly in *Laughter* (1900), was later discovered once more by the Marx Brothers, Buster Keaton, and Charlie Chaplin.

All the characters in Gogol's theater, except Khlestakov, have, like puppets, very small "inner worlds" and big "put on" faces. In contrast to the sparkling richness and invention of the dialogue, which has the wit of a wisecrack and the finality of a proverb, the characters' gestures are limited and mechanically repetitive. Gogol's human fauna grin queerly and cruelly, even those who don't appear on stage and are only mentioned, like the nameless professor who "can't stand up in front of his class without pulling the most terrible faces." And "all the cleverest men are mad, they either drink themselves to death or pull faces that would shame the devil." Gogol's stories and his novel *Dead Souls* are full of those grotesque faces and grins. We are told that Gogol himself used to make horrible faces while reading his works to himself. As for his language, Eichenbaum wrote in the essay on "The Overcoat": "As always with Gogol . . . his phrases exist beyond time, immovable, once and for all: it is a language that could be spoken by puppets." A nose running away and a court clerk strolling around without his nose can be shown only in a puppet theater. Gogol's characters—wrote Eichenbaum—"are like frozen postures."

The first production of *The Inspector General* in Petersburg's Alexander Theater in April 1836 was a personal disaster for Gogol: "they have done *The Inspector*, yet I am sad and fearful." It was not *The Inspector* of his imagination. "My own work seems alien to me, as if it were not I who wrote it." He was most disappointed by the principal actor and wrote in a letter to his friends: "Dur didn't understand Khlestakov at all. He was just one more of the hundreds of buffoons imported from Paris to parade here. He reduced him to a banal liar, a miserable creature that has appeared on the stage for two hundred years, always in the same costume . . . . Khlestakov is not an impostor; he does not lie deliberately, he forgets that he lies and is almost ready to believe everything that slips off his tongue. He is in an excellent mood, everything goes well for him, everybody is listening to him, so he lets his tongue loose and gabbles and blabbers, opens his soul wide, and lies as his heart dictates to him, most sincerely, showing off his true self. . . . Khlestakov does not lie in cold blood, like a theatrical buffoon; he lies with feeling, his eyes glow with the delight he senses in that very moment. It is the most beautiful moment in his life, the most poetic one, the moment of inspiration . . . ."

The same description of Khlestakov, a skinny young man who is almost like a moving void, appears earlier in Gogol's "Notes for the Actors":

> A young man (twenty-three), very thin—somewhat on the silly side and, as the saying goes, there's nobody home. One of those fellows who, in the Civil Service, are called the lamest of lame-brains. He speaks and acts without consideration, utterly incapable of giving attention to any one idea. His speech is jerky, his words pop out in an utterly unexpected way. The more ingenuousness and simplicity the actor evinces in this role, the more successful he will be.

From head to foot Khlestakov is the essence of theater entirely forgotten by the nineteenth century. This poor fellow, who wants to fill his empty stomach, who says whatever pops out of his mouth, mostly about the delights of eating, who lies, tenderly and with inspiration, who like a real Proteus can appear instantly in any role ("there mustn't be anything stiff about Khlestakov") has, in his physique and gestures, much of Harlequin in him.

"Harlequin is perhaps the only character who unites in himself wit and simplicity, shrewdness and folly," Florian wrote in the last years of the triumph of the Comédie-Italienne in Paris. He continues:

> Harlequin, always good-natured, always easy to cheat, believes everything he is told, falls into all the traps set for him; nothing surprises him, everything puzzles him; he has no logic, no sensibility; he loses his temper, is appeased, grieves and is consoled all at the same moment: his joy and his sorrow are both delightful. He is, then, by no means a buffoon, nor is he a serious

person; he is a great child; he has a child's grace, sweetness, cleverness . . . .

(quoted in Allardyce Nicoll, *The World of Harlequin*)

Florian's Harlequin is surprisingly similar to the portrait of Khlestakov in Gogol's letters and in his "Notes for the Actors." The image of the Harlequin comes, of course, from the last quarter of the eighteenth century. Gogol's theater is to the same degree anachronistic and ahead of its time.

3 The oldest and most enduring kind of comic action, from ancient comedy to *commedia dell'arte*, from popular farce to Molière, is a clash between two houses. These two houses may be painted on a backdrop or exist only in the imagination, their inhabitants may look through "real" windows, or appear in rooms that open on stage, but always one of them is a House of Order and Virtue and the other a House of Release and Pleasure. The first is a family house, where respectable citizens of the local society gather; to the other come those who are a threat to the family and social order.

The first house represents Authority and Appearances where, in the name of morality, the father tyrannizes his wife, his son, his daughter. This house guards its image to the outside world and its property. It is this property which inhabitants of the other house— bachelors without a penny, easy girls of uncertain origin, as well as thieves and crooks—are after. Human appetites constitute the law in this second house of deceit and cunning. In old farce and in Renaissance comedy, the bawd and Madam make constant rounds between the two houses. The procuress lives in the house of pleasure and offers her services in the house where pleasure is forbidden; thus, by selling vice for goods, she pays homage to property. A clever slave, a wicked servant, a Harlequin live in the House of Respectability but do not belong to it. Harlequin always serves two masters; the first is himself, the second human nature. The bawd also serves the two masters: money and nature. The procuress and the cunning servant, circulating between the two houses, know the price of sin and the price of virtue.

A classical action in comedy is the assault upon the House of Virtue by the House of Ill Repute. It usually takes the form of a theft: of jewels, a moneybox, a wife, a daughter, a son. From Plautus to Molière, from Machiavelli's *Mandragola* to Pinter's *The Birthday Party*, the House of Virtue is entered by a Stranger, a cheat or a runaway. In ancient comedies and popular farces, thieves and lovers always win. In the most brutal solutions a stranger moves into the family house forever. The young win over the old, a slave outsmarts his master, temptations are stronger than restraints, wit and slyness triumph over authority and power. Human nature is satisfied. The hungry ones stuff themselves at the cost of the well-fed.

Characters in comedy are often reduced to "humors," which are passions, obsessions, or delusions that paralyze reason. In the comical happy ending a father who tyrannizes his family is not only punished but also cured of his "humor." Marriage between the young couple establishes peace between the two houses. But it is an illusory peace. The House of Pleasure wins only to establish a new House of Family. The end of one comedy creates the beginning of a new one. All roles are cast forever, which is one reason why comedy from Plautus to Ionesco has the same stock characters. Since its beginning the lean fellow is against the fat man, and the fat man against the lean one.

In his suggestions on how to play *The Inspector*, written ten years after the opening night in Petersburg, Gogol describes the Mayor's horror—"there is nothing to joke about, his situation is almost tragic"—when he learns how he was cheated, "and by whom! By a pitiful, insignificant creature like Khlestakov." And then he adds: "Khlestakov is, of course, very skinny, all the others are fat."

The props and costumes in these comedies belong to an older time; foods are spoken of whose taste we no longer know. But once we strip away the historical costumes, the facial expressions and grimaces are revealed as our own. The sadness and the stubborn relevance of old comedy resides in unceasing repetition of the same enforced roles—the terrible and the preordained roles—that are foisted upon each of us by family, authority, property, gender, youth or old age.

"Do have mercy and give me any kind of a story, no matter how funny, or sad, it doesn't matter as long as it's a purely Russian anecdote," wrote Gogol to Pushkin in 1835. According to tradition, it was Pushkin who suggested to Gogol the idea for *The Inspector General*. He told Gogol that one evening at an inn in Nizhni Novgorod he was mistaken for a high dignitary from the capital. Vladimir Nabokov, in his brilliant book about Gogol, scorns the naive faith that a work of art must always be somehow traceable to a "true story." Nabokov describes how a certain Russian émigré in the 1870s wanted Karl Marx to meet N. G. Chernyshevsky, the ideological leader of the Russian revolutionary democrats and author of the novel *What Is to Be Done*, who was sentenced for life to hard labor in Siberia. In an attempt to kidnap Chernyshevsky, the Russian conspirator returned secretly to Russia disguised as a member of the Geographical Society. He safely reached the remote Yakutsk region—the mission almost accomplished. He did not, however, foresee one danger: the news spread from town to town that he was a Government Inspector traveling incognito.

It does not finally matter if it was indeed Pushkin who suggested *The Inspector* to Gogol. All he needed was a Russian anecdote, "a funny or a sad one" in which a traditional trickster, a liar from a popular farce, a cheater cheated, a hunter hunted, a drunken beggar who suddenly wakes up in a royal crown, could be transformed into a walking nothing who, after losing everything at cards, checks into a provincial inn without a penny in his pocket, and in two days turns the House of Virtue and Authority upside down.

Historical anecdotes often unveil a whole political system and reveal its hidden nature: a shoemaker from Köpenick dressed up in an old captain's uniform, purchased from a thrift tailor and still smelling of naphthalene, arrested the Mayor, requisitioned a savings-bank cash box, and for three days ruled over Köpenick, one of the largest districts of Berlin, in the year of our Lord, 1906. True anecdotes reveal the necessity of accidents, the evidence of nonevidence, the madness of order and the order of madness.

Several years ago a group of Polish writers and scholars issued the so-called "Letter of the Thirty Four," protesting against censorship. The protest raised a storm. A few days later, at the opening night of a new comedy, one of the signatories ran into the Minister of Culture and Art. "Those irresponsible idiots," the Minister said to him, "passed a resolution against you all. I am just back from the Castle [this Kafkaesque reference was to the new building of the Central Committee of the Party], where your problem was taken up by the Secretariat. The damn fools decided to punish you: you won't be able to publish and travel abroad. But don't you worry, keep cool. They always forget about everything after three months." "Tell me," asked the writer's wife, "have you read the resolution?" "Of course," answered the Minister, "I wrote it."

Some anecdotes suddenly reveal the real in the absurd, and the absurd in the real, the comedy in the nightmare and the nightmare in the comedy. Gogol's *The Inspector* founds a new dramatic genre: the tragic farce.

4 "I've called you together, gentlemen, to let you in on a most unpleasant bit of news. There's an Inspector General on his way here!"

All of them in this country town assume "faces" from the very beginning: the Mayor "even though he is a taker of bribes, carries himself with great dignity"; the judge "has read five or six books and is hence inclined to free thinking"; the Director of Charities is "a very stout, unwieldy, and clumsy man but, for all that, as foxy as they come and a knave." The Mayor's wife and daughter, the inspector of police, the policemen, they all have assumed faces. Even the shopkeepers have shopkeeper mugs. Only Khlestakov does not have a ready-made face. But, even before the Mayor goes to the inn with Dobchinsky, the face of a dignitary from Petersburg traveling incognito is already waiting for him: "he is behaving mighty queer; he's staying here for the second week now, hardly ever sets foot outside the place, calls for everything on credit, and won't lay out cash."

The Inspector General is already discovered in Khlestakov; he alone does not yet know it. Both the Mayor and Khlestakov are terrified of each other and cautiously begin to put on servile and dignified faces. Like Tartuffe and Orgon, who, on their knees, try to outdo each other in their foxy and pious grimaces of converted sinners, the Mayor and Khlestakov compete in making sweet faces of humility and servility. Hence, in this duel of grimaces whoever first makes a threatening face shall win.

Khlestakov uses the standard ploy: "You do not know who I am!" Gogol's great joke lies in the discovery that Khlestakov is who he is not, and he is not who he is. But the Mayor does not learn this soon enough. He is left with his face of fear. "Oh, good Lord, how angry he is! He has found out everything." Poor Dobchinsky summarizes the whole scene in one sentence to the Mayor's wife: "When a high dignitary speaks, you naturally feel scared."

> KHLESTAKOV: I'll take the matter directly to the Prime Minister! *(Thumping the table.)* Who do you think you are, you . . . you—
> MAYOR: *(drawing himself up at attention, with his whole body trembling)* Have pity on me—don't ruin me! I have a wife and little children . . . You don't have to ruin a man.

When Khlestakov tells the truth, when he says that he arrived without a kopeck, that he has not been promoted to any rank, and that his old man has summoned him home, the Mayor does not believe a single word. "Oh, what a fox! Just see what he's aiming at! What a smoke screen he puts up! . . . A fellow doesn't know what side to tackle him from." When after several drinks, Khlestakov promotes himself almost to the rank of Field-Marshal, the tricky old Mayor believes . . . half of it: "Well, now, supposing even half of what he said is true? . . . But then, nobody ever says anything without some added touches. He plays whist with prime ministers and is a regular visitor at Court. . . ."

They fawn on Khlestakov, and he believes them. He climbs higher and higher on the ladder of braggadocio: a while ago he lived on the third floor, now he occupies the elegant first; he was a copying clerk at first (like Gogol himself, for a while), now the Head of the Department is his best friend; a doorman runs after him with a brush to shine his shoes, and then, after a glance at his glittering footwear a group of soldiers take him for a commander-in-chief; an old cook Mavrusha hangs up his coat, and a moment later he is entertaining the most glamorous society in Petersburg.

"You are from the capital, you like to have a laugh at us provincials . . . ." Khlestakov in the House of Good Repute sells his fantasies about the House of Fun. To the greedy souls of provincial bribe-takers, for two dinners and a few hundred rubles, he offers that St. Petersburg where everything is possible, where even to-morrow they can go and put on generals' uniforms, where medals and ribbons are waiting for them together with invitations to the Court. "Do you know why one wants to be an Inspector General? Because, then if one has occasion to travel anywhere, you have aides and state couriers galloping ahead of you everywhere you go, demanding horses! And when you get to a post station there won't be anybody else getting any horses: every other living soul has to wait his turn. All those titled persons, and captains and mayors. But you don't give a good damn, even."

To the equally greedy and vulgar little souls in fat bodies of the wives and daughters of the provincial dignitaries, Khlestakov presents dreams of a glamorous world. "Oh St. Petersburg! What a life!" He entertains the most fashionable guests in the capital. His "staircase alone—is simply priceless." Every night he attends balls and often gives his own. In the morning, while he is still asleep, princes and counts crowd the antechamber of his residence.

Khlestakov believes what he says, and the others believe what he says, and the others believe him, too. The Mayor and the Judge, the policeman Derzhimorda and the Inspector of Police, the Post-master and the Superintendent of Schools, the first lady in this country town and her eligible daughter, they all believe in the same mythical St. Petersburg of pleasures and power. Even Osip, Khlestakov's servant, tossing on the hotel bed and dreaming about kasha with dumplings, sees with his gleaming eyes the same St. Petersburg: "There is no disputing that life in the capital is best of all. You must have money, naturally, but living there is grand and refined—theatres, and trained dogs dancing for your amusement, and everything else that your heart desires . . . ." Osip is right. The Mayor's wife's dreams are in no way different: "We'll belong to the best-mannered society: counts and the whole grand world."

In his famous Moscow production, in December 1926, Vsevolod Meyerhold, as nobody before or after, showed that shimmering dream of St. Petersburg in *The Inspector*. He raised a small provincial town, lost somewhere in vast Russia, to the rank of a capital of the province. The Mayor's wife changes her dress fifteen times in front of the mirror of a gigantic mahogany armoire. From behind the armoire appear a squadron to the Czar's Guard officers, who dance and serenade her on imaginary guitars. A beautiful officer kneels in front of her . . . the Petersburg of all pleasures, as in "The Nevsky Avenue" and "The Overcoat," is frightening and marvelous, almost Kafkaesque, almost surrealistic. "Soups arrive there straight from Paris on a steamer kept in very special pots. As soon as you lift the lid there is an aroma—you've never smelled anything like that on earth before." There are messengers running up and down the streets all the time: "Would you believe it, thirty-five thousand messengers!" The Mayor's wife wants her future boudoir to be so scented with perfume that nobody could enter it without "puckering up the eyes."

Gogol's grim and ludicrous St. Petersburg was to be unexpectedly echoed in the Moscow of Chekhov's *Three Sisters*. There, Moscow is not only the city of Irina's dreams, where life is "beautiful" and "refined," the only place where the talents of General Pozorov's three daughters who mastered three languages could be properly appreciated; it is also their brother Andrei's Moscow, where "you don't know anybody and nobody knows you, yet you don't feel like a stranger." There is also a Moscow which the half-deaf Ferapont heard about from a contractor in a country court, where shopkeepers eat blinis: "one ate forty or maybe even fifty and died." There is a rope stretched all the way across the city in Ferapont's Moscow.

This Moscow of the deaf idiot was born in Gogol's St. Petersburg: a "deaf desert" where there is "no laughter, only fear." Gogol wrote, "do not believe The Nevsky Avenue." In this House of Pleasure "everything shivers and trembles like a leaf." This house of all joys, opportunity and luxury, "where cigars are twenty rubles each," is carpeted with dread. "And what if he wakes up and scrawls a report on us to Petersburg!" That dread is decorated with red and blue medal ribbons, four ranks of the Order of St. Anne and three of St. Vladimir. ("I like Vladimir; Anna of the third rank—that's not the same . . . .") Dread wears frock coats and uniforms with galloons ("and we even didn't put on the uniforms"), parades in boots with spurs, but at home wears felt slippers, and, like a deductive system, is once and forever formalized by consecutive degrees in order of rank: ". . . if somebody with higher rank speaks to me I feel like fainting."

In this masqueraded and disguised dread—in medals, galloons, epaulets, toppers, the three-cornered hats of civil servants and round officer hats with bands—as in a closed structure, all signs are interconnected (a boot implies a rank, a rank implies a boot); in this *écriture* of bureaucracy, as in Chinese characters, all hierarchies and distinctions are enclosed—there were nine ranks of titular councillors alone! Different cuts of coats, height of bows, and size of bribes were prescribed for each of the ranks: "You are not taking according to your rank." The horror of Gogol's world is all in gestures, therefore it is theatrical; this horror is concrete and material, like the whole length of cloth which the policeman takes from the shopkeeper Abdulin instead of the customary two measures.

When in the old comedy a Stranger comes to the House of Decency and Virtue, all masks drop. The father appears to be an old rake, tyrant, and skinflint, his wife keeps her window open for a suitor, their son sells his inheritance to a usurer, the daughter is about to run away with a lover. From the first scene of Gogol's *Inspector*, the Mayor and all the other notables have faces of bribe-takers. Gogol reverses all devices of comedy, one after another. The House of Order and Power itself creates an impostor and, as in a carnival, to welcome his arrival orders the universal masquerade. In all villages and towns of all Saratov provinces, and everywhere between Vistula and Dnepr, at the arrival of a Number One or on the Day of the Great Parade the streets have to be swept out, the windows cleaned. On the eve of the big day, the House of Oppression always becomes the House of Appearances.

In the municipal hospital where, as the Director of Charities assures Khlestakov the patients "recover like flies," a Latin inscription hangs over every bed, and the patients must wear freshly laundered nightcaps. The dog-whip is to be removed from the courtroom, and the geese moved from the waiting room to the kitchen. The Mayor, the clergy, and representatives of the merchants are to participate in the parade.

It is the day when the Mayor forbids the policeman Derzhi-morda to use his fists. "And don't let the soldiers go into the street without anything on: those wretched fellows in the garrison put their coats over their shirts and nothing below." But most important is the thunderous general enthusiasm. Should the Inspector ask questions, the answer must be: "perfectly satisfied, your honor! We're satisfied with everything."

Prince Potemkin, who was a great opera-lover, ordered painted mansions, artificial orchards and neat villages set up along the Dnepr to create the image of a flourishing countryside for Catherine the Great, who wished to sail down the river. Gogol's Mayor, who has probably never been in the theater, only ordered his people to "break up the old fence where the shoemaker lives, and make it look as if we were planning to build something there. The more demolition going on, the greater the proof that the head of the town is an active man."

Gogol's nightmares are always theatrical, but their theatri-cality has perhaps the nature of an autocratic regime in which, as in comic opera, bombastic *buffo* is unavoidably followed by dreadful *serio*. In the mid-1950s I was invited to the presentation of State Prizes awarded to chosen artists, writers, and scholars in Warsaw's Belvedere Palace. The First Secretary, the Prime Minister, the heavy cream of the Party dignitaries and inspectors general attended the reception. When the speeches and toasts were over, and the antique Empire tables emptied of vodka, caviar, hamrolls, pickles, and Coca-Cola, I walked to the window. It was very high, with impeccable classical proportions, overlooking the most beautiful part of old Lazenki Park, which was closed to the public for security reasons. But that evening, thick draperies were drawn and nothing could be seen, so I sat in a chair and began to rock. When I rocked too hard and lost my balance, two heavy hands fell on my shoulders and pushed me back. Hidden behind the draperies were members of the Secret Police.

"My head is haunted by a comedy," Gogol wrote in *An Author's Confession*, the "beztolkovshchina." And to his friends he wrote: "The frightening *beztolkovshchina* of our times fills all of us with a terrifying melancholy." This Russian word, almost untranslatable, means mess, maze, muddle. All these hissing and smacking conso-nants convey a feeling of oppressiveness. Gogol's *beztolkovshchina* is a nightmare. Like the two black and unnaturally big rats the Mayor dreams about the night before the arrival of the Inspector. Prophetic dreams proclaim tragedy. But the Mayor's dreadful nightmare heralds a comedy and provokes laughter in the stalls. In "The Nose," "The Overcoat," and *The Inspector* we find the same frightening and grotesque tragicomedy which we thought was a discovery of the theater of the 1950s, of Beckett's and Ionesco's. The Mayor promises that if he is lucky enough to get out of trouble, he will offer the church a candle, "the world's best yet." But Gogol's nightmare, unlike anyone else's until Kafka, happens in the daylight, so that each detail becomes graphic. "I'll make every damned shopkeeper come across with a hundred and twenty pounds of wax for that candle."

In Gogol's world everything is blown up, as if looked at through enlarging lenses; graphic, shadelessly linear, almost colorless. Noses, bellies, foxy smiles become bigger and bigger and more cartoonlike. Gogol should have been illustrated by Daumier. "The world is both funny and dreadful," he used to write to friends. In *The Inspector General*, everybody is scared all the time. "I almost died of fear," Bobchinsky tells Dobchinsky. "You feel so scared . . . and you don't know why," the Director of Charities says to the Superintendent of Schools. "I still can't shake off the fear," the Mayor whispers in his wife's ear in their bedroom. A corporal's widow, "was found whipped, by herself." She was beaten up by policemen on the Mayor's orders. In this image of the widow who "whipped herself," we glimpse one of George Orwell's visions. At the end of the comedy the word "Siberia" is twice mentioned. This farce begins and ends with fear.

"The official who has arrived from Petersburg with instructions from the Government summons you to his presence. He is staying at the inn." The House of Promotion and Pleasure now becomes forever the House of Horror. "The Inspector General? Has he a moustache? What kind of a moustache?" The inspector announced by a gendarme has a real moustache. The Mayor, the local notables with their wives and daughters stand petrified, eyes wide open and arms stretched, until the curtain falls. Meyerhold first realized Gogol's initial vision in the ludicrous and horrific stage effect of replacing the actors with life-size puppets. The House of Order and Virtue appears as the House of Dread.

The comedy's ending returns to its beginning. The inspector from Petersburg checks into the same inn. In a short while, the Mayor with Dobchinsky and Bobchinsky will rush to invite him, as they invited Khlestakov, to a treat in the hospital, where he will be served delicious butter-fried labardan. Next day, the judge, the Director of Charities, the Superintendent of Schools, and the poor Postmaster will line up in the hotel to offer unreturnable loans to the new Inspector, bending their necks in low bows.

The new comedy begins where the old one ends. Gogol had an amazing and thorough understanding of Molière's *Tartuffe*. Orgon finds his inspector general in the church vestibule, and the Mayor finds his in a wayside inn, but in both masterpieces of comedy the knave and liar from the traditional farce represent the Highest Authority. "A holy man, has he a wig? What kind of wig?" Tartuffe, a *faux-dévot*, behaves himself until his sinful desires get the better of him, like a real devotee and sanctimonious hypocrite, straight out of the Society of the Holy Sacrament. The mask is his face and his face a mask, as Rachmiel Brandwajn perceptively wrote in his essay on *Tartuffe*. A feigned paragon of virtue acts like a real paragon of virtue. An imagined inspector general acts like a real inspector general. The gendarme, who in the conclusion of Gogol's play announces the arrival of the official ("on the highest orders") from Petersburg, repeats in the deep structure of the comedy the function of the Officer of the Guard, who in the end of *Tartuffe* also appears "on the highest orders" in order to save Orgon and to mete out justice to the Impostor. Gogol renders a scathing and merciless interpretation of Molière: in the conclusion to *The Inspector General*, the imagined impostor is exchanged for the real one.

The new comedy begins where the old one leaves off. In this last ingenious transformation of traditional structure, both the Houses of Fear and Horror are one and the same House of Bribery.

5 At the opening night of *The Inspector General* in Petersburg, in April 1836, in the grand loge of the Alexander Theater, the Czar smiled and maybe even clapped politely. The stalls and boxes were filled with princes and counts, governors and heads of departments, and perhaps the same regular circle described by Khlestakov as the "Minister of Foreign Affairs, the French, the British, the German ambassadors, and me."

"It's unlike anything, it's a libellous farce." Pavel Annenkov relates the unanimous opinion of the Petersburg spectators in his memoirs. We have no reason not to believe a member of the Court clique. Two years later, a great Russian actor M. S. Shchepkin, the Mayor in the first Moscow production, wrote to his friend I. I. Sosnitsky, who played the Mayor in Petersburg: "The audience, struck by something entirely new, laughed a lot. And still, I expected a better reception. I was quite astonished, but a certain person from high society gave me very amusing reasons: 'How can you expect the play to be better received when half of the audience consists of those who take and the other half of those who give.' "

Gogol gave *The Inspector* an epigraph from a folk proverb: "Don't blame the mirror if your mug is crooked." Great comedies are always mirrors. But Gogol's *The Inspector* is the first and probably the only comedy which whenever performed realizes its theatrical function as a mirror. When at the end the Mayor and the other notables stand immobile like huge puppets, audience and stage change roles. At the opening night in Petersburg, the house was full; both Houses of good and ill repute took place in the audience. "What are you laughing at? You are laughing at your own selves!" This extraordinarily brilliant line, shouted straight at the audience by the enraged Mayor, Gogol added after the first performance.

Writers and journalists were also present at that historical first night. What the stomping Mayor yelled in rage was addressed to them as well. "It's not enough to be made a laughing stock—there will be some scribbler, some ink-slinger, who will put you in a comedy." Among all those scribblers, "the damned liberals," hidden modestly in a dark corner was, perhaps, Ivan Vasilyevich Tryapichkin, to whom Khlestakov sent the letter describing the whole adventure, and asking him to use it in one of his columns: "Give 'em all a punch as they deserve." Had he not sent the letter, his fraud would not have been detected so soon.

In *The Misanthrope*, Molière's Célimène was ruined by a very similar passion for composing satirical portraits (of "personages from society") which she would then send in letters to her friends. The poor copying clerk in Gogol's comedy has, like Célimène, the soul of a writer and is brought to ruin by his ambition and meager literary talents. "I want to go into literature myself," he writes to Tryapichkin. "After all, one wants some spiritual food." Khlestakov may dream of watermelons that cost seven hundred rubles, Field-Marshal outfits, residences crowded with counts and princes, but his real reveries concern something else. "I am often in literary circles . . . on friendly terms with Pushkin. I must confess I live for literature." Khlestakov in his dreams is the author of a comedy. And what a comedy! It was he who wrote *The Marriage of Figaro*!

"There is nobody who for a minute—or even for a number of minutes—has not changed or is not going to change into a Khlestakov, although naturally he is reluctant to admit it. We even make fun of this habit—but only, of course, when we discover it in somebody else," wrote Gogol in a letter to a friend in May 1836. Flaubert wrote the famous statement *"Madame Bovary, c'est moi."* But Gogol's sudden identification with Khlestakov is even more unexpected and puzzling. "Even the smart office of the imperial guard," Gogol continues in the same letter, "even the eminent head of the family, even our brother, the sinful man of letters, will sometime turn into a Khlestakov."

Khlestakov became an inspector general in spite of himself, but this inspector in spite of himself is also the author of a comedy in spite of himself. After all, he did send a story about the inspector general in spite of himself to his friend Tryapichkin. The inspector general in spite of himself is the author of the comedy, but the author of the comedy is also an inspector general in spite of himself. The actors of the comedy (which mirrors the customs of the time), its *real* actors, sit in the audience; and barely does the comedy end than they begin to play it again in real life. Great comedies not only begin where they end; their first nights are often the beginning of a new comedy, which repeats and confirms in real life the text played on stage. *Tartuffe* was banned after its first showing in Versailles, which was attended (like *The Inspector General*) by the King and characters who were the doubles of those depicted in the play. During the next five years Molière had to fight with the Orgons and Tartuffes to realize the greatest of his comedies.

The least expected and most amazing theme of *The Inspector General* is the story of the origin of the comedy, which is written right into the play. The beginning and ending of the intrigue are made up of two letters intercepted and read on the stage: the first of these announces the arrival of the real inspector and the second is the unmasking of the false one. But in the second letter, the inspector in spite of himself is already the author of the comedy about the inspector in spite of himself.

"Each work, each novel," writes Tzvetan Todorov in his essay about *Les liaisons dangereuses*, the epistolary novel by Choderlos de Laclos, "tells, through its narration of events, the story of its own genesis, its own story. . . . Each novel tries to draw us into itself; and we can say, that it really does begin where it ends. For the existence of a novel is the last link in its plot and there, where the told story, the real-life story ends, that is where the story of its narration, of its literary history, begins."

The performance of a comedy is the last link in its plot even more so than in a novel. "The story of its narration" is the comedy which plays itself. The comical aspect of a story is then the story of the comedy. The day after the premiere of *The Inspector General*, Gogol also found himself in Khlestakov's shoes and playing a double role: that of inspector general and libeler. Except that the stage on which he found himself was not a provincial town, but Petersburg and all of Russia. The author of the comedy, *The Inspector General*, became the Great Inspector General. In spite of himself.

Upon Khlestakov's departure the Mayor sends for a blue Persian rug and puts it in his carriage. On this "magic carpet," as Nabokov calls it, the inspector in spite of himself makes his volatile exit backstage to the silvery sound of the horsebells and to the coachman's lyrical admonition to his magical steeds: "Hey, you my winged ones!" In a similar coach driven by a troika, Chichikov was leaving Russia at the end of the first part of *Dead Souls*, and so was Gogol himself, "our brother, the sinful man of letters," frightened by his own *Inspector* only three months after the opening night. "Tell the coachman they'll be given a ruble each, and—make 'em go fast, fast as *feldyegers*, and let 'em sing songs . . . ." Before the departure, in June 1836, he wrote to a friend: "Oh, not ever to be in one place for longer than two days. I would like to be a courier, a stage coachman, a messenger. I'm going abroad. A comedy writer should live far from his country." Khlestakov was the inspector in a country town for only two days. And he, too, had to run away.

The great inspector in spite of himself was suddenly seized by a panic. "They are all against me: government men, policemen, shopkeepers, men of letters. Together, they hiss at my play. I, myself, begin to abhor it." Gogol was scared of the accusations of the court clique that he had wanted to strike higher than the provincial bribe-takers and that he had slandered all of Russia. He was equally terrified by the voices of the enthusiasts who had acclaimed him as a democrat, a liberal, an implacable critic of autocracy; but most of all by those who like Belinsky saw in him "a poet of real life," the author of a Russian *Marriage of Figaro*. As everyone knows, *The Marriage of Figaro* was written by Khlestakov, "our brother, the sinful man of letters." In the early 1840s, isolated and debilitated by chronic ill health, Gogol underwent a crisis that marked a new phase in his life, labeled by some as mystical. "The royal subject of the czar" began to denounce his own masterpieces. In 1846, in *Addition to the Dénouement of the Inspector General*, he declares as the author of the comedy, "Do look attentively at the town described in the play. Everyone knows there isn't such a place in the whole of Russia."

In 1945, I toured China with a group of Polish writers. Our hosts were rather reluctant to take us around the streets. But one morning in Shanghai they let us out of the park. Two ragged children, a girl of maybe four and a boy of seven, came up to us, begging. "Centuries of hunger," I said to our guide, "cannot be erased in five years." He gave me a severe grin. "Take a good look, comrade, at these children. There are no such children in the whole of China."

IBSEN READ
ANEW

1   In the first scene of *The Misanthrope* Alceste rushes into Célimène's
drawing room and, in keeping with an old French stage tradition,
knocks over a chair. In the last scene he leaves never to return. *The
Misanthrope* may be read as bitter comedy or as tragedy. Alceste
abandons society either to wander off into a no man's land or to kill
himself. But had he taken Célimène to his house in the country,
Molière's play would have had a fitting epilogue in Strindberg's *The
Father*, or better yet in his *Dance of Death*, in which a Scandinavian
Célimène hangs old theatrical trophies above her marriage bed or
buries them in a chest. *The Misanthrope* prefigures Strindberg, but
its affinity with Ibsen is even greater.

   Like Alceste, who in the first scene of Molière's play rushes
into Célimène's drawing room, so Nora, in the first scene of Ibsen's
play, rushes into her "doll house." She too leaves alone in the last
scene, reversing the traditional resolution of comedy, in which a
wedding or the reunion of an estranged couple takes place. Like
Molière, Ibsen breaks the rules of the genre, but he inverts the
situation: the woman leaves, not the man; the wife, not the husband;
and she exits into the world, not the desert. *A Doll House* is the first
comedy whose "happy" resolution is a broken marriage ending with
the wife's departure.

   In both tragedy and comedy the turning point is the recognition scene which precedes the final resolution. In all the *Electra*

plays a sister recognizes her brother, a mother her son, behind the mask of the Stranger. In all comedies of error, from Plautus to Shakespeare and Molière, twins recognize each other, or a brother recognizes his sister beneath a man's disguise. And in the comic quid pro quo—from the ambiguous *Alcestis* of Euripides, in which the wife returns as a beautiful veiled stranger, to *The Marriage of Figaro*—the husband rediscovers his wife in the guise of the Stranger. But in *A Doll House* the traditional signs of tragedy and comedy are inverted.

At the outset of Ibsen's play the "strangers" are still outside Nora's house. "Them? Who cares about them!" she says. "They're strangers." In the last act, after the masked ball, Nora casts off her Sicilian costume but doesn't go to bed. She dresses to go out again. "Tonight I'm not sleeping." She won't even wait until morning: ". . . for eight years I've been living here with a stranger . . . . I can't spend the night in a strange man's room." In this new recognition scene the wife discovers the Stranger in her own husband. Hidden beneath the manifesto of women's emancipation—a theme which in itself had created such an outrage one hundred years ago—lies a provocative comedy of marital life, a new *physiologie du mariage*, after Balzac.

Throughout the play Nora secretly indulges in macaroons despite her husband's interdiction. Does she eat them because, like a child, she hankers after sweets? Why is her husband so strict about macaroons? One thing is clear: there's too much talk of macaroons in this "doll house." Nora has been married eight years, has three children, and is at least twenty-five years old. Her secret—hence exciting—munching of sweets seems a repetition and a displacement of those forbidden pleasures and solitary satisfactions of the child's bedroom. Nora's sole confidant is Dr. Rank. Only in his company does she feel at ease, and she even goes so far as to "put a macaroon in his mouth." Rank alone knows her inner thoughts:

NORA: Now there's just one last thing in the world that I have
an enormous desire to do. . . . It's something I have such
a consuming desire to say so Torvald could hear.
RANK: And why can't you say it?
NORA: I don't dare. It's quite shocking. . . . I have such a huge
desire to say—to hell and be damned!

In Act II Nora prepares her costume for the masked ball. Once again Rank is present. The maid has brought in a large box. I remember such boxes in my grandmother's room. They contained hat ribbons, long suede gloves, lavender-scented handkerchiefs, a small silver hook for fastening buttons on ankle boots, and white stockings from some ball of long ago.

NORA: Look here. Look.

RANK: Silk stockings.

NORA: Flesh-colored. Aren't they lovely? Now it's so dark here, but tomorrow—No, no, no, just look at the feet. Oh well, you might as well look at the rest. . . . *(Hits him lightly on the ear with the stockings.)* That's for you. *(Puts them away again.)*

RANK: And what other splendors am I going to see now?

NORA: Not the least bit more, because you have been naughty.

In stills from turn-of-the-century German and Scandinavian productions of *A Doll House*, Nora wears ankle-length skirts and white blouses with lace ruffles at the neck. When she goes out, she wears a hat with ribbons tied beneath her chin. She is always corseted. It would be difficult to imagine Nora in any other costume, although we readily set Greek and Shakespearean plays in periods besides their own. *A Doll House* retains a distinct *fin de siècle* flavor. Ibsen's comedy of manners—perhaps even more so than Chekhov's—depends as much on those evocative nineteenth-century details like oil lamps, top hats, and long dresses, as on character, plot, and dialogue. The nineteenth-century audiences of *A Doll House* were shocked when Nora showed Rank her stockings, for at that time the secrets of the female body began at the ankle. If Nora shows her knees, the scene loses its impudent effect.[1]

At the masked ball Nora, costumed as a Sicilian peasant, is to dance a tarantella. She is disguised. The word "disguise" is used repeatedly in Act II, and always with special emphasis. In one of his brilliant essays Northrop Frye describes three elements or "periods" in Shakespearean comedy. First comes "a somber and gloomy period" of strict rule, of discipline and fasting under the domination of an authoritarian father or husband. The second period is one "of license and confusion of values represented by the carnival . . . , the phase of temporarily lost identity . . . usually portrayed by the stock device of impenetrable disguise . . . . Third is the period of festivity itself."

---

[1]"Ibsen's play *A Doll House* is often costumed as if it took place in 1900 or even later, but it was published in 1879. The state of women's consciousness developed a good deal between those dates, and so did their clothes. To dress this drama up as if it were a late Shaw play, pregnant with the nascent sense of modern female power and independence, is ridiculous. Its action is contemporary with the suicide of Anna Karenina (1876), and it should look so and look as if it is felt so, if it is to have its proper impact" (Anne Hollander, *Seeing through Clothes*).

This third Shakespearean period does not exist in Ibsen. But the first two are graphically presented in *A Doll House*.

The rehearsal of a dance takes place in Act II. Nora "snatches the tambourine up from the box, then a long, varicolored shawl, which she throws around herself, whereupon she springs forward." In this scene, the most theatrical Ibsen ever wrote, the stage directions are even more important than the dialogue. Rand accompanies Nora on the piano, Helmer plays the director by showing her how to dance. But Nora will not obey. She dances ever more wildly. Attempts to stop her are fruitless. "Her hair loosens and falls over her shoulders; she does not notice, but goes on dancing."

A tarantella is a popular dance of Southern Italy performed by villagers who believed dancing rapidly until exhausted would offset the poisonous bite of the tarantula spider. In this dance of life and death Nora achieves an ecstasy she has never known before. Suddenly she turns pale, and the rhetoric of "emancipation" vanishes from the stage. Once again Ibsen reverses the traditional signs. The "disguise" is no loss of identity—rather it is the unexpected and sudden regaining of an identity heretofore unknown. But perhaps Northrop Frye is also wrong. Maybe it is the same with the girls in Shakespeare who discover their hidden Eros while disguised as boys. Nora, in her dance, is freed without her knowing it. She is now her own body and soul.

Nora again dances the tarantella in Act III, this time offstage, at the masked ball. She is enthusiastically applauded, "although the performance," says her husband, "may have been a bit too naturalistic—I mean it rather overstepped the proprieties of art." He uses what was still then (1879) a new word—"naturalistic"—and opposes Nora's passion and fury to "art." "Art" for him means bourgeois decency: Nora, in her "naturalistic" dance, does not break the rules of art but defies social convention: ". . . you dance as if your life were at stake." For the first time, Nora stepped out in public without a "corset." And this new Nora is whisked home by her husband after she dances. "An exit should always be effective." Ibsen's heroines always exit dramatically. Nora leaves her "doll house" slamming the door.

A Doll House marked the beginning of a new theater that changed not only the drama but also the stage. The stage had not been ready for naturalistic drama. Doors painted on canvas "rocked at the slightest touch." When Nora slams the door at the end of the play, "the whole house shakes," wrote Strindberg in his famous foreword to *Miss Julie*. "Real" doors with "real" doorknobs were first introduced in Scandinavian theater—even before André Antoine's innovations in stage design—at the Stockholm premiere of *The Wild Duck* (1885), which was also famous for displaying a wash basin and a chamber pot on stage.

In both *The Misanthrope* and *A Doll House*, the entire action takes place in a closed room. The only difference is that Célimène's aristocratic salon has been replaced by a bourgeois parlor whose windows, if one could open them, look out not on elegant carriages arriving from Versailles or the Louvre, but on the corner of a narrow gas-lit street in Christiania. Onstage is the "doll house"; offstage is what Ibsen called the "raw world." From this "raw world" Ibsen draws the themes and obsessions that will haunt his plays throughout his career: bankruptcies and betrayals, blackmail and fear of public censure, young women of modest means who are given away in marriage to old widowers, legitimate and illegitimate children who have to be reared.

Onstage is a drawing room, offstage is a mailbox. This new dramaturgy requires new props. In *A Doll House*, the small objects of everyday life create dramatic tension: an ordinary mailbox fulfills the same dramatic function as Desdemona's handkerchief. This mailbox, unopened for thirty-one hours, contains a letter with either a sentence of death or a miraculous reprieve. The mailbox is a new medium for suspense, and facilitates the classical postponement of the denouement. When finally opened, the mailbox will be found to contain not a compromising love letter, but a forged note. To save her husband, Nora had borrowed money without his consent by forging her dead father's signature. Ibsen was the first to discover the props of a new marital comedy. The husband has the keys to the mailbox. *A Doll House* came after Balzac.

2 In the second half of the nineteenth century, the novel—history of manners, platform for social reform, confessional for women—became the leading literary genre. This bourgeois epos, particularly after *Madame Bovary* (1857) and *Anna Karenina* (1876), achieved the artistic and social respectability and the importance that the theater had lost after the Romantic period. Ibsen restored them to the theater. For twenty years, from *A Doll House* to *When We Dead Awaken*, his plays challenged the novel's preeminence as a forum for depicting social concerns. But this realistic drama could challenge the new prose epic only after a new dramatic was discovered. The history of two or three generations, told in hundreds of pages, with the setting moving back and forth from the exteriors to the streets and landscapes, had to be condensed into two days separated by one night, and the action confined to one bourgeois parlor.

This new bourgeois drama found its model, strangely enough, in Greek tragedy, whose prologues recall the past and foreshadow the future and whose action, limited to five episodes, begins at dawn and ends at dusk in one and the same place. Among the patterns of classical tragedy one stands out as being particularly flexible: the homecoming. It is repeated from *Electra* to *Hamlet* to Pinter's *Homecoming*. Ibsen uses this model twice: in *Ghosts* and *The Wild Duck*.

Critics have often compared Mrs. Alving to Oedipus, and the Alving house atop the gloomy fjord to the House of Atreus in the *Oresteia*. All playwrights with the exception of Shakespeare and Racine wilt when compared to Aeschylus and Sophocles. Yet such comparisons have interpretative value. Ibsen brought fatum into the House of the Alvings. Fatum as a technical term is the "higher necessity" which, in addition to realistic motivation, governs the fortune and misfortune of the tragic protagonist. It is not easy to introduce fatum into a bourgeois parlor furnished with a sofa and comfortable armchairs, even if the rainy fjord is visible through French windows. In *Ghosts*, Ibsen replaces the Greek Furies, who tracked down murderers by following their bloody trail, with the spirochetes of syphilis.

In the Renaissance, syphilis was regarded as the result of original sin—the poisonous worm in the apple plucked from the tree of the knowledge of good and evil. In the Victorian period, syphilis was not only a shameful disease, it was thought of as a fitting punishment meted out by a Puritan God to the impure. The God of the Old Testament punished sinners to the tenth generation. As a hereditary disease, syphilis was a stigma and, like cancer today, aroused *odium* and *angst*. It was a pollution, as *miasma* was to the Greeks. "The infection," Mrs. Alving says to the pastor, "came right within our own four walls." It kills her son.

Comedy ends with marriage, tragedy with death. But aside from this "biological" opposition between these two genres, there exists another opposition, more substantial, which we might call "anthropological." [2] In the tragic model, the Father is more powerful than the Son, and symbolically kills him. In the model of comedy, the Son is more powerful than the Father, the Daughter than the

---

[2] " . . . if society is to go on, daughters must be disloyal to their parents and sons must destroy (replace) their fathers" (Edmund Leach, *Claude Lévi-Strauss*).

Mother. Free from the burdens of the past, the Son and Daughter in comedy leave their parents' household to establish their own—symbolically killing their parents. In tragedy, the past impinges upon the present, demanding of each new generation reparations for the sins of its forefathers. The ghost of Hamlet's father symbolically kills Hamlet: "Adieu, adieu, adieu! Remember me."

Ghosts are found not only in polluted blood. "It's not only what we inherit from our fathers and mothers that keeps on returning in us," says Mrs. Alving. "It's all kinds of old dead doctrines and opinions and beliefs . . . . They must be haunting our whole country, ghosts everywhere—so many and thick, they're like grains of sand. And there we are, the lot of us, so miserably afraid of the light." Marx wrote almost the same lines in the beginning of his *The Eighteenth Brumaire of Louis Bonaparte* (1852): "The tradition of all the dead generations weighs like a nightmare on the brain of the living." The past paralyzes: physically, as in the case of Osvald, Captain Alving's son; and morally, as in the case of everyone in the old house atop the misty fjord. The past transforms them into the living dead: ". . . we are ghosts, all of us."

But *Ghosts* has two endings, not one. In the manifest tragic ending the mother holds a vial filled with poison beside her dying son's head. At the end of the play's hidden comedy, Regina, Captain Alving's illegitimate daughter, leaves the stricken household. She is the second woman in Ibsen who abandons her home to live on her own. Strong and healthy, Regina is free of remorse and of the ghosts of the past.

> My spouse bore me a blighted boy,
> Our slavey pupped a bouncing bitch.
> Paternity, thy name is joy
> When the wise sire knows which is which.
>
> Both swear I am that self-same man
> By whom their infants were begotten.
> Explain, fate, if you care and can
> Why one is sound and one is rotten.

Joyce wrote his "Epilogue to Ibsen's *Ghosts*" after seeing the play performed in Paris in 1934. It was a time when the French theater was witnessing the triumphs of Giraudoux and the first plays of Anouilh. Ibsen had never been, and was never again to be, as demode as he was then. Tragedy seemed no less bombastic and artificial than opera, and it seemed bearable only when subject to parody or burlesque. But Joyce's witty poem is intended not just to make fun of *Ghosts*. It is also an interpretation which reverses a model through "de-montage" or, to use a more fashionable term, "deconstruction."[3]

In the prologue to Plautus's *Amphitryon* Mercury tries to appease the disappointed spectators who came to see a comedy but are presented with a tragedy: "Don't worry. I am a god and for you I will transform tragedy into comedy without removing a single comma." Mercury, master of transformation and sponsor of alchemists, is the patron saint of Joyce. In Joyce's "Epilogue," the incorrigible Captain Alving returns from the dead as a merry ghost to reread *Ghosts* as a comedy. Or, in keeping with Plautus's Mercury, as a "tragico-comedy":

> The more I dither on and drink
> My midnight bowl of spirit punch
> The firmlier I feel and think
> Friend Manders came too oft to lunch.

Although twenty-eight years have passed since Pastor Manders sent Mrs. Alving back home, she still dotes on him. She wants Osvald to be the pastor's spiritual son, and she does not want him to inherit anything from his father; she even imagines that Osvald resembles Manders, "No, it's nothing like him, not at all. To me, Osvald has more of a minister's look about the mouth." Here Ibsen hints at a darker play than *Ghosts*, a play he was never to write.

Yet Osvald is his father's son. At the end of Act I, Mrs. Alving and Manders overhear him struggling with Regina in the dining room. "Osvald! Are you crazy? Let me go!" Twenty-two years before Mrs. Alving heard these same words from the same dining room when Regina's mother was protesting Captain Alving's advances.

In nearly half a century I have seen seven performances of *Ghosts* on various stages and in various languages. But each time this

---

[3]The oldest and most beautiful image of deconstruction can be found in Enûma elish, the Babylonian book of genesis (Second Millennium).
"O Lord,
Command destruction and construction, and may both come true.
May your spoken work destroy the constellation, then speak
    then speak again and may it be intact."
He spoke, and at his work the constellation was destroyed.
He spoke again, and the constellation was [re] constructed.
The gods, his fathers, seeing [the power of] his word, rejoiced,
    paid homage: "Marduk is king."
(Thorkild Jacobsen, *The Treasures of Darkness: A History of Mesopotamian Religion*).

scene was enacted, it conveyed a sense of horror. The past returns to haunt Mrs. Alving. "Those two . . . have come back." But neither the director nor the audience has reason to share Pastor Manders's indignation and Mrs. Alving's dread. Through the partly opened door Regina's low, sensual laugh should be heard. It is the only moment in the play when we hear laughter in the gloomy household. When Mrs. Alving invites Regina to share a half-bottle of champagne with Osvald (nothing better marks Ibsen's sharpness in characterization than that half-bottle of champagne—Mrs. Alving's feelings are equally half-way), the young couple's candlelit "engagement" party resembles a funeral repast. "There is a positive odor of spiritual paraffin," Henry James has written of Ibsen, with infallible taste.

In Greek tragedy, myth sanctioned fate, the predestination by a "higher necessity." There are no myths of gods in *Ghosts*. The sanction for tragic necessity and for its metaphysics is Puritan theology. And for this reason Osvald alone is stricken with syphilis-fatum. No one else—not even Captain Alving's wife or his mistress—is physically afflicted. Paralysis punishes the son for the "sin" of his father. If Pastor Manders had literary talent, he could have written his own *Ghosts*: it would have been a didactic "tragedy" about a rakish captain, and about a woman who read books, lost the faith, failed to fulfill her role as wife and mother, sent her son to Paris, the capital of sin, blessed his incestuous union with his own half-sister, and, finally, out of pity, was ready to give him poison. God refused the pay-off: the orphanage, whose founding is a hypocritical act of penance, is destroyed by fire, ". . . this is God's fiery judgment on a wayward house!"

Throughout his career, Ibsen had both Manders and Kierkegaard under his skin. Until the very end he grappled, not always victoriously, with them. The traces of his struggles are found in all his plays, from *Ghosts* to *When We Dead Awaken*. This inner conflict resulted in the strange nexus of exasperating flatness and moral tension that characterizes his plays. The incongruity beneath the surface of his tightly constructed dramas, the puzzling omissions and dark holes in his relentless dialogue in which everything is said except what is most important—these are at once the strength and weakness of Ibsen's dramaturgy. It is a dramaturgy that never lets itself be reduced to any one narrow ideological interpretation, such as the progressive Fabianism that Bernard Shaw sought to impose on it.

In *Ghosts*, Puritan theology is deflated by Pastor Manders's hypocrisy and cowardice. But the stage has its own idiom, no less potent than plot and dialogue, which sustains an atmospheric tragedy. In the last scene, white mountain peaks and glaciers illuminated by the rising sun are projected onto the glass doors of the veranda by a magic lantern. The rainy fjord, the cold whiteness of glaciers, and the sun rising above this inhuman landscape at the hour of death are laden with traditional symbolism. The atmospheric climax stands for a "higher necessity." Symbols that have been thrown out the door return through the windows. *Ghosts*, like many of Ibsen's later plays, has a dual setting: a bourgeois parlor cluttered with furniture, where a realistic and contemporary "family drama in three acts" takes place, and the primeval and archaic world of elemental forces of nature offstage. The characters seem unequal to the play's tragic pathos. Mrs. Alving attains only a momentary and incomplete self-awareness. For this Tragic Mother, there is no maturity and liberation other than despair. Two different plays coexist in *Ghosts*: Joyce's ironic lines ridicule the "ghosts" and uncover a comedy hidden in the *Ghosts*.

The protagonist of this comedy is Regina, "that splendid girl so alive with health and beauty." She takes everything that remains from Captain Alving's bequest and the remainder of the dowry that the cripple Engstrand, her legal father, received for marrying her mother. Like Jean the valet in Strindberg's *Miss Julie*, she learns a smattering of French to pursue a career in the world. "A poor girl's only got her youth; she'd better use it—or else she'll find herself barefoot at Christmas before she knows it."

When finally "this long horrible farce ends," the Captain Alving Memorial Orphan's Home will be transformed into a brothel for seamen: Captain Alving's Home. But Regina does not plan to return to Little Harbor Street; if she does, she will return as a Madam. She is a prototype of Frank Wedekind's Lulu (1891). This most gloomy of Ibsen's dramas contains in embryo the naturalistic farce and the anti-bourgeois grotesque theater of the next two decades.

3 The theme of "the homecoming" recurs in *The Wild Duck*. Gregers Werle returns to his father's house on the day before his father's wedding. The past is buried and forgotten. The son comes back to unearth it. Fifteen years earlier, while his mother was seriously ill, his father had had an affair with their young housekeeper. When she became pregnant, he gave her away in marriage to Gregers's old schoolmate. Old Werle gave Gina's husband money to study photography and to set up a studio. At the play's opening, Gina, Hjalmar, and fourteen-year-old Hedvig are living happily in this studio.

Such is the prologue of *The Wild Duck* as contemporary comedy of manners. The tragedy will be played out in the ensuing four acts, during the next forty-eight hours, in the same studio. In this tragedy, the past returns to kill: Hedvig, the victim of a recalled past and of a truth that serves no one, shoots herself with an old pistol. *The Wild Duck*'s tragic plot has the son return to avenge his mother. The sacrificial lamb is his father's illegitimate daughter—his own half-sister.

In *The Wild Duck*, characters from a bourgeois comedy act out a tragedy. Therefore they must also play some additional mythic parts. Hedvig is a new Iphigenia who sacrifices herself to regain her father's love. The masks of Greek Erinyes represented dogs' heads. Gregers Werle is the envoy of the dark past, the "truth" hunter, like the ancient Furies: "If I could choose, above all else I'd like to be a clever dog . . . the kind that goes to the bottom after wild ducks when they dive under and bite fast into the weeds down in the mire." This "clever dog" has an archetypal stigma of ugliness and in the comic plot leaves his room smelling of soot, having forgotten to bolt the stove door shut.

The characters of the comedy can act out their tragedy only if a "symbolic place" other than the realistic setting has been created. In *Ghosts*, and even more dramatically with the "white horses" seen through the windows in *Rosmersholm*, a locus for the fatum is provided by the "offstage" landscape. The most significant dramatic invention in *The Wild Duck* is its stage design. The play's "symbolic place" is the loft: "The room, which is fairly spacious, appears to be a loft. To the right is a sloping roof with great panes of glass, half hidden by a blue curtain."

The loft is both onstage and offstage, partly visible and partly invisible. The shade is pulled up twice. For the first time in Act II, at night:

> The doorway opens on an extensive, irregular loft room with many nooks and corners, and two separate chimney shafts ascending through it. Clear moonlight streams through skylights into certain parts of the large room; others lie in deep shadow.

And again in Act III;

> . . . morning sunlight shines through the skylights. A few doves fly back and forth; others perch, cooing, on the rafters. Chickens cackle now and then from back in the loft. . . . [Hjalmar] pulls a cord; inside a curtain descends, its lower portion composed of a strip of old sailcloth, the upper part being a piece of worn-out fishnetting. By this means, the floor of the loft is rendered invisible.

The "invisible" part of the loft is invariably symbolic. What can be seen of the loft—"the wonderful adjoining room"—belongs to the comic plot of *The Wild Duck*. In this "real" place Gina keeps her poultry and pigeons. Here old Ekdal re-lives his past as a hunter by tracking down rabbits with an old pistol. On Sundays, father and son play handymen there and work at various odd jobs. For Hedvig, this loft is an enchanted world of strange and useless objects—as in Alain-Fournier's *Le grand meaulnes* (1913), a world of broken cuckoo clocks and old picture books. But for Gina "the green world" of her daughter, husband, and father-in-law is just one more room to clean and air out.

GREGERS: I, for my part, don't thrive on marsh gas.
HJALMAR: Oh, don't start that rubbish again!
GINA: Lord knows there isn't any marsh gas here, Mr. Werle; every blessed day I air the place out.

Two "lofts" are contrasted in this brief exchange: the realistic loft and the loft of dark symbols, the loft of the comedy of manners and the symbolic loft of lies and redemption. Gregers transforms the realistic loft, which is part chicken coop, pigeon house, and warren into an underground inferno, a swamp giving off deadly fumes like poisonous lies. He changes the loft, in which a fourteen-year-old girl keeps an injured duck in a basket, into the "depths of the sea":

HEDVIG: But to me it sounds strange when someone else says "depths of the sea."
GREGERS: But why? Tell me why?
HEDVIG: . . . because it's only an attic.
GREGERS: Are you so sure of that?
HEDVIG: *(astonished.)* That it's an attic!
GREGERS: Yes. Do you know that for certain?
HEDVIG: *(speechless, stares at him open-mouthed.)*

My interpretation of this "slippage" into symbolism owes a lot to Mary McCarthy's brilliant piece on *The Wild Duck*, which, written in the mid-fifties, still contains some of the most illuminating pages on Ibsen. Symbols possess a blurred quality, and are easily misused, in both a semantic and moral sense. Green, in the middle of the color spectrum, has traditionally symbolized both rebirth and decay; it is the color of grass growing in spring as well as the color of rotten meat. Gregers sees the seaweed and rabbit feed in the "realistic" loft as the "depths of the sea" from which there is no escape and as the swamps in which one drowns. "I wouldn't say you're wounded; but you're wandering in a poisonous swamp, Hjalmar. You've got an insidious disease in your system, and you've gone to the bottom to die in the dark."

The visible and invisible parts of the loft, the realistic place and the symbolic one, correspond to two levels of language, two opposed systems of signs. The first is that of everyday language, "low," concrete, rich in details, in which manners and customs, even the prices of food and services, are important, as in the beginning of Act II, where the vocabulary of stage directions matches that of dialogue:

> GINA: *(lays her sewing aside and takes a pencil and a small notebook from the table.)* Do you remember how much we spent for butter today?
>
> HEDVIG: It was one sixty-five.
>
> GINA: That's right. *(Making a note.)* It's awful how much butter gets used in this house. And then there is so much for smoked sausage, and for cheese—let me see—*(Making more notes.)* and so much for ham—hmm. *(Adds.)* Yes, that adds right up to—
>
> HEDVIG: And then there's the beer.
>
> GINA: Yes, of course. *(Makes another note.)* It mounts up—but it can't be helped.
>
> HEDVIG: Oh, but you and I had no hot food for dinner, 'cause Daddy was out.
>
> GINA: No, and that's to the good. What's more, I also took in eight crowns fifty for photographs.

The second language in *The Wild Duck* is "lofty" and figurative; it exchanges real situations and unpleasant conflicts for their symbolic equivalents:

> GREGERS: My dear Hjalmar, I suspect you've got a bit of the wild duck in you.
>
> HJALMAR: Of the wild duck? What do you mean?
>
> GREGERS: You've plunged to the bottom and clamped hold of the seaweed.

Or, as in old Ekdal's last words, just before the play ends: "The woods take revenge." The forest of symbols is never neutral, never innocent. It demands sacrificial victims. Hedvig identifies herself not with the wild duck she keeps in a basket, but with the "wild duck" turned into a ritual victim by the murky symbolists. Hedvig is not only a symbolic victim; she is also a victim of symbolism.

The invisible part of the loft and the ambiguous symbols of the play's second level of language introduce the metaphysics of tragedy into the disgusting realistic comedy. They transform a trivial farce into a drama with a sinister ending. Shakespeare's method was different. The "tortures of the cruel world" and the long "cold night" which "turns us all to fools and madmen" belonged to a world in which one could call heaven, even if it was empty, or appeal to a moral order, even if it did not exist. In *The Wild Duck*, the characters of the bourgeois comedy do not mature into tragic roles. They eat herring and drink beer; they even have sturgeon and Tokay, as at the reception in Werle's house. And when afterwards they play blind man's buff, the game is not meant to symbolize moral blindness; it provides entertainment after a good supper.

The dramatic incongruity in *The Wild Duck* is finally a moral inconsistency. Nora's prototype was a young Norwegian woman, a novelist and playwright. She contracted debts so that her consumptive husband could go to Italy. When the time came to repay them, she forged a note. She then went to Ibsen for advice, and he, like Mrs. Linde in *A Doll House*, suggested she reveal everything to her husband. The consequences were disastrous: her husband assumed sole custody of their children, and committed her to an asylum. There is much of Ibsen in Gregers Werle with his "acute case of moralistic fever." *The Wild Duck* is a cold shower for Nora enthusiasts, if not a personal reckoning for Ibsen.

But this reckoning is not carried through to the end. Gregers is not entirely compromised. Mary McCarthy was right: Gregers, the thirteenth at the table, is like the avenging Furies; he inspires dread. Tragic fate in *The Wild Duck* recalls the sacrificial lamb with fake bathos. Hedvig's suicide is a pathetic affirmation of the Puritan morality which views hereditary diseases as punishments for the sins of the forefathers, and according to which the past always returns to haunt the present. As in *Ghosts*, Kierkegaard's shadow looms large over *The Wild Duck*. But only his shadow, not his greatness.

The schism between the pathetic and the ludicrous in *The Wild Duck* is even deeper than that in *Ghosts*, although it is more hidden. To uncover it, we must have recourse once again to radical interpretation. Hedvig shoots herself in the hidden part of the loft: the "dual" scenography permits "the wild duck" to remain unseen until the very end. Yet another ending is possible. Hedvig could return to the stage holding in her arms the wild duck she has killed. The symbol would then become a prop. The "sacrifice" would have been accomplished, but in a modest and convincing way, half ironic, half sad within the limits of the moral status of the characters. The very ending of this "untragic" *Wild Duck* would have Gina once again airing out the loft.

I do not recommend this ending to *The Wild Duck*. The piercing of the tragic bathos is intended only to uncover its bitter comedy and another dramatic pattern, one which Chekhov will discover and, after him, Friedrich Dürrenmatt and Max Frisch in their "adaptations" and continuations of Ibsen's themes.

The example of Chekhov is probably the most relevant. *The Sea Gull* was written in 1895–96, a little more than ten years after *The Wild Duck*. The use and symbolic function of the water bird in the title seems modeled on Ibsen. Like a sea gull, the young Nina is associated with a lake, and like a sea gull, she is fated and doomed. Trigorin asserts quite clearly at the end of Act II: ". . . a young girl like you lives all her life beside a lake; she loves a lake like a sea gull, is happy and free. A man comes along by chance, sees her, and having nothing better to do, destroys her, just like this sea gull here."

The young Treplev, having fallen in love with Nina, writes symbolic plays for her and performs them on a little stage which, when the curtain rises, reveals the view of a lake. When Nina becomes infatuated with Trigorin, the lover of Treplev's mother, the son shoots a sea gull and lays it at Nina's feet. "Soon, in the same way, I shall kill myself," he says.

Here for the first time a symbol was "reified," transformed into a prop. Chekhov's dramatic strategy is to force us to forget the prophecy which is fulfilled at the end quite unexpectedly. Chekhov cautions us not to believe in symbols. Nina says in this scene: ". . . I can't understand you, it's as if you were talking in symbols. This sea gull, I suppose, is another symbol. But, forgive me, I don't understand."

But in the end Nina begins to believe in symbols, and has symbolically identified herself with a sea gull. When Trigorin, with whom she had lived, threw her over, she wrote him letters and signed them "Sea Gull." In the last act, after all her defeats both as actress and as woman, she returns to the lake to meet Treplev for the last time. "I ought to have been killed. . . . I am a sea gull. . . ." When she leaves late at night in the direction of the lake, the force and logic of the symbol make us believe that Nina will kill herself. But it is Treplev who shoots himself—with the same gun that had killed the sea gull. At the very end, just before the sound of the shot offstage, Shamrayev, steward of the estate, takes a stuffed sea gull from a cupboard. For the second time a symbol has been changed into a prop. Through this reduction of symbols into props the bitter human tragedy, ironical and *non-symbolic*, was presented by Chekhov in a previously unknown and poignant way. Chekhov learned much from Ibsen, both from his strength and from his weakness.

4 Chekhov wrote: "If in the first act a gun hangs on the wall, in the last act it must go off." In laying down this dramatic precept, he must surely have had *Hedda Gabler* in mind. Hedda inherits two pistols from her father. She fires the first one over Judge Brack's head when he approaches the house from the garden; and again at the end, when she shoots herself. The other pistol is fired offstage. It kills Eilert Lövborg. But the two pistols in *Hedda Gabler* are not only props exploited by Ibsen with iron-clad dramatic logic and preordained consequences; they also have sexual undertones. A Scandinavian Madame Bovary, well read in romantic novels, gives Lövborg a pistol: "use it now . . . and beautifully." But the fatal shot wounds him "in the stomach—more or less," and is fired in the parlor of the red-haired Mademoiselle Diana.

Ibsen's setting for *Hedda Gabler* is striking. The action takes place in a spacious salon with French windows which open out on a veranda and a garden in the "fashionable part of town," not a fjord. The windows are curtained; the theater had already learned the advantages of gaslight.

In the first scene, Hedda orders the curtains drawn. She can't stand sunlight. This is our first glimpse of her character. The salon is spacious and the furniture arrangement makes it possible for two separate conversations to be carried on at the same time. The old-fashioned *a parte* is no longer necessary. Chekhov borrowed this "contrapuntal" dialogue from Ibsen and masterfully refined it.

The crucial part of the stage design is the room in the background, with a huge portrait of "a handsome, elderly man in a general's uniform" hanging on the wall behind the sofa. In the last scene Hedda will enter this room, draw the curtains, and shoot herself in front of her father's portrait. Hedda Tesman, two months pregnant, kills Hedda Gabler. The inner room, whose only exit leads to the salon in the foreground, is at once the concrete and the symbolic setting of the conflict between the Father/superego and the id. By shooting herself, Hedda kills the shadow of her Father and the child she never wanted. The "shadow" of the father kills the daughter. In contrast to the earlier dramas, *Lady from the Sea* and *Rosmersholm*, where the prehistory of the conflicts, traumas, and sexual complexes festers beneath the surface, and though continuing to grow they are never seen, in *Hedda Gabler* nothing remains unspoken.

In this case study of a neurosis, the mother's place is left empty. Hedda was raised by her father, who would have preferred a son. She rode horses and learned to shoot guns. In school, like a tomboy, she pulled her girlfriends' hair. She can barely resist pulling Thea's blond locks in Act II. In the last *Hedda Gabler* I saw, in Bochum in 1977, Peter Zadek directed the scene of Hedda's and Thea's drinking bout with distinct lesbian undertones. It is an extreme though not arbitrary reading of the text. In this record of sexual neurosis, the inversion and displacement of libido are intended. Thirty-year-old Hedda Gabler is frigid.

General Gabler's daughter not only wants to rule in a man's world. Unable to assume her female sexual role, she escapes by playing out the male one in her imagination. She demands that Lövborg initiate her into masculine rites and describe his visits to the red-haired Diana. Imaginary sex is vicarious. Hedda, rejecting the traditional roles of wife and mother, is condemned to live vicariously, full of the frustration and sense of emptiness which she calls deadly boredom. Madame Bovary's love affairs with shallow men were substitutions for the romantic ecstasies she read about in contemporary novels. For General Gabler's daughter these flights and escapes are ruled out. She has only her inner room "with its heavy curtains and her father's portrait."

It is not only sexual fulfillment that Hedda strives for through imagination. Until the very last scene, all her passions and hatreds are realized only by acts of substitution. The manuscript of Lövborg's new book is twice called his and Thea's "child"; Hedda commits a substitute "infanticide" by burning it in the fireplace. The pistol shot above Judge Brack's head was a substitute murder and a substitute sexual act. Fear paralyzed her twice before: once when she was afraid to shoot Lövborg for his aggressive advances, and then a second time when she was afraid to sleep with him. Handing the pistol to Lövborg is murder by intent: the shot that kills him, in keeping with the logic of the dramaturgy, symbolically castrates him as well.

In coded messages, myths, dreams, and unconscious acts, opposite terms are interchangeable: they assume the guise of their antitheses. As in Racine and Chekhov (although in Chekhov it is deeply hidden), the appeal of death in Ibsen disguises itself as the pulse of life, the instinct toward self-destruction is masked as libido. *Hedda Gabler* appears to return to the realistic technique of the earlier dramas, but along with *Rosmersholm*, it marks the beginning of Ibsen's last cycle of plays, from *Little Eyolf* to *When We Dead Awaken*, each of which repeats the theme of sexual frustration leading to self-destruction. With the exception of his final masterpiece, *John Gabriel Borkman*, in all these plays the balance between the realistic world and its symbolic projection is broken.

In his biography of Ibsen (1957), Michael Meyer entitled his chapter on *Hedda Gabler* "Portrait of the Dramatist as a Young Woman." *"Madame Bovary—c'est moi,"* Flaubert once wrote, and Hedda Gabler is in some sense Ibsen's alter ego. The psychoanalysis of Hedda would no doubt become the merciless psychoanalysis of her author. But in psychoanalytic interpretations of the author or of his work Ibsen's invention and artistic discoveries are usually neglected, and what is even more important, the historical context, the customs and atmospheric realism of the *fin de siècle* are altogether lost.

Ibsen never read a page of Freud. Neither did Strindberg. In the early 1890s Freud began his first methodical studies of hysteria; in 1895 he announced his first analysis of dreams; and he used the term "psychoanalysis" for the first time in 1896. The Scandinavian Miss Julies and Heddas were finding their dramatists in Strindberg and Ibsen while the Viennese Julies and Heddas were finding their analyst in Freud.

In his preliminary notes for *Hedda Gabler* Ibsen wrote: "Men and women don't belong to the same century." Freud could have written this. Balzac, in his introduction to *La comédie humaine*, wrote about two opposing realms: the *pays légal*, constituted by laws, hierarchal authorities, and bureaucracies, and the *pays réel*, one of cooking and fashions, beliefs and superstitions. Almost concurrently, Ibsen and Freud showed that there is yet a third *pays*, a "sexual" realm in which men and women live side by side, but in different centuries. Perhaps the beginning of the sexual emancipation of women from the upper classes became more visible and dramatic in Scandinavia and cosmopolitan Vienna where feudal structures persisted longer and began to crumble violently only toward the end of the nineteenth century. It is this sexual tension that Strindberg later characterized as "the war between the sexes." Arthur Schnitzler could here be summoned as another literary witness. Ibsen has often been read through Freud. It would be illuminating to read Freud through Ibsen, Strindberg, and Schnitzler.

From this perspective, *The Interpretation of Dreams* (1899) appears surprisingly like a grand, realistic novel of manners, a collection of dramas of the waning of the "Belle Epoque." Perhaps even as the greatest novel of the turn of the century. In this new "physiology of marriage" sexual and social discrimination against women is shown in dozens of dream examples—before marriage, outside of marriage, and within marriage. But the sexual failure of women in roles still dictated by a patriarchical family has its counterpart in the sexual failure of men and the sexual neuroses of children, both legitimate and illegitimate. All the failures of the conjugal bedroom are transmitted to the taboos and prohibitions of the nursery. Perhaps the Oedipus and Electra complexes are universal, but *The Interpretation of Dreams* and Ibsen's play show them at work only in bourgeois society. In both Freud and Ibsen the parental home is hell. Freud considered his dream-symbols universal. However, in his *Interpretation of Dreams* women indulge in reveries of top hats and pistols.[4] We need not even look at the stills of Ibsen performances of the nineteenth century to realize that these presumably universal dream-symbols were stamped and shaped by the costumes, uniforms, and manners of the period. The exchange mechanism between the remnant of wakefulness and the realm of dreams may be universal but Freud's "Egyptian Book of Dreams" is also a testimony to the society that produced "Art Nouveau." One can see the Secession Angels of the *fin de siècle* as much in Freud as in Klimt. Czesław Miłosz writes in his *Treatise on Poetry*:

> Secession angels
> Sat in the dim waterclosets of their parents' homes
> Pondering the link between sex and the soul,
> Healing their sorrows and migraines in Vienna
> (Dr. Freud is from Galicia from what I have heard).
> And Anna Csilag's hair kept growing and growing,
> The chests of hussars were decked out with braid.
> [trans. Lillian Vallee]

5 *The Master Builder* ends with a fall from a tower. The tower is invisible. It is offstage. Only the steps leading to it are visible. The fall is both real and symbolic: it is a fall from the tower and a sign of the fall. Solness's fall resolves two conflicts, two plots, which started long before the beginning of the play.

Solness built his first house on ashes and rubble. It was on the site of his wife's house which had been destroyed by fire. Their twin sons died a few months after that fire, and Solness's wife never

---

[4]"The hat has been adequately established as a symbol of the genital organ, most frequently the male, through analyses of dreams . . . . In phantasies and in numerous symptoms the head also appears as a symbol of the male genitals, or, if one prefers to put it so, as a representation of them . . . " (Freud, "A Connection between a Symbol and a Symptom" [1916] in *Character and Culture*).

approached him again. The disaster marked the beginning of his career as a master builder. But it also brought guilt. Solness had seen a crack in the chimney in the attic long before the fire but told no one about it. The crack was not the cause of the fire, but Solness is plagued by guilt, as though he had dreamt of his father's or mother's death only to have the dream come true. In Puritan and pietistic morality one is always responsible for one's thoughts and intentions. "I feel there's almost a kind of beneficial self-torment in letting Aline do me an injustice. . . . it's rather like making a small payment on a boundless, incalculable debt—."

The Solness's marriage is dead; husband and wife are kept together only by a sense of duty and the need for self-torment. His "guilt" and her "responsibility" for the death of their children have reduced sex to ashes: there is no more desire, no renewal. Remorse becomes a sickness, a paralyzing trauma. The Kierkegaardian analysis of conscience needs only the change of terms to become pre-Freudian analysis.

In *Fear and Trembling*, some of the most superb pages Kierkegaard ever wrote, Isaac's trauma is compared time and again to the experience of a child weaned from its mother's breast. In Kierkegaard trauma and the memory of guilt are changed into a symbolic abscess, unconscious but always festering. Just as in Ibsen. Just as in Freud.

Still another source of remorse emerges from Solness's past, and it will lead to his fall. Solness built a tower atop an old church in a provincial town ten years earlier. When it was completed he climbed to the top to hang a wreath. People below were cheering, and schoolgirls in white holiday dresses were waving flags. The thirteen-year-old daughter of the local doctor was among them. When Solness stood at the top, she felt ecstasy for the first time. She heard harps playing. That same evening Solness put his arms around her and kissed her. He called her his princess. He promised to return in ten years to give her a "kingdom."

Solness forgot his promise, but Hilda Wangel didn't. One morning, exactly ten years later, she walks into his workroom, "dressed in hiking clothes, with shortened skirt, sailor blouse open at the throat." The knapsack she carries contains only her underthings. To make her more presentable in town, Solness's wife buys her a skirt and a jacket.

Hilda left home never to return. Dressed in the "hippie" style of that time, she is the first teenage runaway on stage: she is aggressive, without scruples, and all too aware of her charms. Even if she had not yet read Nietzsche in her little Norwegian village, she belongs to that generation determined to live dangerously. It is for her that Solness will climb the tower: it's all so "terribly thrilling . . . ."

Hilda Wangel is twenty-two or twenty-three years old when she meets Solness for the second time. Born in 1870, she is almost the same age as Frida Uhl, Strindberg's second wife, and only two or three years younger than Dagny Juel, Edvard Munch's model and mistress, also a doctor's daughter from a small Norwegian village. Strindberg met Frida Uhl, or at least introduced her to the famous Berlin tavern, "Zum Schwarzen Ferkel," in 1892 when modern artists and writers began meeting there. That same year Ibsen completed *The Master Builder*. Edvard Munch brought Dagny Juel, who later became Strindberg's lover, to the "Zum Schwarzen Ferkel" tavern in the spring of 1893. It was here that Strindberg, accompanying himself on a guitar, sang ballads, and here that Stanisław Przybyszewski, the "brilliant Pole" whom Dagny Juel later married, to her misfortune, played Chopin. The innocent trolls from the Scandinavian forests who possess Solness and Hilda were transformed in the Tavern of the Black Suckling Pig into new, but more venomous modernistic demons of the "naked soul" and the "blind cosmic will."

Frida Uhl and Dagny Juel belong to the first generation of emancipated German and Scandinavian women. In 1882, when Hilda Wangel, dressed in white, waved her flag at Solness as he stood atop the tower, co-education was introduced in the public schools of Norway. That same year women were admitted to the university in Christiania. Here, in 1885, the first co-educational "bohemia" emerged. It was also at this time that Dagny Juel came to Christiania. She was among the first women to cast off corsets. In 1888, when she stayed briefly in Lund, her mode of dress incited public outrage. Many years later people remembered her for having taken off her stockings—her famous green ones—at the "Zum Schwarzen Ferkel" tavern. Two generations, grandfather and granddaughter, meet in Solness and Hilda.

Hilda Wangel walked into Solness's workroom on September 19. This date, the only exact date in *The Master Builder,* was a private code that at the time could be understood by only one person other than Ibsen. As Michael Meyer tells us, under 20 September 1889 Ibsen wrote a line from *Faust* in Emilie Bardach's album: "*Hohes, schmerzliches Glück—um das Unerreichbare zu ringen!*" ("Oh, high and painful joy—to struggle for the unattainable!"). Emilie was then eighteen years old, Ibsen sixty-one. He met her at Gossensass, in the

Tyrol, where he was spending his summer vacation. He saw her for the last time on 27 September. A few hours after they parted, Emilie, on the express train to Vienna, wrote in her diary: "He means to possess me. That is his absolute will. He intends to overcome all obstacles." Ibsen called Emilie his princess and promised to carry her off as Solness promised Hilda. Later he wrote tender yet discreet letters to her. In his last letter, he told her never again to write to him. Fifty years later Emilie Bardach confessed that Ibsen had never even kissed her. She never married. Perhaps in Gossensass, on 19 September 1889, she heard harps playing for the first and last time.

Biographical criticism is often considered shallow and limited: what is more, it is unfashionable. But sometimes it is illuminating. From the double perspective of biographical data and contemporary social life, we can see the artificiality of *The Master Builder*'s symbolic ending, as well as its moral falsehood. In the prosaic situations of real life, as in the realistic content of the play, Ibsen/Solness had only two options: to take Emilie/Hilda to Spain, Italy, or the "Zum Schwarzen Ferkel" in Berlin, or to send her home. Their "honeymoon" would probably have led to sexual disaster on the very first night and to their parting the next morning. Their trip together would then have been a comedy more virulent than even *Playing with Fire*, written by Strindberg a year after Ibsen's play. In his real-life ending there would be no harps playing, and the Scandinavian "trolls" would have been dismissed forever.

"You arrange the drama . . . ." Ibsen did. He had the Great Builder climb a tower and fall. But one can fall symbolically only from symbolic towers. Symbolic towers exist only offstage, like the "wild duck" in the loft covered with fishnetting. The fall from the tower is the Great Fall and a substitution. The Great Fall is a claim for the great absolution and a testimony of vanity out of measure. The erection of the tower, the ascent, and the fall belong to an old and lasting symbolic tradition having two semantic fields: the sexual and the religious. What is most interesting is the way they have always stood for each other.

In the second century A.D. Lucian of Samosata wrote in *The Syrian Goddess*: "In these propylea there stand phalli thirty fathoms high. A man climbs on one of these phalli twice a year and remains on its summit seven days. And it is from this summit that this man can enter into closer conversation with the gods and pray for the welfare of all Syria." Solness first built houses for God, then for people, and finally decided to build houses with towers at the top of which he could talk to and compare himself with God: "And when

I stood right up at the very top, hanging the wreath, I said to him: Hear me, Thou Almighty! From this day on, I'll be a free creator— free in my own realm, as you are in yours."

Perhaps the most graphic example of the sexual "tower" is the marvelous hyperbole in Rabelais's *Gargantua and Pantagruel*: the cloister's belfry, whose "very shadow is fecund." Hilda hears harps for the second time when Solness again stands atop the tower. She whispers: "Now, now it's fulfilled." The question is: for whom?

Nevertheless, the dual symbolism of Solness's "tower" may have a more concrete and contemporary provenance. In 1890, when Ibsen submitted the manuscript of *Hedda Gabler* to his publisher and was preparing to write his next play, the Eiffel Tower was completed for the opening of the World's Fair in Paris. It was one of the greatest events of the end of the century. Almost at once, the Eiffel Tower became a two-fold symbol: it stood for man's prowess rising above the New Babylon, and it was a monstrous phallus.

The Eiffel Tower was the new Tower of Babel, but this time it was not destroyed by God. In Ibsen's symbolism we have not only the erection of a tower, but also the biblical Fall. Perhaps Joyce, in *Finnegans Wake*, was the first to discover this biblical symbolism. Solness the "bygmaster" is the "bourgeois meister who sought to touch the heavens with his tower and was humbled."

The fall from the tower, like all signs, has manifest and hidden meaning. The manifest meaning is punishment for the challenge thrown at heaven: "His mill went right on grinding." In this image of a jealous and vengeful God from Greek myths and the Bible, there is once again the Puritan emphasis on guilt. But Solness's fall has another hidden message. In Freudian terms, falling from a tower is a displacement of the fear of impotence.

Solness's fall is at once an exaltation and a cover-up of actual conflicts: the elevation of Solness and the sublimation of his defeat. The pathos is beyond the measure of his character, although perhaps not beyond the measure of Ibsen's own inflated alter ego. Here, as in *The Wild Duck*, dramatic falseness leads to unearned tragicality. And once again the "deconstruction" of this bathetic tragicality is perceptive and justified.

In Dürrenmatt's *The Visit*, after the town has been bribed with Klara Zachanassian's money and the lynching has taken place, a great feast begins in Güllen. A brass band plays. Men, women, and children all dressed in holiday clothes sing, dance, and wave flags. In the last act of *The Master Builder*, just before the end, "Out in the street, faintly visible through the trees, a crowd of people has gathered. Distant music of a brass band is heard from behind the new house." And only a moment before the builder falls from the tower "ladies on the veranda wave their handkerchiefs, and shouts of Hurray fill the street below."

Not a single word of Ibsen's text need be changed. It is enough to advance these stage directions some twenty or so lines closer to the end of the play, immediately after Solness's offstage fall. Have the brass band come on stage then and play dance music. This time even Hilda would hear no harps. The tower has been erected; nothing can interrupt the feat now. But now the climax is for others. Contained within this bathetic drama with its crack in the chimney is a bitter comedy of "disguises of the soul," of exaggerated roles and poses. The dramatists of coming generations will see this in Ibsen and continue writing in this vein.

6 Mary McCarthy described *The Wild Duck* and *Hedda Gabler* as "near masterpieces." Perhaps. But Hedda Gabler is certainly the greatest female role that Ibsen invented. John Gabriel Borkman is the greatest male role in his theater. And the play that bears his name—Ibsen's penultimate drama—is the only one without a fracture and the only one in which Ibsen is not self-indulgent.

John Gabriel Borkman is Ibsen's *Endgame*. It is a play about the end of the epoch of great conquerors, the end of great passions, the end of the family and the end of life. A play about the last of the great "captains of industry" who, with capital hidden in underground vaults, wanted to extract all the ore in the mountains and the sea. Like a Balzacian hyperbole that condenses the history of a generation, here, John Gabriel Borkman, the son of a miner and uncrowned king of finance, embezzled millions entrusted to him, was under arrest for three years, spent five years in prison, and for the next eight years shut himself in his room, a voluntary prisoner, refusing to come out until his last night when the action of the play unfolds. In the same hyperbolic mode, an epitome of the "human comedy," John Gabriel sacrificed one woman to further his career, exchanging her for a bank presidency and marrying her twin sister for money. He murdered love in one; he destroyed the other.

From the dead marriage only cold hatred remained. Hatred between husband and wife and between twin sisters ensued. For eight years, not a single word was spoken between husband and wife, between the sisters, or between the man and the woman who had loved him once. Disasters do not cool hatred. In this frozen household lives John Gabriel's son. The two women, his natural and adoptive mothers, now fight over him. The latter had raised the seven-year-old boy after Borkman was sentenced. Now she returns to claim him. His real mother wants her son to fulfill a "mission," to transcend his father's guilt, and to restore grandeur to the family. His adoptive mother wants him to share her last years with her. The father wants his son to leave the house with him and to start life anew together.

Young Borkman does leave the house that same night, but without his father. He goes away, but not to his old aunt's rose- and lavender-scented rooms. He would have found them as stifling as his mother's house. He goes away, but not to fulfill any "mission." He wants only to live and be happy. "I'm young! . . . I want to live my own life! . . . Just live, live, live!" He goes away with a divorcée ten years his senior, in a horse-drawn sleigh heading south for Italy. They take with them fifteen-year-old Frida, the eldest child of Borkman's clerk who lost his job and savings after Borkman's bankruptcy. They take her because, as the divorcée observes, "men are so variable . . . and women likewise. . . . it'll be good for both of us that he, poor boy, has someone to fall back on."

Ibsen's setting in *John Gabriel Borkman*—two rooms, one above the other—is the core of the drama, and is repeated by Sartre, consciously or unconsciously, in *The Condemned of Altona* more than half a century later. Sartre's play is also about the end: the end of Hitler's Third Reich and the end of the great German family von Gerlach, steel barons and owners of Europe's biggest shipyards. The father had given Himmler property next to the mills for a concentration camp. To atone for his father's deed, the son went to the Eastern front and, in this merciless drama, tortured captured partisans. Upon his return he shut himself away in his room for thirteen years and said not a word to his father, who listened every night to his son's footsteps coming through the ceiling: "That is all they have left me of my son—the sound of his two shoes on the floor." In Ibsen's drama, "a sick wolf" paces "his cage up in the salon."

For the last of Ibsen's imprisoned doubles, the only exit is into death. The long and uninterrupted night, this "winter's tale," ends outside the house on a snow-covered road. Here, John Gabriel, deposed but still undefeated ruler, dressed in an old-fashioned cape and felt hat, is walking with a cane. He meets Frida's father, who is limping and who has lost his glasses in the snow, having been hit by the sleigh carrying Frida and young Borkman to sunnier climes.

In the last scene Borkman walks up a mountain to a small clearing high in the woods surrounded by dead fir trees. "The house and the open land are lost to view. The landscape, with its slopes and ridges, alters slowly and becomes wilder and wilder." But in this finale there is no need for canvases painted with mountains and fjords descending from the arc of the proscenium. As in the long journey blind Gloucester made with his son Edgar up the imaginary cliffs of Dover in *King Lear*, all the stage directions here are in the dialogue.

> ELLA'S VOICE: *(heard from within the trees, right).* Where are we going, John? I don't know where this is.
>
> BORKMAN'S VOICE: *(higher up).* Keep following my footprints in the snow.
>
> ELLA'S VOICE: But why do we need to climb so high?

This climb to a mountaintop through deep snow is a dramatic pantomime like the one in *King Lear*. The traditional staging of the scene, with all the tools and devices from the naturalistic theater, is the product of a poor reading of *John Gabriel Borkman*, an instance of theatrical myopia. Unlike *Ghosts*, this play does not require magic lanterns to project images of mountains and glaciers in the morning sun. Landscape here is evoked by two contradictory voices: Borkman's and Ella's. He, sinking into his madness as into the snow, creates the landscape. She annihilates it—a landscape of madness and of dreams of grandeur:

> BORKMAN: *(stops where the clearing falls off at the left).* . . . You see how the land lies before us, free and open—all the way out. . . .
>
> ELLA: The dreamland of our lives, yes. And now it's a land of snow. And the old tree is dead.
>
> BORKMAN: *(not hearing her.)* Can you see the smoke from the great steamers out on the fjord?
>
> ELLA: No.
>
> BORKMAN: I can. They come and they go. They make this whole round earth into one community. . . . *That's* the thing I dreamed of doing.
>
> ELLA: *(softly).* And it stayed a dream.
>
> BORKMAN: It stayed a dream, yes. (*Listening.*) Hear that? Down by the river, the factories whirring! *My* factories! All the ones *I* would have built! Can you hear how they're going? It's the night shift. Night and day they're working. Listen, listen! . . . Don't you hear them, Ella?
>
> ELLA: No.

There are two endings to this *Endgame*. A sleigh with silver bells carries off the young, the "children of paradise," the "soft" generation, into an operetta-like world of happiness and endless delight. A sleigh carrying Frida and her future lover knocks down her father, a bookkeeper and author of a tragedy in verse, written in his youth, which he never stopped improving and rewriting. Another father is also left in the snow. But John Gabriel Borkman, who after his downfall locked himself in his room for eight years, as in another prison, will once again attempt to rise. He is the last of the "hard" generation, the power-hungry, the ruthless ones who are ready to trample over anyone who stands in their way, even as they destroy themselves. "And so I prophesy this for you, John Gabriel Borkman—you'll never win the prize you murdered for. You'll never ride in triumph into your cold, dark kingdom!"

As in Kierkegaard, "all or nothing." "Nothing" remains in Ibsen's last masterpiece. The last King Lear goes out into a frozen world, and his heart breaks. There is no pity, or purification. "It was a freezing hand of metal that seized his heart." But even this metaphor is too pathetic for Ibsen:

> ELLA: It was more probably the cold that killed him.
> MRS. BORKMAN: *(shaking her head)*. . . . the cold? The cold—that killed him a long time back.

Two old women, one of whom had taken Borkman away from the other twenty years earlier—twin sisters, one of whom is dying of cancer, can finally embrace each other over Borkman's corpse: "we two shadows—over the dead man."

7 In 1900 the eighteen-year-old Joyce wrote about *When We Dead Awaken* in his first published essay, "Ibsen's New Drama": "One cannot but observe in Ibsen's later work a tendency to get out of closed rooms. Since *Hedda Gabler* this tendency is most marked. The last act of *The Master Builder* and the last act of *John Gabriel Borkman* take place in the open air. But in this play the three acts are *al fresco*. . . . And this feature, which is so prominent, does not seem to me altogether without its significance."

Ibsen's first six prose plays are set in "closed rooms"—from *The Pillars of Society* to *Rosmersholm*, and once again in *Hedda Gabler*. After *A Doll House* comes a house of *Ghosts* and then, in *An Enemy of the People*, a house whose window panes have been shattered by stones. A marriage ends with the slamming of a door in Nora's house and, in *Hedda Gabler*, with the shot Hedda fires to kill herself behind the heavy curtains of the inner room. The family house is a prison in *The Master Builder*.

Into the Rosmers' gloomy house, where, as in *Ghosts*, laughter has never been heard, and through whose windows one can see "white horses rushing out of the darkness," comes a deadly messenger: the wife's young nurse. And once again the drama ends with an exit from "closed rooms" into death. Rebecca West and the man whose wife she drove to her death, but with whom she has never slept, will throw themselves from the footbridge into the millrace. Of all of Ibsen's women only the simple Gina in *The Wild Duck* seems happy and reconciled to her role as wife, just as she had been reconciled to her role as her master's mistress. But her marriage can be saved from disaster only by Hedvig's suicide.

In Ibsen's ten plays from *Ghosts* to *When We Dead Awaken* there are twelve corpses, either suicides or characters who abandon their homes to meet with inevitable death. In these ten dramas there are three incestuous relationships: twice between brother and sister (in *Ghosts* and *Little Eyolf*), unconsummated, but close to it; and a complete incest, even though unconscious, between Rebecca West and her father in *Rosmersholm*.[5]

Nine-year-old Eyolf walks on crutches. He had fallen out of bed while his parents were losing themselves in the heat of passion. Later, the Rat-Wife led the boy out of the house and he drowned in the fjord. His crutches are at first nothing but a prop; only later, after they are seen floating on the water, do they become symbols. Eyolf's mother had wanted to get rid of her son; his lame leg stood "as a wall" between her husband and herself. The lame leg recalls Oedipus. But in *Little Eyolf* the signs are inverted. A mother "kills" her son.

In the model of tragedy, parents destroy their children. In *Ghosts*, a father "kills" his son; in *The Wild Duck* a brother "kills" his half-sister as remission for his father's sins; in *Hedda Gabler*, in which Hedda shoots herself beneath General Gabler's portrait, a father "kills" his daughter; in *Rosmersholm*, an incestuous father "kills" his incestuous daughter; in *Little Eyolf*, a mother whose son has killed her husband's sexual desire, "kills" the crippled son.

Such a reading of signs shows Ibsen's dramas to be as merciless as Greek tragedies. Into the houses of Ibsen's imagination descend the ghosts of Oedipus, Electra, Orestes, and Iphigenia. Wearing top hats, bowlers, and fedoras, carrying parasols and baskets with cold cuts or beer, they enter Ibsen's "tasteless parlours," as Henry James called them, his salons and dining rooms, drawing rooms and kitchens. But these ghosts are not prepared for their tragic roles.

---

[5] See Freud,"Some Character-Types," in *Character and Culture*.

The summoning of Greek shadows reveals, once again, parallels between Ibsen and Freud. The ghosts of Oedipus, Orestes, and Electra haunt Freud's marital bedrooms and children's rooms. In "closed rooms" the same unchanging drama unfolds and repeats itself between father and daughter, mother and son, sister and brother. The Greek phantoms in Freud also sport contemporary clothes, and their sinister signs can range from pistols to crutches and stilts to prostheses and broken glasses, and even to cracks in chimneys.

Racine's tragedies are also full of "closed rooms." The parallel between Ibsen and Racine, whose heroes are rendered bare by the transparency of his alexandrines, may seem puzzling at first, but the "closed rooms" in the emperor's palace also have no exit. Racine's stage is an empty but enclosed place. The sounds of heavy footsteps in the forum, or of the clash of arms of mutinous legions never reach the palace. Only voices come from the outside: the voices of spies and confidants, friends and traitors. In this empty space, Caesar the Father is ever present, even after he has been murdered or, like Theseus, descends to the underworld. His presence/absence haunts parricides and matricides, incestuous sons and wives. And the way out of the emperor's palace leads only to death.

In the "closed rooms" of Ibsen's houses sex is traumatic. Marriage ends with sexual disaster, first for the wife and then for the husband, or for both husband and wife at once. Hedda Gabler is sexually paralyzed by her father, as is Rebecca West. All wives in Ibsen except Gina are sexually stricken by their husbands: Nora and Mrs. Alving, Jan Rosmer's wife, Solness's and Borkman's. And nearly all husbands are sexually paralyzed: Rosmer, Solness, and Allmers in *Little Eyolf*.

The Lady from the Sea is the first of Ibsen's prose plays to take place almost entirely outdoors. This "near comedy," anticipating Chekhov, is the only Ibsen play in which a wife returns after abandoning her husband and in which a dead marriage is revived. But this homecoming is made possible only by the intrusion of romantic icons: a siren cast out of the sea and a long-lost sailor, nameless and homeless, with a red beard and burning eyes, who returns like a ghost from the north to enable his fiancée of long ago to renounce him and go back to her elderly husband.

Two acts in *Little Eyolf* also take place *al fresco*. In the last, a married couple whose crippled son has drowned in the fjord return home to care for abandoned children from the nearby village. But dead eros is not revived, and theirs is a homecoming on crutches.

In *Rosmersholm*, *The Master Builder*, and *John Gabriel Borkman*, each exit from a "closed room" ends in death. The last act of *The Master Builder* and of *John Gabriel Borkman*, and all three acts of *When We Dead Awaken* take place outdoors. Ibsen's last three doubles—the uncrowned king John Gabriel Borkman, the great Builder Solness, and Rubek, the greatest of all sculptors—all die outdoors. Dying onstage is different from dying offstage. Corpses onstage are never resurrected, not even symbolically.

In *When We Dead Awaken* four characters, two couples—the sculptor and his model whom he has never touched, his wife and her new companion—climb higher and higher up the mountain. In the last act they are already in the clouds, at the edge of a precipice, on a snow-covered Alpine slope. The sculptor and his muse die in an avalanche amidst thunder and lightning. The sculptor's wife Maja, the eternal woman, and her companion, a hunter of animals, go back down the mountain to mankind. In the double allegory of this "Dramatic Epilogue in Three Acts" one can see the two alternatives present in Ibsen's plays almost from the very start: the opposition between *Brand* and *Peer Gynt*.

Almost every photograph of Ibsen from the 1880s on shows a stout, elderly man with a top hat pulled down to his ears, dressed in a high, starched collar with a white tie, a jacket, and always carrying an umbrella. Huge white sideburns frame his round face. Ibsen brushed them often and meticulously; he carried a small brush and mirror in the crown of his hat. In a picture taken of Ibsen at the turn of the century, he is walking down an empty street with his back to the camera, in his top hat, a long black coat with padded shoulders, and carrying his inseparable umbrella. In a black and white lithograph by Edvard Munch, done in 1897, only Ibsen's head is portrayed. His forehead is high and wide. His thin lips are tightly shut, one eye is half-closed, the other stares penetratingly at the viewer. His white hair and sideburns are disheveled. His imposing head is illumined by beams from a lighthouse. Ibsen's two powerful opposing sides are bodied forth by these two images: an old man walking down an empty street with his back to us, and a prophet facing us in the beams of a lighthouse. The angry, bitter Ibsen, free of illusion, who turns his back on us, may be closer to our own age.

WITKIEWICZ,

OR

THE DIALECTIC

OF ANACHRONISM

1 Stanisław Ignacy Witkiewicz was born in 1885. If alive today, he would be almost a hundred years old. I met him fifty years ago, four or five years before the Second World War. I was then a student, and Witkiewicz sometimes dropped by as a guest in the seminars given by the Philosophy Department of Warsaw University. I knew his two novels and some of his plays that had been published or were circulating in manuscript copies. I saw many of his paintings; Witkacy (the name he created for himself from the first part of his last name and the last part of his middle name) was very popular as a painter. He made portraits at a low price and often gave them away free of charge. Later on I met some of his personal friends, or rather his "ex-" friends; Witkacy called them his "ideological enemies." He had the practice of keeping a numbered list of his acquaintants, and whenever he lowered the position of one of them, he would inform him about it with an "official" letter. Once as an annual, or semestrial, assignment, I wrote about his theory of Pure Form. Later on he invited me to his house. He showed me his collection of canes of famous women, artists, and politicians. There were among them, if I remember correctly, the little cane of Maria Curie-Skłodowska and the umbrella of the great pianist Ignacy Paderewski, who, after the restoration of Polish independence, became the prime minister of the first Polish government.

I was under the spell of Witkacy; however, I was more fascinated by his personality and himself than by his creative work. I knew that he was an extraordinary and splendid man, but at the same time I had not the slightest doubt that his extravagance and splendor belonged to another time. To the future? No! To the past. Witkacy as a man, writer, and artist seemed to me like a dazzling relic from the very beginning of the Twentieth Century who had strayed into the present.

It would not be worth mentioning this opinion of a young Polish student from before the war were it not for the fact that it was currently shared both by young intellectuals and mature writers. By definition a precursor is one who swerves away from his own time. Between the wars, Witkacy was the most eminent writer in Poland and one of the most interesting in Europe. But he was also—and this may be more astonishing—one of the most original precursors of the intellectual and artistic climate of the 1960s, of its style and thought. And not only in Europe, but in America as well. Witkacy, who came too early, seemed to his contemporaries to be a man who came too late. It would be worthwhile to devote some attention to this phenomenon of the precursor who swerves away from his time or, to be more precise, to the problem of the dialectic of anachronism and innovation.

Witkiewicz had the rare gift, even among painters, of a rapid grasp of resemblances. His portraits resembled their models, even those paintings—the most expensive according to his price list—which were made under the influence of narcotics, and which were visionary and deformed. At that time the leading school of painters in Poland were the postimpressionists, for the most part students of Pierre Bonnard. The younger or more "modern" painters continued the experiments of the constructivists and cubists; they rigorously practiced abstract painting. Max Ernst and the surrealists were still at that time almost unknown in Poland. Witkiewicz was somewhat slighted by painters; they considered his painting "literary," and this "literariness" was very badly regarded by artists at that time. The postimpressionists and the post-cubists as well were preoccupied with form, quality of color, and composition; they were not interested in qualities that were extrinsic to the painting. According to them, Witkacy—the theoretician of Pure Form—was painting old-fashioned, figurative pictures. For them even his visions were illustrations.

I think that this perception was quite right. From today's perspective, the connections that link Witkacy's painting with the

English Pre-Raphaelite school and with the Viennese Secession are obvious. The cold blue tones, the violet and rose colors in Witkacy's pastels, his unreal, ghostly lighting derive from Arnold Böcklin's painting; his thin, vanishing, and undulating stroke, like the unfolding coils of a snake, is more ornamental than pictorial and comes closest to the style of Edward Burne-Jones. But what was generally considered in the twenties and thirties as passé became a live inspiration a quarter of a century later.

The Viennese Secession, anathemized as "the epoch of the decline of taste," has come back triumphantly into fashion in furniture and perhaps most of all in posters. It has become a new tenet of style. Witkacy's portraits and compositions often strikingly call to mind the psychedelic posters which have become a new art form for collectors. Witkacy's faces, which emerge from a colorful mist with their magnified eyes, their grimacing mouths, and all their striking resemblance to their models, are first of all the portraits of a "soul." There is always tension and anxiety in them, a puzzling absence; they are returning from a "trip" to beyond.

Witkacy used the term "Pure Form" for the particular metaphysical quality in painting and poetry which cannot be dissected into primary elements. He called it "the one in the many" or "the mystery of existence." It is not astonishing that this was misunderstood by painters; for them, form consisted of lighting on a surface and the balance of colors, and not of any "metaphysical tension."

For philosophers, Witkacy was an interesting, sometimes fascinating amateur; for writers, he was a painter who, as an amateur, dabbled in literature and the theater. Today Witkacy is more and more often described as a "Renaissance man," as one of the most universal European minds. In his own time, despite the great spell and fascination which he exerted, he was considered a dilettante; he did not fit into the intellectual and artistic community, which was divided into professions and highly specialized. Nobody scoffed at the pretensions of artists to superhumanity and independent morality with more force than Witkacy. But in life, especially for the benefit of his friends, Witkacy often very readily put on the mask of a demon. He proclaimed in his theory that modern art is more and more compelled toward perversity, which meant the use of provocation and shock. In addition, he defended the right to perversion in life. This "demonism," which was so characteristic of many generations of the European bohemia, seemed, in the years between the two wars, frightfully old-fashioned.

As a young man, Witkacy walked through the streets of Zakopane in a Pierrot costume; he liked to disguise himself until the end of his life. He adored all forms of social and intellectual provocation; he treated life as a game and a play; certainly he had much in common with Oscar Wilde. But now, from the perspective of a greater distance of time, it becomes obvious that although he practiced his life as a play, the genre of the play was tragedy acted out as a farce.

Witkacy was, or acted (the adopted mask is also the face), the role of an aristocrat among the bohemians, and a dandy among the bourgeois. All these personal patterns—of a liberated artist, of an artist at odds with society, of an artist misunderstood by the philistines—seemed extremely *fin de siècle*. The new personal pattern, which was more and more generally adopted between the Spanish Civil War and the outbreak of World War II, consisted of conformism with political movements and of the attitude of an "engaged writer." With all its simplicity, the diagnosis of Julien Benda in his famous book *The Betrayal of the Intellectuals* was basically accurate. Of course the "engagement" was understood by intellectuals in various ways. Some considered that the function of a writer was that of Agitator; some, of an Ideologist; others thought, finally, that participation in the power apparatus or the preparation of a revolution was the only important intellectual and moral experience of a twentieth-century writer. The best examples of these attitudes were: the adherence of the majority of the French surrealists to the Communist movement, the participation of André Malraux and many Anglo-Saxon writers in the Spanish Civil War, Bertolt Brecht's political and didactic theater, and, on the side of the "Establishment," Jean Giraudoux as minister and Paul Claudel as the French ambassador in the United States.

Just as Witkacy did not fit into any of the intellectual and artistic milieux that were becoming more and more specialized, so he did not fit into the division of the political left and right. Nor did he have any liberal illusions. His basic nonconformism resulted from his historical experience and implied something different. It occurred earlier, and it will occur later. Witkacy saw the "naked soul" in its Russian version, a new Sodom, a new Apocalypse, and later one of the ends of the Western World, when he was a cadet in the elite Pavlovski regiment of the czar's bodyguard, and then, at the time of the February Revolution, elected political commissar by his regiment.

Witkacy's nonconformism is probably closest to that of Aleksandr Blok, Lev Shestov, and a large part of the pre- and post-World

War II Russian revolutionary intelligentsia. His rejection of established values, moral rules and tradition was repeated on American university campuses nearly thirty years after his death.

The main road of the Berkeley campus of the University of California ends at the intersection of two streets: Bancroft and Telegraph. On this corner, in the fall of 1969, when I came there as a visiting professor of drama, a man with a hoarse voice and a middle-aged woman would sing psalms every day about noon. Next to them barefoot girls and long-haired, disheveled boys wearing strings of beads over colorful shorts would sell the *Berkeley Barb*. Two hundred feet toward the center of the campus there is a square with a fountain between the Student Union and the wide, amphitheatrical steps of the administration building; here stand the tables of the various student groups and organizations. And here you could buy a red booklet with Mao Tse-Tung's maxims, sign a protest against the war in Vietnam, enroll in several political parties or in the sexual freedom league. Psychedelic leaflets with the same flowery, serpentine designs invited you to attend a Baptist service, to join a nudist group, to take judo lessons, or to devote yourself to either Christian or Buddhist meditation. This little square on the Berkeley campus, where every day numerous scenes from Witkacy's plays were performed with few changes by young boys and girls who had never heard of their author, was one of the most sensitive barometers of the intellectual ferment of American youth. One could find similar squares, although perhaps less intense and colorful, on other American campuses; and similar symptoms of ferment could at that time be found in Swedish, English, and German universities.

The atmosphere of the Berkeley campus resembled most, I think, the Russian universities before the 1905 revolution. Not only were the long locks of the boys and the short hair of the Russian female revolutionaries and suffragettes similar, but also the furs worn over shirts, trousers tucked into high boots, or, in summer, sandals on bare feet. Similar, also, was the use of sartorial means to demonstrate abnegation and scorn for accepted forms. But all these similarities are not the most important. Each generation of artistic bohemia since Romanticism has performed some kind of masquerade. The costume was like a uniform; it attested membership in a clan. For a long time the cape has been the uniform of a painter, just as the bowler has been the uniform of a London stockbroker.

More important than clothes and hairdo are the similarities of moral and ideological appeals. In the Russian universities at the beginning of our century, the followers of Tolstoy's belief in nonresistance to evil attempted to convince the apologists for terror that any form of violence was immoral. Socialists disputed with Anarchists the need for the political activization of the masses and scoffed at individual heroism as if it were without political significance. The Russo-Japanese War laid bare the weakness of Czarist Russia. The old religions were coming back, and new ones were born; the adherents to Buddhist Nirvana tried to convince the Old Believers of the new light coming from the East. At the universities the causes of free love and equality of sexual rights for women were advocated; hashish was smoked, ether was inhaled, and the first drug mystics appeared. Most of the time they drank, of course, vodka; but it was a Slavic way of drinking vodka: full of passionate discussions, of "stripping one's soul" and intimate confessions—drunken nights like trips down to the bottom.

All historical analogies are true only up to a point, and are only one means of interpretation. It is easier, however, to understand Witkacy's swerving from his time and the contemporaneity of his theater—so striking today—if we compare even for a moment the ideological ferment of the sixties with the Russian universities at the beginning of the century, the similar revolt against the establishment by the children of the same establishment, the contempt of the intellectuals for professional politicians, and the basic nonconformism of the artistic milieux.

2

LEON: But let's not have any dramas à la Ibsen, with all that tragedy business about the various professions and the shortcomings of each. I'd rather have a cold-soup tragedy or a meat-with-all-the-juices-cooked-out-of-it tragedy à la Strindberg.

MOTHER: Nothing's sacred to you. You treat Ibsen and Strindberg just the same way you treat me. Is there any greater work of genius in the whole world than Strindberg's *The Ghost Sonata*?

[Witkiewicz, *The Mother*]

Witkacy in his plays and manifestos continues the destruction of naturalistic theater exactly from the point where Strindberg stopped. The same is true for Antonin Artaud. One of the first plays performed in Artaud's theater was Strindberg's *A Dream Play*.

Witkiewicz and Artaud never met; they may never have even heard of each other. But the similarities in their theatrical visions and the posthumous impact of their work are striking. Artaud issued his first manifesto on the Theater of Cruelty in 1932: in that same year Witkiewicz's treatise on narcotics appeared in print. The first volume of Artaud's collected works was published in 1956, and in the sixties his *Theater and Its Double* became the bible for those in America and Europe who sought for the new theater, and Artaud himself became the precursor and the ultimate incarnation of a prophet and theatrical guru. The first edition of Witkiewicz's collected plays appeared in 1962, and since then he has become one of the most frequently produced playwrights in Poland, and known to theatrical audiences throughout the world, from Paris to Hawaii, and from Alaska to Caracas. Before Witold Gombrowicz, Witkiewicz was the most original and universal Polish writer of the twentieth century.

In *An Introduction to the Theory of Pure Form in the Theater* (1919), Witkiewicz wrote: "Is it possible, even if only for a short period, for a form of the theater to arise in which contemporary man, independent of dead myths and beliefs, could experience the metaphysical feelings which ancient man experienced through those same myths and beliefs?" One of the most frequently quoted lines from Artaud is amazingly similar even in its rhetoric to Witkiewicz's exhortations published almost fifteen years before Artaud's "The Theater and the Plague" (1933): "And the question we must now ask is whether, in this slippery world which is committing suicide without noticing it, there can be found a nucleus of men capable of imposing this superior notion of the theater, men who will restore to all of us the natural and magic equivalent of the dogmas in which we no longer believe" (in *The Theater and Its Double*).

Witkiewicz firmly believed that when, as a result of indus-trialization, an individual becomes more and more absorbed by the uniform society, religion and then philosophy will become unable to express the mystery of existence which will arouse "metaphysical feelings." Only art will still be able to inspire an audience with fear and trembling. And, above all, the theater, which should become, as for Artaud, a "double" of dream: "On leaving the theatre, the spectator ought to have the feeling that he has just awakened from some strange dream, in which even the most ordinary things had a strange, unfathomable charm, characteristic of dream reveries, and unlike anything else in the world" ("On a New Type of Play").

Neither Witkiewicz nor Artaud realized how much they in-herited from symbolists. Flaubert once called literature "the mysti-cism of those who no longer believe." For Paul Claudel, Arthur Rimbaud was "a savage mystic" (*"un mystique à l'état sauvage"*). In the period of symbolism religious language was absorbed by the rhetoric of literary criticism and poetical manifestos, where we find on every page prophets and heretics, conversion and initiation, grace and revelation.

This religious vocabulary passed into theatrical programs. E. Gordon Craig might be the first to have used it. For the last decade Jerzy Grotowski has been the best example of its abuse. His basic terms are "holiness," "sacrifice," and "profanation." His actor must be a saint and a martyr in this new Mass, which is profane but metaphysical. It was not by chance that in his *Towards a Poor Theatre* Grotowski quoted from this sentence by Artaud: "And if there is still one hellish, truly accursed thing in our time, it is our artistic dallying with forms, instead of being like victims burnt at the stake signaling through the flames." This line could have been written by Witkiewicz, almost in the same words—"hellish" is truly Witkacian. Artaud's victims burnt alive are counterposed to, yet also compared with, the modern artist "dallying with forms."

The theory of "Pure Form" in painting and theater is at the core of Witkiewicz's aesthetics. Only through "Pure Form" can the Insatiability and Strangeness of Existence be revealed. Only "Pure Form" can provoke the Metaphysical Shudder. This too sounds very old-fashioned. But translated into "deep structure" it becomes unexpectedly modern. "Pure Form," "one in many," is "significant structure." The metaphysics and the "essence" of art were for Witkiewicz a system of signs independent or disconnected from the referent:

> . . . What is essential is that the need for the psychology of the characters and their actions to be consistent and life-like should not become a bugbear imposing its particular construction on the play. . . . In the theatre we want to be in an entirely new world in which the fantastic psychology of characters, who are completely implausible in real life . . . produces events which by their bizarre interrelationships create a performance in time not limited by any logic except the logic of the form itself of that performance. ("On a New Type of Play")

In 1915, in Zurich's Cabaret Voltaire, Tristan Tzara would clip an article from a morning paper, then cut out all the words, mix them in his hat, and finally put them back together randomly to make a poem. On some other evening, Francis Picabia took an alarm clock apart, and then out of all the tiny bits made an "object-dada." During the following fifty years all the clocks of all the arts were taken apart, to the last spring, to the last screw. Young boys and retired men have always enjoyed fiddling with clockwork: this *bri-*

colage, so beautifully analyzed by Lévi-Strauss, became for the Dadaists the new aesthetics, or if you will, the rule of anti-aesthetics.

The Dadaists decomposed sentences into words which, disconnected from their primary function and meaning, created new arrangements. In the deconstruction and the remodeling of the clock-parts the relations of continuity and contiguity were changed. In the permutation discovered by the Dadaists and practiced by the surrealists, the sign is severed from its former significance. In Artaud's vision, the icons of Greek, Elizabethan, and Far Eastern theater are reconstructed according to a similar *bricolage:* the rites, gestures, and magical formulas from various cultures and epochs meet together to forge a new unity, connected and disconnected at the same time. Witkiewicz and Artaud both believed in the theater of pure signs which induces the "metaphysical shudder."

One more of Artaud's statements might have been written by Witkiewicz, and again almost in the same words: "Without an element of cruelty at the root of every spectacle, the theater is not possible. In our present stage of degeneration it is through the skin that metaphysics must be made to re-enter our minds." And of all Artaud after more than a quarter of a century this program of physical exercises in metaphysics has been the most influential.

In the fifties and sixties almost all student and artistic "underground" theater in Europe and America had adopted as their program the "through the skin" formula. Theater seemed to be a "sacred place," where Paradise Lost could be, at least for a short while, regained. Theater was to replace not only religion but also revolution. In the theater which had a "through the skin" impact, instant sex and instant rebellion were to be the new liberation.

"We must unleash," wrote Witkacy as early as 1920, "the slumbering Beast and see what it can do. And if it runs mad, there will always be time enough to shoot it before it's too late" ("On a New Type of Play"). But this "slumbering beast" was shot too late.

Witkiewicz, like Artaud, was convinced that in societies bored by automatization, art in order to shock must be violent. But Witkiewicz had a different view from Artaud about violence, or as he called it the artistic perversity. For Artaud, the rebirth of the theater implied the destruction of the written play. "No more masterpieces!" Elizabethan dramas should be "stripped of the text" and retain "only the accouterments of period, situations, characters, and action."

It is no accident that Büchner's *Woyzeck* was among the plays Artaud proposed in his "First Manifesto." Woyzeck is the first tragic hero who stammers. He is beyond or above language, beyond the rhetoric of madness and disgrace. And here again, by the fascination of madness or even of stupor as "being different," Artaud and Witkiewicz converge.

"When choosing my destiny I chose insanity." Witkacy took this line from a poem by his personal friend, Tadeusz Miciński, a modernist Polish poet and dramatist, as the motto for his novel *Insatiability*. For Artaud madness was fate and a personal choice, a part of his own life, his own Golgotha, a testimony to be proclaimed as the gospel. He did not wish to be healed, and he did not seek refuge in suicide. "I have lived for nine years in an asylum. Yet I have never suffered from the obsession of killing myself. But I know very well that every morning after talking with the psychiatrist I had the irresistible urge to kill myself, because I well knew that I could not strangle him."

In an early Witkacy play, *The Madman and the Nun* (1923), a poet confined to an asylum and freed by the nurse for one night from his straightjacket kills his psychiatrist with a pencil. But like his later suicide this murder is only "theatrical," and at the end of the play everyone reappears alive and unharmed: the real madmen are only the psychiatrists and attendants. In this mocking finale with its farcical shock, the differences between Artaud and Witkiewicz's life-experience and dramatic vision are clearly seen. Witkiewicz suffered repeatedly from deep depressions and in his youth sought Freudian treatment. But he was "healthier" than Artaud, or perhaps just "cooler" and with fewer illusions.

Artaud told Jean-Louis Barrault in 1935: "Tragedy on the stage is not enough for me. I am going to carry it over into my life." Witkacy knew very well that tragedy became farce in a civilization condemned to be dead-alive. Witkacy finally proved himself to be a writer of comedy—a writer of comedy often unexpectedly prophetic.

3　There is a long theatrical history behind characters who, after their death, come back on stage in order to haunt living people or to give them moral lessons. The dead come back on stage both in Shakespeare and in other Elizabethan theater, both in Romantic and in modern drama. The dead come back either as ghosts or as hallucinations. The ghost is a metaphysical statute; the hallucination is a psychological situation. But both imply, in the properly theatrical sense, that the ghost or hallucination can be seen only by some of the characters on the stage, that it behaves in a different way from the "living" characters, it speaks differently, it moves differently, it often wears the costume of a ghost, and if it does not have a costume, then it still must have some special traits or marks.

The theatrical tradition of the behavior of ghosts was probably undermined for the first time by Strindberg. In *The Ghost Sonata* the dead Consul, wrapped in a winding-sheet, comes out of the door of the house where he died the day before to look at the flag flying at half mast and to count the poor who came to his funeral. Only the Student, however, sees him. A young girl, whom many years ago Company Director Hummel had seduced and drowned, appears as a Milkmaid in the first scene; she does not speak, but she behaves normally. She even gives a cup of water to the Student. At the beginning only he sees her. The Milkmaid will, however, appear in the same act for a second time; she will raise her arms like one who is drowning and gaze fixedly at her murderer. The metaphysical statute of these apparitions is ambiguous in Strindberg's play; maybe they are ghosts, maybe only hallucinations. From the theatrical point of view, however, they no longer have other worldly attributes.

But it is only in the plays with "corpses" by Artaud and Witkiewicz that the dead characters come back on stage in an ordinary manner. In *The Water Hen* the heroine who is shot in the first act comes back in the second as though nothing had happened. In the third act, she is shot once again, but this time definitely. In *The Mother,* old Mrs. Eely dies in the second act. In the third act she lies in state, but this does not hinder her from appearing simultaneously as a person thirty years younger and, moreover, pregnant, expecting the birth of the hero of the play. The "first" Mother who is lying in state turns out to be a dummy. In *The Madman and the Nun* the corpse of a murdered psychiatrist, which has been removed by hospital attendants, comes back after a while, smiling, with the murderer who had hanged himself in the previous scene. His corpse is still on stage and is, of course, a dummy. The same thing happens in Artaud's pantomime *The Philosopher's Stone,* where Harlequin, who has been cut in pieces a moment ago by the jealous Doctor, jumps up from the operating table and immediately has sexual intercourse with the Doctor's wife, Isabella. After a while a baby is shaken out from her skirt who resembles the doctor as closely as two peas in a pod. The Harlequin who was tortured on the operating table was, of course, a dummy. The resemblance between Artaud's and Witkiewicz's plays which use corpses is all the more surprising since Artaud could in no way have known Witkacy's work. The theatricalization of corpses is very important in the history of the contemporary, avant-garde theater; the centuries-old convention of portraying the return of the dead in European theater was completely broken.

In the Chinese theater, when the hero dies or is killed he drops and lies flat for a moment and then runs off the stage. He has died, thus he has ceased to exist, and consequently he cannot be present on the stage even as a motionless body. For a European spectator this convention seems surprising at first, yet it does not lack theatrical logic. The actor acts the role of a character, but it is impossible to act the role of a corpse; at most it is possible to simulate it. But to simulate a corpse means, in theatrical language, to pass from the technical devices of "acting" to "pantomime." The only difference is that it is a pantomime with no gestures. After the curtain calls, the corpses get up to bow before the audience; they might just as well have got up earlier.

Nor do the dead in the Japanese Noh theater—the dead who return to haunt the living, or to revenge themselves, or to reward their benefactors—follow the theatrical representation of a European "ghost." They behave, as far as I know, like characters who are alive, that is, according to the same theatrical convention of gestures and without any change in makeup. In the Bali theater, ghosts and demons are represented as huge and lurid puppets. Artaud wrote in *The Theater and Its Double:*

> There is in the truly terrifying look of their devil (probably Tibetan) a striking similarity to the look of a certain puppet in our own remembrance, a puppet with swollen hands of white gelatine and nails of green foliage, which was the most beautiful ornament of one of the first plays performed by Alfred Jarry's theater.

The theater in which the dead are puppets and in which the dead get up and walk—the theater which breaks away from the convention of European drama—originated in the fascination with the Oriental theater. Artaud saw the Bali theater during the colonial exposition in Paris. The Chinese opera and the Japanese Noh fascinated Brecht, too. From the Oriental theater he adopted the ways in which the mask was used, the semantic makeup, and pantomime acting as the basic means to produce the effect of estrangement.

For a foreigner who does not know the language it is primarily a visual theater of gesture, costume, and movement, a true theater of Pure Form. But this theater of Pure Form is at the same time a ritual and a liturgy. Artaud understood this theater in exactly the same fashion, as pure spectacle and as sheer ritual, and he opposed it to the deadness of the European stage. In his chapter "Metaphysics and the *Mise en Scène*" from *The Theater and Its Double,* Artaud wrote: "In any case, and I hasten to say it at once, a theater which subordinates the *mise en scène* and production, i.e., everything in itself that is specifically theatrical, to the text, is a theater of idiots, madmen, inverts, grammarians, grocers, antipoets and positivists, i.e., Occidentals." In its style, choice of words, and terms, this statement surprisingly resembles Witkacy's theories about the theater of Pure Form.

"The last part of the spectacle," wrote Artaud about the Bali theater, "is—in contrast to all the dirt, brutality, and infamy chewed up by our European stages—a delightful anachronism. And I do not know what other theater would dare to pin down in this way *as if true to nature* the throes of a soul at the mercy of phantasms from Beyond."

These "throes of a soul at the mercy of phantasms from the Beyond" are expressions Witkacy might have used, and they could characterize his painting and his theater. Witkacy's Theater of Pure Form and Artaud's Theater of Cruelty were to serve as the last places where metaphysical experiences which had been banished from philosophy and had become dead in religion could be expressed.

Both in Witkiewicz and in Artaud we find the same infernal fusion, the same explosive combination of two notions, or rather of two visions, of the theater. One of them is the theater of ritual and liturgy, the theater of metaphysical transports, in which the "Mystery of Existence" will shake even the unbelievers. The other is the theater of violent physical action in which spoken language, gestures, movements, and objects are not only a system of signs, but have their own pure theatrical value, just like a hieroglyph or Chinese ideogram which not only has a meaning but is an image as well.

In fact, these are two entirely different notions of theater, although both in Artaud and in Witkiewicz they are tightly interlaced like two fibers in one cord. From the perspective of another half century, it becomes clear that one of these visions was an illusion. The magic counterpart of dogmas does not exist once you cease to believe in them. Ritual and liturgy in theater are either mockery or profanation. This very profanation of ritual we can find in the theater of Genet, who is the only one to draw all of the consequences from Artaud's Theater of Cruelty.

In the real theater created by Witkiewicz, there are no metaphysical transports, nor is there any mystery of existence. And perhaps that is the reason why this theater became understood so late.

Witkiewicz's theater is sometimes bitter, but always scoffing. The unquestionable significance of his plays consists in its historical perspective, in the perception of the end of civilization fatally threatened by the egalitarian revolution coming from the East and by Western consumerism and mechanization. This mechanization not only produces a society of automatons, but also impels the automatons to direct even those who had invented them. Witkacy's catastrophism only apparently belongs to the Nineteenth Century. In fact, it was the perspicacious and appalling vision of an inevitable clash between the civilization of computers and the levelers' revolution. For Witkacy the Nineteenth Century ended once and for all in 1917. In this perspective, all that followed was grim and grotesque.

4   The characters in Witkiewicz's plays speak a special language—all of them the same one, even servants, children, and executioners. It was the language of the literary and intellectual café in Cracow, Vienna, Prague, or Berlin, in the years between the First and Second World Wars. In this café all are friends: the famous artists and celebrities are mentioned by their first or nicknames. The café has its own personal idiom as language.

In almost all of Witkacy's plays a friend of his youth, Bronisław Malinowski, is either one of the leading characters or is mentioned under the most fantastic nicknames. Witkacy had accompanied him on a 1914 expedition to Ceylon and Australia. After a few weeks Witkiewicz suddenly returned to Europe and Russia after an emotional and still mysterious breakup with Malinowski.

Edmund Leach, a British anthropologist, wrote recently that the real and unexpected novelty in Malinowski's famous work, *The Sexual Life of Savages,* was the radical departure from the naive evolutionism of Puritan anthropologists, who believed that the progress of civilization leads directly from the mating of savages in the jungle to Victorian marriage, and looked in horror at the indiscriminate games of boys and girls in Melanesia. But Malinowski traveled to the tropics with quite different experiences. Like Witkacy, since his early youth he had many friends among poets and painters. Like Witkacy he was fascinated by Gauguin. In New Guinea and on the Trobriand Islands he discovered Gauguin's "paradise" under the rays of the tropical sun. The sexual practices of "savages" neither shocked nor amazed him. They were probably for him amazingly similar to the Bohemian life of artists in Munich and Paris or maybe even in Cracow.

In the epilogue to Witkacy's first novel, *The 622 Downfalls of Bungo*, which appeared only posthumously, we find under the name of the Duke of Nevermore a sharp biographical sketch of Malinowski:

> The Duke was deported to New Guinea after scandalous crimes he committed in the back streets of Whitechapel with various lords. However, he wrote such a brilliant work about the perversions of the apparent savages, who lived there, contemptuously called Papuas, that he returned to England as a Member of the British Association for Advancement of Science and as a Fellow of the Royal Society. Later his life was a series of wild and incredible triumphs . . . .

Even more characteristic is a "bibliographical" footnote to this "brilliant work about the perversions: *The Golden Bough of Pleasure* by Edgar, Duke of Nevermore; Cambridge University Press." Witkacy was the first and for a long time the only one to read Malinowski's *Sexual Life of Savages* as the new Frazer, but this time *The Golden Bough* of pleasure. I think it was an extremely good reading.

The second real character transferred from the artistic café into his novels and plays was Leon Chwistek, painter, philosopher, and famous logician. In this prewar café where prominent mathematicians met with artists and *le beau-monde,* the most "perverse" sexual proposals could be communicated in technical, philosophical terms. "A pragmatist" was a common insult. On the cover of one of Witkiewicz's works one could read: "he was struggling with the suffocating mist of the major problem of General Ontology. . . . " That was exactly the language of Witkiewicz's characters.

In his *Water Hen,* the Duchess of Nevermore's footman announces: "Her Grace requests that you come to the table." But, besides the footman, the Duchess had also a husband (another fantastic alter-ego of Malinowski) who was torn apart by a tiger in Africa. "He was reading Russell and Whitehead's *Principia Mathematica* after his entrails had been torn out by a tiger. He was a hero. He was fully conscious when he said he'd duped you into a metaphysical flirtation. He called it a psychopath's metaphysical flirtation. Yet, he wasn't a madman himself."

The characters in Witkiewicz's plays are disguised in fantastic or historical costumes, scattered around the world from great metropolis to Malayan jungle, with their sophisticated names, titles, and nicknames. They all belong to the same social circle, and seem only for a moment to have left the table reserved for them. Even Pope Julius II and Richard III in other of Witkacy's plays come from the café in central Europe.

In translation, Witkacy's allusive names often lose their flavor and venom, such as the Duchess of Nevermore's *nom de guerre,* Water Hen. In the beginning of the play she is standing under the street lantern. In the Polish original she is called *Kurka wodna,* which (with a slight alliteration) sounds like "kurwa," a whore. Only the French translation of the title—*Poule d'Eau*—is congenial. *The Water Hen* is the third play, after Ibsen and Chekhov, to use the name of a water bird as a title. But in Witkiewicz all symbolical meanings are definitely lost, and what remains is nothing but a brutal and vulgar sexual connotation.

Just as in *commedia dell'arte* the parts in Witkacy's theater are unalterably fixed: this perverse chess game is played once and for ever with the same characters. This unalterable "typology" has been repeatedly and most precisely analyzed by Polish critics. The most important, frequently the hero of the play, is "Titan," often a mathematical genius or metaphysically insatiable artist. "Insatiability" is for Witkacy a word full of metaphysical meaning. Like "cruelty" for Artaud, "insatiability" characterizes in some way the psycho-climate of Witkacy's theater.

The Titan endures all the pain of limitation of individual existence; he is burned out by his permanent urge to perform; he finds no outlet for the energy exploding within him; he cannot sleep, foam bubbles from his mouth. Witkacy loved the devices and tricks of the fair and the popular theater, and even provided the recipe for theatrical "foam."

Bored with themselves and the automatic world, Titans become the most cruel dictators simply to fill time with action. They carry on gigantic financial operations or found subversive organizations to rule the world through terror. They murder, rape, and torture without scruple solely in order to experience a metaphysical shock. In the end all Witkiewicz's Titans deflate like pinched balloons.

Female demons are the Titan's partners. Sexually insatiable, they promise the most perverse pleasures. They demand greatness from the males, just to eat them alive like a praying mantis during copulation. These great "demonesses" are usually the wives of English lords, financial sharks, or Russian princesses. Common female demons come from a bourgeois background and are not so well read in Husserl and Cornelius. The female demons entangle their artistic paramours with their tentacles and suck their blood like succubae. The super-demons are insatiable and indestructible like Wedekind's Lulu, the modern incarnation of mythic Lilith. The demonic ten-year-old Tadzio comes to *The Water Hen* also directly from Wedekind's *Earth Spirit*. The other young demons are the ten-year-old "piggies," dressed up like little angels, lascivious and perfidious, the predecessors of postwar Lolitas.

Between the Titans and the artists circulate scoundrels and fops. The scoundrels are young and of "low origin," either metaphysical or common. The metaphysical ones muffle the strangeness of existence with cruelty and swindles. The common ones want money, women, and power. They have strong shoulders and no qualms. Eddie in Sławomir Mrożek's *Tango*, "Last Tango in Warsaw," the modern Fortinbras killing the modern Hamlet, comes from the family of Witkiewicz's common scoundrels. Fops, gigolos, and little swindlers pretend to be artists, but are always ready to do the dirtiest jobs. In Witkiewicz, after the departure of Titans and demons, only scoundrels, fops, Lulu, and monstrous matrons remain.

In Witkiewicz the characters torture themselves physically and mentally, indulge in gigantic orgies, and use terrifying narcotics. Mass executions follow fascist coups and social upheavals. Titans and female demons, or candidates for the roles of Titans and demons, slaughter each other and wind up in suicide. Plots in these dramas often seem like the most unexpected mélange of Marquis de Sade's *Justine* with Jarry's *Ubu Roi*. We do not know if Witkiewicz read Sade, but once more we find the amazing analogy with Artaud, who in "The First Manifesto" announced: "We shall stage . . . a tale by the Marquis de Sade, in which the eroticism will be transposed, allegorically mounted and figured, to create a violent exteriorization of cruelty, and dissimulation of the remainder."

The torments and poisons, orgies, sexual perversions, and executions are always "theatrical" in Witkiewicz. The action is a spectacular "make-believe," devoid of credibility. But in this great *buffo*, in this perfidious and metaphysical Grand Guignol, one theatrical sign is not empty, and has always its frightening *serio*. It is the vision of the ineluctable, final and total destruction.

In this Central European café the real "geniuses," genuine artists and charlatans meet; governmental journalists and opposition deputies walk in and out; the wives of Jewish lawyers and physicians in their expensive furs sit next to Russian princesses, genuine or phony, with their enchanting daughters, also genuine or fake. Lulu was always there, at her separate table. Scoundrels and fops, metaphysical and ordinary, would sit with snobbish socialites, looking greedily around the house.

Since the early thirties, regular customers of this Central European café were either murdered or dispersed to all the corners of the world, by fascist putsches, military coups, witch-hunting, antisemitism and nationalistic upheavals, and finally invasion and occupation, both Nazi and Stalinist. Witkacy was among the first to understand that this literary café of male Titans and female demons was entering its final hours and soon would be turned into "goulash" and dragged into the "gulag" by real history.

Witkiewicz, like George Orwell—but the Orwell of *Animal Farm* rather than *1984*—was a "catastrophist" with an astonishing clarity of vision. He predicted that a permissive society of the rich and satiated would be threatened not only by the "levelers" and fanatical fundamentalists from Russia, the Far East, and Africa, but also that this civilization—always fragile and more and more universally alienated—would be defenseless against madmen and psychopaths. In a world which has become a "global village" madness is contagious and could easily be universal. In this mega-village everything happens simultaneously, and everything is possible.

5 In Witkiewicz, the congruity of the nineteenth-century dramatic structures was torn apart as abruptly as the coherence of nineteenth-century social and political systems. The way the characters meet in the most distant parts of the world is more unexpected and accidental than the encounters among words which Tristan Tzara was pulling out of the hat. Terrorist attempts, communist revolutions, fascist coups appear in Witkiewicz's plays without any realistic motivation.

And, because of this lack of internal congruity, and apparently rational probability, Witkiewicz's plots have unexpectedly begun to approximate reality in the second half of our century. For the same reason Sade and Jarry have also come to mirror TV news.

The Form as cruelty has become cruelty without form. Since the sexual practices which Malinowski observed in New Guinea have become the usual evening pastime not only among "Bohemians," but among respectable managers and even middle-class wives and husbands—interrupted only by acts of violence viewed from the comfort of one's TV chair—the theater of the "metaphysical Strangeness of Existence" has unexpectedly become the black comedy of manners. We are not only spectators in Witkiewicz's realistic theater, but some of us, unknowingly, have also been its supporting players for quite a long time.

In the summer of 1965 at a cocktail party in an Oxford college I was introduced to Aleksandr Kerenski. I could hardly conceal my surprise that he was still alive. Indeed, he was in perfect shape. He wore a ring with a four-carat diamond with which, in November 1917, disguised in women's clothes, he had left the Winter Palace in Petersburg to flee the Bolsheviks. At the time I met him he was traveling to all the great libraries in Western Europe and America, where between ten in the morning and noon he read memoirs and documents dealing with the nine months from February to October when he was a Premier of the Provisional Government. He was still curious to know what mistakes he had made during those nine months.

In 1954, eleven years before my visit to Oxford, I was invited as a member of a Polish writers' delegation to China to a party given by Chou En-Lai in honor of the Dalai Lama. In those days the road from Warsaw to Peking was shorter than to Vienna or West Berlin. Among the small number of guests were Nehru's aunt and sixteen Balinese dancers of astonishing beauty. The Dalai Lama looked like a precocious child—he was then no more than eighteen years old. With his head shaved, dressed luxuriously in yellow and red, the nail of his little finger extremely long, he made me think of an altar boy disguised in the bishop's ceremonial clothing.

During the party, we played hide-and-seek, and when it was my turn to be blindfolded I found Nehru's aunt unexpectedly in my arms. The Dalai Lama did not participate in the game. Later, at the window overlooking the Emperor's Gardens we saw him feeling up one of the Balinese dancers. Chou En-Lai knit his bushy brows, clapped, and announced: the party is over.

During the evening in Oxford I called the Dean of the College: "I think I am the only one here who has met both Kerenski and the Dalai Lama." At one o'clock in the morning a telephone woke me up. "You are not the only one," said the Dean, "My friend, an archeologist who two weeks ago returned from India, met the Dalai Lama, who had escaped from Tibet after the Chinese invasion, in one of the northern provinces almost at the foot of the Himalayas."

Among the contemporary Witkiewicz plots, this is one of the most innocent. In 1961, or perhaps 1962, when President Kennedy was still alive, Onassis invited the First Lady for a yacht cruise on the Mediterranean. Her sister, Princess Lee Radziwill, married to one of the several Radziwills scattered all around the world, was there, and also present was super-diva Maria Callas, a few artists, a number of scoundrels, metaphysical and common, and undoubtedly a handful of fops, not counting Onassis's bodyguards and CIA and KGB agents disguised as sailors. More than one of the Witkiewicz dramas was enacted during that cruise.

In 1968 I came to Princeton to participate in a colloquium on the future of the world, with delegates from three continents. During the last evening on the hotel terrace I saw an old colleague from Poland, of a good Jewish family which had broken with him when he had ended up in jail (not for too long) after he had been caught with communist leaflets. We were then both at the university. He left Poland before the war, and later became an expert on the Soviet Union and China, publishing a journal in Washington which earned him well-deserved esteem among kremlinologists and pekinologists.

Now, at this international conference in Princeton, with only a few tables between us, there he was, stocky, his head balding, his belly well formed, his face like a big egg with a golden tooth glittering, sipping wine with a middle-aged woman almost two heads taller than he and chestnut haired. Her face seemed strangely familiar, but I did not recognize her until they both walked by my table, holding hands, towards the park. My Warsaw friend—the "red-haired Semite" in Witkiewicz's terminology—disappeared into the bushes with Svetlana Alliluyeva, Stalin's daughter, that evening in Princeton.

In the first act of Witkiewicz's *Water Hen,* written in 1921, we have a large, octagonal lantern, with green glass shades. This lantern, writes the author, can be painted silver, very fancy. Antique dealers hunt now for this kind of gas lantern under which, in my youth, whores would wait for customers. They have now become art-deco items and are on display in museums. In the same play the Father says: "We've got to drink away three abortive generations. Maybe I'll still become a revolutionary admiral, but those others— ugh, what a comedown." *The Water Hen* takes place between Art Nouveau's gaslights and the revolution of 1917. The revolution marks the end of this world, but, the destruction is ludicrous.

Marx wrote in *The Eighteenth Brumaire of Louis Bonaparte:* "Hegel remarks somewhere that all facts and personages of great importance in world history occur, as it were, twice. He forgot to add: the first time as tragedy, the second as farce." Witkiewicz seems to have been the first to understand that the destruction of his world will be a farce. And even more: a time is coming in which only farce will have the appearance of tragedy. *The Water Hen* ends with a game of whist at the card table.

> FATHER: Two diamonds. Banging away in fine style. Your bid, Mr. Specter.
>
> SPECTER: Two hearts. The world is collapsing.
>
> TYPOWICZ: Pass.

For Witkiewicz *The* Revolution occurs always in 1917. Orwell, born in 1903, belongs to the next generation after Witkiewicz. The decisive experience for understanding the communist "Utopia" was for him the massacre of anarchists and idealistic revolutionaries by Stalinists in Spain during the Civil War. For Witkiewicz, the crucial experience remains 1917. But in the last of his plays, *The Shoemakers* (1934), it is not revolution that ends the play. The play ends with the end of revolution. In the Epilogue, two high-level Apparatchiki, dressed in elegant English-made suits, appear on stage accompanied by Hyperworkoid, "carrying his copper thermos bottle."

> COMRADE X: Listen Comrade Abramowski: I'm abandoning the idea of nationalizing agriculture for the time being, not because I am making any compromises. . . .
>
> COMRADE ABRAMOWSKI: Of course not: you can just justify it ideologically and make them understand that this is purely a provisional measure. . . .
>
> COMRADE X: Only as much compromise as is absolutely necessary—understand, ab-so-lu-te-ly necessary.

The Shoemakers proved to be a prophetic play. In December 1941 when the military junta seized power it was acted out all over Poland. "The great days for ideologies have come to an end—you know, when you could stuff yourself with mayonnaise, and be an ideological Bolshevik, and find consolation in utopian dreams even though you were down to your last bowl of soup, and feel that you're somebody even though you're rotting in excrementalia. No one individual is going to come up with a new utopia—the new social order will come about all by itself, by spontaneous combustion, explosion, eruption . . . ."

6 In January 1947, for the last time, Artaud appeared publicly in Paris, at the Théâtre Vieux Colombier. He was supposed to read his last poems. The evening was called "*Tête-à-tête.*" The theater was sold out. But Artaud did not read any poems. The notes he had prepared fluttered from the podium to the floor. He began to wave his arms like a drowning man. At length and in detail he recounted the horror of electric shocks. He began to stutter, cried out a few unintelligible words. He sobbed and fled.

I do not know if Ionesco was in the audience, but I am sure that his Orator in *The Chairs*—who can only moan, rattle, and scribble illegible words on a blackboard, is a portrait of Artaud. He arrived to stand in front of the empty rows of chairs, occupied by invisible spectators, to tell them—what is most important. But he was a deaf mute. On that wintery afternoon in Vieux Colombier, Artaud became a sign of the theater that "can only be from the moment when the impossible really begins."

On 18 September 1939, Witkiewicz slashed his wrists and took poison. German troops had for a week been shelling the outskirts of Warsaw. A day before the radio announced the crossing of the eastern Polish border by the Soviet Army. Witkiewicz had once survived the Apocalypse in 1917 and did not want to face it again. In his novels and plays the end of the world to which he belonged is presented as a farce. All suicides in his plays were fake; only his own was genuine. Yet his own suicide is as much a part of his own theater as Artaud's last, speechless appearance is of his.

Until the outbreak of the Second World War, Witkacy was understood only by a few—maybe because we were all still *before*, while he was already *after*.

ON GOMBROWICZ

1

FACE
AND
GRIMACE

Even the best party becomes a hell if you cannot leave it. Throughout the war in German-occupied Warsaw, a curfew was imposed. An invitation to a party was an all-night invitation. Apartments were small: two, three, rarely four rooms. At each good party there is something of a "happening"—but imagine a happening performed and then repeated with tiresome regularity from ten P.M. till six A.M.

In occupied France a curfew was also enforced. Sartre's play *No Exit* probably originated from a similar experience. Guests crowded into a small apartment, drunks among drunks, clearheads among drunks, drunks among clearheads tell themselves their idiotic stories, push themselves into an increasingly grotesque psychodrama from which there is no exit and in which no one plays himself, nor the role that he would choose. He is cast by others. He is cast by the situation. As in Witold Gombrowicz's preface to *The Marriage,* "Being united, people impose upon one another this or that manner of being, speaking, behaving. . . . Each person deforms other persons, while being at the same time deformed by them." Arthur Rimbaud's *"Je est un autre" ("I* is somebody else") is in Gombrowicz a *gueule* put on me, and my only recourse is to make an even worse *gueule*—to grimace—an even more horrible and shameful *gueule* on others.

In the winter of 1943 in occupied Warsaw, I was invited by a young actress to an all-night party. Toward morning, strange sounds reached me from the next room. I opened the door a crack and noticed two young men kneeling opposite each other. They were banging their heads against the floor, and then, at the count of three, they raised their heads and mimicked each other, grimacing in the most sinister way. It was a duel of grimaces until the opponent had been completely wiped out, until a face was made against which there could be no counter-face. All faces were permissible: intimate and sexual, professional and political, ideological and historical. The face of a virgin, of a queer and of a bridegroom, of a patriot and of a traitor, conservative and radical, Churchill's face and Hitler's face and finally the face of Father, the face of King, and the face of God. I can't remember any more whether there was an appropriate answer to the face of God. It was already daybreak and I left.

One of the two young men engaged in this duel of grimaces was Jerzy Andrzejewski, the other Czesław Miłosz.[1] It is not so important that it was specifically these two writers who knelt opposite each other and made horrible faces that winter night of 1943—but even then they were both possessed by Gombrowicz. Not only these two. Already there were a few of us who had been infected by Gombrowicz, or more precisely by *Ferdydurke*.

> "The two contestants will stand facing each other and will make a series of faces. Each and every constructive and beautiful face made by Siphon will be answered by an ugly and destructive counter-face made by Mientus. The faces made will be as personal and as wounding as possible, and the contestants will continue to make them until a final decision is reached."
>
> He fell silent. Siphon and Mientus took up their positions. Siphon tapped his cheeks, Mientus rolled his jaw, and Bobek, with his teeth chattering, said:
>
> "You may begin!"
>
> At these words reality burst from its frame, unreality turned into nightmare, the whole improbable adventure became a dream in which I was imprisoned with no possibility of even struggling. It was as if after long training a point had been reached at which one lost one's own face. It would not have been surprising if Mientus and Siphon had taken their faces in their hands and thrown them at each other; nothing would have been surprising. I muttered:
>
> "Take pity on your faces, take pity on my face, for a face is not an object but a subject, a subject, a subject!"

Ferdydurke was published in Poland in 1937. In this novel we have the whole Gombrowicz. It is still his most important book.

---

[1] Jerzy Andrzejewski (1909–83), author of *Ashes and Diamonds* (London, 1982), *The Gates of Paradise* (London, 1963), and *The Appeal* (New York, 1971), is probably the most important novelist of postwar Poland. Both Andrzejewski and Miłosz were very active in the literary resistance movement during the war in Nazi-occupied Warsaw.

Out of the duel of grimaces in *Ferdydurke* later developed the Gombrowiczian theory of social behavior and particularly of aggression and mutual debasement. This duel contains Gombrowicz's entire theater.

The unexpected source of this duel of grimaces in *Ferdydurke* is Rabelais's *Gargantua and Pantagruel*. In the second Book, a Great English Scholar named Thaumast comes to visit Pantagruel in Paris. He challenges Pantagruel to a philosophical disputation. The subjects of the disputation, however, are so lofty and deep that they are beyond verbal articulation. It is advised, therefore, that this scholastic debate before doctors and students of the Sorbonne be expressed in grimaces.

> And then, everybody being present and listening in dead silence, the Englishman raised his two hands high in the air, one at a time, clenching the extremities of his fingers into the shape known in the Chinon country as the hen's arse; and with one hand he struck the other with his nails four times, then opened his hands and with the palm of one struck the other a resounding slap. Joining them as before, he struck twice, and then four times more, opening them as he did so, then brought them together and stretched them out in front of him, as though he were devoutly praying to God.

In this duel, Panurge, who substitutes for his master, Pantagruel, outgrimaces his opponent.

> . . . Panurge placed the two master fingers at each side of his mouth, stretching his mouth out as far as possible and displaying all his teeth, while with his two thumbs he pulled down the lids of his eyes, making a face that was quite ugly, or so it seemed to those present.

Thaumast cannot make a more horrible face and so concedes defeat.

Gombrowicz ranked Rabelais among his masters. And it seems odd that in the many, not just essays, but entire books about Gombrowicz, written not only in Poland but even in France and Germany, no one has pointed out Rabelais's influence. A few critics, making use of Mikhail Bakhtin's categories, have noted carnival elements in Gombrowicz's view of the world, but these carnival inversions and indecent proposals have their source and model in *Gargantua*. Gombrowicz's mug and backside are straight out of Rabelais's epic work. In Gombrowicz's theater even more important are gestures. Terrible faces, obscene proposals, pointing fingers, hiccups, and all the other indecorous voices of the flesh, derive from Rabelais. This observation ought to be singularly useful to directors of Gombrowicz's plays.

Rabelais, however, is only half the tradition. What could be more theatrical than attaching noses, and making faces at others? And what could be more Molière? Obviously this Molièresque Gombrowicz or Gombrowiczian Molière (Gombrowicz was always for me more in the tradition of Molière than Shakespeare) is perfidious and turned around. But, in fact, it is not so remote from modern interpretations of Molière as it might seem. Molièristes, even the most dignified among them, have recently become more and more concerned with the problem of face and mask.

Tartuffe is a mask, but does a true face of Tartuffe exist? He is not what he pretends to be and what he pretends to be is someone else. He performs, but what happens if he performs faultlessly? He pretends, but what happens if he pretends perfectly? He wears a mask, but what if he never takes it off? A perfect impostor is a living contradiction. He has become his role. He no longer has a face; the mask is his face. Tartuffe is a fake saint. But the fake saint is the true Tartuffe. Tartuffe plays: lies and pretense are his truth as an actor. "The falsest of appearances joins the truest being. . . . The result is . . . that in order 'to be true' the actor must play false." I quote from Sartre's Introduction to Genet's *The Maids* and *Deathwatch*.

Molière's Tartuffe is not a perfect impostor. He plays badly. He overacts. His mask falls off. Tartuffe is not just a hypocrite, a *faux dévot,* he is an *apparent* hypocrite, a *faux faux dévot.* Hypocrisy is already a role—that is, a fake; a false hypocrite is a role on top of a role, a face on a face, impurity on impurity. Pure Gombrowicz! "Their truth is their lie," writes Sartre about *The Maids,* "and their lie is their truth." And once again: "the fake is true and the true can be expressed only by means of the fake."

In his preface to *The Marriage,* Gombrowicz writes: "The characters in this play do not express themselves directly; they are artificial; they are always acting. The play is thus a waterfall of masks, gestures, shouts, grimaces. . . . It should be played 'artificially,' but never at the expense of the normal human quality that is discernible throughout the text."

The mask falls off for the first time; Damis secretly observes Tartuffe's seduction of Elmire and tries, unsuccessfully, to tell everything to Orgon. Tartuffe kneels. He confesses his guilt. He makes a face on a mask, truth on a lie, which is a new face.

Do you trust my pious face?
Ah, no, don't be deceived by hollow shows;
I'm far, alas, from being what men suppose;

Though the world takes me for a man of worth,
I'm truly the most worthless man on earth.

> [trans. Richard Wilbur]

And now Orgon is on his knees. For each pious contortion of Tartuffe, a pious contortion of Orgon. He will surrender everything—his wife, his daughter, his house—if only Tartuffe remains. The two fat men now kneel opposite each other and distort their faces in foxy grimaces. The devout face of Tartuffe is countered by the even more devout face of Orgon, and this in turn by the super-face of Tartuffe. Tartuffe and Orgon engage in a duel of grimaces, humility and dignity, like Siphon and Mientus in *Ferdydurke*:

> [Siphon] burst into tears, pious, bitter tears, floods of tears that reached the heights of remorse, revelation, and ecstasy. Mientus burst into tears too, and sobbed and sobbed until a tear trickled down to the end of his nose—whereupon he caused it to drop into a spittoon, thus reaching a new level of disgustingness. This assault upon the most sacred feelings was too much for Siphon . . . [he] beat a hasty retreat, recomposed his features, and once more elevated his eyes towards heaven. He advanced one foot slightly, slightly ruffled his hair, caused a lock to droop over his forehead, and froze into a position of unshakable unity with his principles and ideals; then he raised one hand, and pointed towards the stars. This was a powerful blow.

Ultimately, who puts a face on whom in Molière? Tartuffe on Orgon or Orgon on Tartuffe? All Tartuffe's grimaces are for the benefit of Orgon. Orgon is his audience. For Orgon he lies prostrate in church, casts his eyes to heaven, and lasciviously distorts his face when Dorine appears to him with bared breasts. In Gombrowicz's anthropology, *cul*, backside, butt, the pink fanny of the baby, and *gueule*, face, grimace, mug, are key concepts. In Gombrowicz's system, the backside and the *gueule* are as important as in Sartre, *"en soi"* and *"pour soi."* However, this pink bottom and mug *(pupa* and *gęba* in Polish) are much more palpable, physical, concrete. Tartuffe's faces, all his holy faces, serve to bring about Orgon's final "bottomification." Of all comic characters, Orgon is the most perfect embodiment of Gombrowicz's infantile cruelty, fanny-pink and soft-fresh. Orgon is necessary for Tartuffe, but Tartuffe is even more necessary to Orgon. Without Tartuffe, Orgon, Père Orgon, could never become Père Ubu. Tartuffe is his raison d'être, his philosophy and justification. If there were no Tartuffe, Orgon would have to invent him. For Orgon, Tartuffe is a deputy of God, but for himself, he preserves the role of a deputy of the king. Without a God in the house, he could never have become a domestic tyrant.[2]

Orgon and Tartuffe are created by and for each other. Each alone is incomplete, unfinished, in the Gombrowiczian sense, immature. Tartuffe is a starving cheat, Orgon a frustrated tyrant. Each needs a grimace from the other. They ascend on each other's faces. However, their imagined patterns and models, that of a perfect hypocrite and a family tyrant, are also inadequate, unsuccessful, and apparent. Authenticity does not arise from faces only. When the Sun King (the "King" of comedy appears as *rex ex machina* for a happy ending and consequently is also a fake) orders Tartuffe to be led out under guard, Orgon will remain alone. All his grimaces have fallen off; he has no face at all.

"Le monde n'est composé que des mines," wrote La Rochefoucauld in his *Maxims*. During my first year at Yale, I lived in the guest suite in one of the colleges. Every Friday there was a mixer. At five o'clock chartered girls arrived, tightly packed in chartered buses. In the buses they had changed from girls to Dates. They had the smiles of dates, voices of dates, hairdos of dates, panties of dates, and bras of dates. They brought sex along with them, putting on sex like sweaters and bell-bottomed pants because dates must be sexy. The boys were no longer boys. They lost all their charm, simplicity, and freshness; grimacing, they reacted to the artificial female faces with even more artificial male faces. In mutual degradation and imposing their fanny-pink maturity on each other, the boys and girls practiced the obligatory ritual of Friday dating. Till two o'clock in the morning. The mixer lasts with terrifying American punctuality and precision. Everything planned in advance—coffee, drinks, dinner, dancing, petting, and the good-night kiss.

La Rochefoucauld said: "The world is composed entirely of grimaces." Gombrowicz reverses this sentence; the grimace is the first and material reality of the world. Each ceremony, ritual, and initiation, which in his terminology he calls "Form," is a Face. Form originates from mutual deformation, imposing on each other female-male faces, adult-immature faces, faces of the Son, of the Father, of

---

[2]Lionel Gossman, *Men and Masks: A Study of Molière* (Baltimore: The Johns Hopkins Press, 1963): "Orgon is bent on using Tartuffe as much as Tartuffe is bent on using him . . . . Orgon sets himself up against society as the only true Christian in it. The function of Tartuffe is to guarantee Orgon's superiority to everybody else."

the King. Form arises from mutual immaturity and the urge for mutual debasement.

Gombrowicz, like Genet, is fascinated by ceremony. As in Genet, theater is ritual, but ritual performed and repeated on stage. Thus, ritual is at the same time a counter-ritual, an aping of ceremony, therefore a repetition of faces by actors. In this mutual distortion and mockery, the actors create their social roles. To be somebody means for Gombrowicz to be inflated by the form, and therefore deformed. To be somebody is to be somebody or something else, inauthentic.

In *The Marriage,* Gombrowicz uses the logic of nightmare. Dreaming, we are ourselves and not ourselves. We are ourselves because we dream. We are not ourselves or we are not fully ourselves because we are dreamed. Our body is also limited, concentrated in one part: arm, leg, member. It is a deformed corporality. We are lighter or heavier. Our freedom of movement is restricted. We cannot get out of our own dream. The dream is real, because it is we who dream, but at the same time, the dream is an illusion because it is only a dream. In dreams our relation with others and with our own ego is degraded, immature, compromised. Id has no face. Everyone in the dream gets his face from the dream. The dream is composed only of faces. In his *Journal (1957–1961)* Gombrowicz writes: "Is there anything strange in the fact that the dream (which is a discharge of the anxieties of the day) shows to Henry the ruin and degradation of his parents, his fiancée, his home? Is it so strange that in this dream, dreamed in an inn, there appear drunkards, and that these drunkards begin to harass the father when he forbids them to get at Molly? Is it not logical and in harmony with the situation that the father, mad with fright, proclaims himself—to escape the touch of the drunkards—untouchable king? And that Henry feels that the miracle will be sustained or turned into a farce depending on him-self—is this not a feeling we have in many dreams?"

When the Drunkard in the key scene of *The Marriage* points his erect finger at the Innkeeper-Father, Henry kneels, and by kneel-ing creates the dignity of the Father and the obedience of the Son. The Father is King, because the King is Father. However, the King is not complete without God. Therefore, the Father of the King is God the Father. The Father now sinks to his knees. They kneel before each other, like Orgon and Tartuffe, like Mientus and Siphon, like Andrzejewski and Miłosz. They kneel and trade grimaces: the face of the Son, the face of the Father, the face of the King, the face of God the Father. As in Molière, Tartuffe conquers in this scene. He assumed the face of god: "In all things let the will of Heaven be done." In *The Marriage:*

> HENRY: . . . *(He gazes around with distrust and kneels down.)* . . . I am kneeling before him and he is kneeling before me. This is a farce! What an old copycat he is! *(With increasing rage.)* How disgusting!
>
> FATHER: Wait a minute! I'm kneeling in the wrong direction. *(Kneels down with his back to HENRY.)* I kneel down before the Lord! I address myself to the Lord! I commend myself to Almighty God, to the Holy Trinity, to His inexhaustible goodness, to His mercy most holy, His protection most sublime . . .

Now the Innkeeper-Father points his finger to heaven. Like Tartuffe, like Siphon in *Ferdydurke,* like the Drunkard a moment ago. In Gombrowicz ceremony is parody of ceremony, ritual, a mockery of ritual. Taking an oath one raises one's fingers. I raise my fingers and I am somebody else. "I do," I am king. "I do," I am president. "I do," I am judge. "I do," I am sworn witness. "I do," I am married. The Innkeeper transformed into Father, Father into King, King into God the Father, in turn transforms Henry into the Prince; and Molly, the wench from the inn, sport for the drunkards, becomes the immaculate bride. The marriage can now take place. But before this happens the King-Father will be dethroned, and Henry himself will proclaim himself King. This role is also ready-made. The Usurper is King Ubu.

In Gombrowicz's theater, as in Genet's, ceremony is mockery. The Black Mass is an insult to a god in whom one still believes. If there is no God, there can be no blasphemy. For Genet the impossibility of fulfillment, the grimace before the mirror, the gesture in empty space or in a locked cell is tragic. For Gombrowicz this absolute impossibility is grotesque. Gombrowicz's theater is more vulgar, physical, and coarse. Siphon's erect finger, the Drunkard's huge finger which he points at the Father, the King's finger raised upwards—each has its glaring phallic imagery. Gombrowicz is close to *dell'arte,* the farce, and Molière, and what is probably more striking, to young American playwrights.

The American motel also has its liturgy and ceremony: silence, cleanliness, hygiene, and respect for civilization are required in it. It is for married couples; they must sign the guest register. Purity, sanity, and morality are guarded by the proprietor.

In Jean-Claude van Itallie's play, *America Hurrah,* a huge puppet with a vacuum cleaner stands on the threshold of the room. She is waiting for the American couple. They arrive. He and she. Two puppets. They close the door and methodically, systematically with American precision, they demolish everything in the room. They tear comforters and sheets, break the armchairs, smash the television set, pull out the shower in the bathroom. They write obscenities on the walls, draw female-male genitals. Then they tumble into the unmade bed.

For this theater, Gombrowicz is a forerunner. He is fascinated by degradation, destruction, debasement, and by all that is shameful, low, and physical, things that are natural and therefore called unnatural. The attempt to rebuild order and bring about the solemn ceremony of marriage is degraded and destroyed by universal stupidity and aggressiveness, personified by the chorus of Drunkards shouting, "Pig! Pig!" This need for shame and artificiality is clearest in Gombrowicz's attitude to Woman. Before becoming the bride the girl must be debased, must be a wench in the inn, must lose her virginity, to have this "virginity" artificially restored by ceremony. As in the case of Genet, Woman becomes sexually arousing only when mated with masculinity, when she has been part of another man, when another man is still fresh in her. The girl in the girl must be destroyed, must be made to resemble the farmhand as much as possible.

> HENRY: All the same, who knows whether it is
> possible . . . whether in general it is possible for a man
> to fall in love with a woman without the co-operation,
> without the intermediary of another man? It may be
> that in general man is incapable of responding to a
> woman except through the intermediary of another
> man. Might this not be some new form of love? Before,
> only two were needed, but today it's three.

The Marriage ends in catastrophe. Just as remnants of day pass through dreams, the most nonrealistic work contains fragments of reality, a sphere of meaning which can be explained directly and simply.

The Marriage could take place anywhere or nowhere at all, but this particular Henry begins to dream in France. The hero not only has a name, he is a Polish soldier during World War II. We can even set the action precisely—in June of 1940 after the defeat of France near Dunkirk, where the routed Polish units desperately awaited evacuation to England. A return to Poland was impossible for years. For more complex reasons, personal and political, the return to Poland seemed impossible for the émigré Gombrowicz when in 1946, in Buenos Aires, he was writing *The Marriage*. The Poland that he had left in 1939 no longer existed. This impossible return to a real Poland is transformed in his dream into a possible return to an unreal Poland. As Poland becomes more artificial and anachronistic, the more real becomes the return. And so, the manor and the inn, the relics of old country life, and finally the feudal archetypes of Prince and Usurper. It is certainly not accidental that Act III of *The Marriage*, showing the grotesque cruelty in Henry's reign, is like Jarry's *Ubu Roi* in its texture and atmosphere. As in *The Marriage*, the action of *Ubu Roi* takes place "in Poland, that is, nowhere." However, even in fiction and dream, this return to the most unreal of homes and the most unreal of marriages cannot be fulfilled.

The Marriage ends with a funeral march and Henry imprisoned. As in Genet's *The Maids*, Solange and Claire can only kill Madame in a symbolic ritual gesture. To kill or sleep with her they have to play her. In reality, the poor maids sleep together or poison each other. The pressure of reality is stronger than any fiction, and the only real return to Poland that Gombrowicz could imagine was a return to prison.

In 1942 after the defeat of France, in the most hopeless of the wartime winters, the drunken night parties in Warsaw sometimes ended in a duel of grimaces from *Ferdydurke*. But this game could not change anything; it was only a grimace at a blacked-out window, beyond which spread the night of occupation. *The Marriage* has a bitter taste, Polish and universal.

2
ALBERTINE
ETERNALLY
YOUTHFUL
Each theatrical encounter with Gombrowicz yields a discovery. In *Ivona* there was actually little need to discover Shakespeare, so close was he to the surface, often like a too persistent echo. In *The Marriage*, I discovered Molière and the duel of grimaces from Rabelais's *Gargantua*. In *Operetta* I suddenly saw the unexpected, Aristophanes. *Operetta* ends with an apotheosis as does Aristophanes' *Birds*, where the Bride from Heaven ("Miss Universe" in Arrowsmith's translation) floats down from Olympus. "O youthful nudity, nudely youthful, O nudity of youth, youthfully nude!" Albertine, whom two pickpockets kidnap from the castle of Himalay during the confusion that ends the masked ball, steps out of a coffin naked.

In Aristophanes, obscene gestures alternate with lyric, the low mixes with the high, the vulgar with the lofty and the scoffing with the urbane. Aristophanes was ashamed of nothing, neither the gods nor the phallus. He was not afraid of seriousness or laughter. Each time I read Gombrowicz or see one of his plays, I admire his boldness. He was not afraid of kitsch. The low genre in the theater was always the operetta as in television the soap opera. Gombrowicz was not afraid of the low.

In *Operetta*, the last of his plays, Gombrowicz displays all the daring of Aristophanes in mixing "the monumental idiocy of the operetta . . . with the monumental pathos of history: an operetta mask concealing the bloody visage of mankind, contorted by a ridiculous pain." Thus once again we have the great Gombrowiczian juxtapositions: face and grimace, "bottom" and "mug." This time, however, in this operettic idiocy, the whirlwind of history will scatter the aristocratic guests at the masquerade ball in the castle of Himalay and reveal the terrifying costumes of the past. The rebellious lackeys will bring about a revolution as they did in Zygmunt Krasiński's masterpiece of Polish Romantic drama, *The Undivine Comedy* (1835). But the operatic revolution of Gombrowicz is in a Marxist-terrorist mode.

Before that happens, however, Gombrowicz's "mug" and "backside" return in new operettic disguise. Count Charmant is smitten with Albertine, "a marvel of a lass." It is Sunday and there is a promenade on the square in front of the church. In a moment Mass will end and Albertine will leave the church with her parents, and, as usual, will sit down on a bench. But Count Charmant cannot sit down next to her because, alas! he has not been introduced. But he finds a way out. His faithful valet brings along a pickpocket, but on a leash just in case. The pickpocket is to sneak up to Albertine and filch her locket. Count Charmant is to snatch the locket away from the thief and, with a great show of gallantry, return it to Albertine.

Albertine is even more sluggish than Ivona, Princess of Burgundia. She sits down on the bench with her needlework and immediately falls asleep. But before he steals Albertine's locket, the pickpocket slips his hand into her bosom. Albertine is aroused in her sleep: from now on she desires nudity. Count Charmant wants to dress her, but she wants to be undressed. And undressed and undressed and undressed. She is still asleep in her naughty dream where she is being touched. She parts her lips and legs. She is now one with her desire and that desire is the hand of the pickpocket. In

Gombrowicz's private mythology, which intoxicated many of his followers, the mating couple is the Victorian boardingschool girl and the stable boy. The stable boy is the low and forbidden which attracts and arouses. Strindberg was the first to dramatize attraction by shame in *Miss Julie*.

Once again, within the "idiocy" of the operetta the high and low return. "High" is the operettic "idiocy" somewhat elevated to the skyscraping Himalayas by Gombrowicz's sarcasm ("the aristocracy does not possess a single peculiarity which might distinguish it from the common people, except for one, but one which is decisive— namely, that it is the aristocracy. And what, ladies and gentlemen, is the aristocracy? It's the aristocracy, pure and simple"). And what is "low"? To Gombrowicz, with his fascination with making faces and gestures, theatricality first of all is the debasement. Even though it was years ago, I still remember how Gombrowicz would say to me: "You cannot understand this, my dear Kott, your origins are too humble."

But what is low in Gombrowicz? The "low" is the gentleman professor who has been converted to Marxism and revolutionary theory, constantly vomiting while the revolutionized lackeys, who once licked their masters' shoes to a shine, kick him mercilessly in the backside (Gombrowicz, when writing *Operetta*, told one of his friends that the professor was modeled on Jean-Paul Sartre). The "low" is also the Count and Baron taking off their pants after the mock duel, and the unleashed pickpockets who, at the end of the ball, throw themselves upon the aristocratic guests in the Himalay castle, pinching and tickling them.

This unmatched corporeality in Gombrowicz's *Operetta*/anti-operetta derives from the folk carnival or the Roman *ludus,* in which the high is exchanged for the low and the lower half of the human body takes revenge on the upper. At the end of Act II, however, the whirlwind of history sweeps the guests out of the carnival costumes. In this libretto (which displays the imagination and freedom of Aristophanes), the last act is set after the "revolution" on the ruins of the Himalay castle, which is Gombrowicz's derisive transformation of Krasiński's Ramparts of the Holy Trinity. It is at this time that under the "mask of the operetta," "the bloody visage of mankind, contorted by a ridiculous pain" shows itself. Even here, in a style that is quite pathetic for Gombrowicz, "pain" is "ridiculous." It is a "grimace" that mankind is making.

The theatricality and plasticity of Gombrowicz's imagination is striking not only because it derives from the carnival masquerade in which the world is turned upside down, but because it has also absorbed and transformed the later experiences of surrealism and seems to be the chronological counterpart of the sinister drawings of Topor. *Operetta* was written in 1967. Since then, one can see not only the oldest comic tradition from which Gombrowicz sprang, but also its unabashed novelty.

In Act III of *Operetta*, after the revolution, the Prince "with a big lampshade on his head concealing his face makes believe he is a lamp." A theatrical wind blows onstage. The Prince-Lamp says: "It's the wind of history!" The Princess of Himalay, "on all fours," is a table "covered with a tapestry." Hufnagel the revolutionary, astride the vomiting Professor, gallops to the head of the division of rebelling Lackeys. The Priest "emerges from a pile of debris. His cassock is pinned up in such a way that it looks like a blouse and skirt. On his head is a large woman's hat; in his hand an umbrella."

In spite of appearances (and the clichés of many "theater experts"), Gombrowicz owes almost nothing in this stage vision to Witkiewicz. Witkacy's settings and costumes are from the much earlier periods of Constructivism and Cubism. Gombrowicz's vision, on the other hand, attracted, and maybe even in its own way, shaped the theater and imagination of Tadeusz Kantor. In terms of theatrical material, Kantor is more Gombrowicz than Witkacy. The symbolic relationships between "philo, ideolo and meta" are translated into "materialistic" or, better, "material" relationships, into concrete detail: stage objects and action, the relationship of actor to mannequin and their mutual degradation.

Act III of *Operetta* is full, maybe even too full of "heavy" symbolism: the end of the old world, revolution, judgment of the Nazis, etc., but that "contorted visage of mankind" is illustrated in the "light" symbolism of the carnival in which people vomit, kick, run around, ride, disguise and unmask themselves, and talk gibberish. The old world is tossed into the coffin. That "coffin" is from the symbolist theater of Stanisław Wyspiański (who wrote at the turn of the century), and, if my memory serves me well, in the coffin were the ashes of the king. In Gombrowicz, out of a coffin as out of a bathtub (perhaps the stable boys stole an old prewar bathtub from the Himalay castle and carried the sleeping heroine in it) steps the nude Albertine. Gombrowicz's optimistic finale is a distinct retort to Witkiewicz's catastrophic vision in the ending of *The Water Hen*.

Operetta ends, as does *Birds,* with the triumph of Eros. And just as in *Birds,* this triumph is also undercut by mockery. Albertine is divested of her clothes as of the vanishing past and is freed from Form by what remains at the bottom: the two pickpockets.

Stefan Rudnicki, who directed *Operetta*, has directed all three of Gombrowicz's plays. Two of these I have seen only in his theater: *The Marriage*, ten years ago in Rochester, and *Operetta*, just recently in Greenvale on Long Island. I was able to see *Ivona* twice; once in Paris in 1965, under the innovative direction of Jorge Lavelli, with costumes and scene design by Krystyna Zachwatowicz. I remember how together we combed all the Parisian flea markets, secondhand shops, and automobile junkyards in search of old pipes, broken-down cars and various kinds of scrap metal. Krystyna's scenography for *Ivona* astonished Paris critics; they had never seen anything like it on stage. But I had seen *Ivona* earlier in Warsaw, in the Teatr Dramatyczny, at the first post-thaw premiere with the unforgettable Barbara Krafft. My God, that was more than a quarter of a century ago, and almost a half century (minus a trifling five years) has passed since the writing of *Ivona*. Stefan was my student at the Yale School of Drama in 1966–67 and that, too, was almost twenty years ago. Time passes too quickly and only Gombrowicz remains eternally youthful. Along with all the Albertines.

IONESCO,

OR A PREGNANT

DEATH

We all know that we shall die. But Ionesco knows it even as he eagerly reaches for a menu in a restaurant. Even while he eats, he knows he is dying. Each of Ionesco's doubles, the Bérengers in his comedies, knows it too. Not only is death constantly present in everything Ionesco writes, but it is present as *dying*—one's own and other people's, universal and incessant.

"When the bells toll for a funeral I am overcome with a mysterious anguish, a sort of fascination. We know all the people who die." This is one of the earliest entries in "Scattered Images of Childhood" from Ionesco's *Fragments of a Journal*. A few pages later, he writes ". . . when I was four or five years old I realized that I should grow older and older and that I should die. At about seven or eight, I said to myself that my mother would die some day and the thought terrified me." And once again: ". . . the only thing one can know is that death is there waiting for my mother, my family, myself."

Many years later, in his reminiscences of the Vaugirard Square, close to where he spent his Parisian childhood, Ionesco wrote: "When memory brings back a picture of that street, when I think that almost all those people are now dead, everything does indeed seem to me to be shadow and evanescence. My head spins with anguish. Really, that *is* the world: a desert of fading shadows" (*Notes and Counter Notes*). And the following two lines, which could have concluded

Bérenger's long monologue at his last meeting with the Killer: "It's to Death, above all, that I say 'Why?' with such terror. Death alone can, and will, close my mouth"(*Fragments*).

Ionesco's double in *The Killer* says: "We shall all die, this is the only serious alienation." In *Fragments of a Journal* we read: "The human condition is beyond bearing." And further: "I cannot understand how it should be that for hundreds and hundreds and hundreds of years men have accepted life and death in these intolerable conditions: have accepted an existence haunted by the fear of death, amid war and pain, without showing any real, open, decisive reaction against it. . . . We are caught in a sort of collective trap and we don't even rebel seriously against it."

One could go on and on citing such quotations, but they are tiresome in their monotony: death is the process of dying, there is no cure for it and no reconciliation. It is as if there were nothing else to say. Ionesco had intended to write his dissertation at the Sorbonne on "Sin and Death in Poetry after Baudelaire." He never completed his thesis. Smitten by death, he became an author of comedies.

According to the simplest definition, comedy is a spectacle which evokes laughter. "Nothing is more difficult," wrote Molière, "than to amuse *les honnêtes gens*." But who are *les honnêtes gens* now? You and me: we all laugh at Ionesco. The comic power of *The Bald Soprano, The Lesson,* and *Amédée* compares only with that of Chaplin's early films. They arouse and continue to arouse loud laughter.

What kind of laughter is it, and what is its object? "When I say: is life worth dying for? I am still using words. But at least they're comic" *(Fragments)*. In other words, dying can be amusing when it is talked about or performed. "For my part," Ionesco explains in *Notes and Counter Notes*, "I have never understood the difference people make between the comic and the tragic. As the 'comic' is an intuitive perception of the absurd, it seems to me more hopeless than the 'tragic.' The 'comic' offers no escape. I say 'hopeless,' but in reality it lies outside the boundaries of hope or despair. . . . For it seems to me that the comic is tragic, and that the tragedy of man is pure derision."

The tragic is a source of metaphysical consolation. The tragic without metaphysics—ordinary dying which nothing will justify, the absurd without hope—is ridiculous. "Pure derision," writes Ionesco. And where does it occur? On stage. The *ridiculous-tragic* is a theatrical genre. In 1960 he wrote: "But when these older writers use the comic and mix it with the tragic, in the end their characters are no longer funny: it is the tragic that prevails. In my plays it is just the opposite: they start by being comic, are tragic for a moment and end up in comedy or tragi-comedy." Ionesco called *The Bald Soprano* an anti-play, *The Lesson* a comic drama, *The Chairs* a tragic farce. In *Victims of Duty,* Nicolas explains to the Detective: "No more drama, no more tragedy: the tragic's turning comic, the comic is tragic, and life's getting more cheerful . . . more cheerful."

"Tragicomedy" would in this case be a misleading term. The "cheerful life" Nicolas envisions for the Detective is a "tragic farce." Using Aristotelian terms, we would say that terror is to be accompanied by laughter rather than by pity and compassion.[1] The tragic hero must first perform his role clownishly. As a result, the terror of his tragic situation is revealed for a moment, only to be overcome by laughter so that life can become "more cheerful" again.

Ionesco has been transforming the *ridiculous-tragic* into the *tragic-ridiculous*, both in his reflections, and in his plays from *The Chairs, Jack, or the Submission* and *Amédée*, to *The Killer* and *Exit the King*. This dual exchange of theatrical signs, the inverted sequence of the tragic and the ridiculous, seems to give the formula for tragic buffoonery. The best and perhaps the oldest description of this theatrical genre was given by Peter Quince in *A Midsummer Night's Dream* after he assembles his actors for the first rehearsal. "Marry, our play is ' The most lamentable comedy and most cruel death of Pyramus and Thisby.' "

The "most cruel death of Pyramus and Thisby," as the long title indicates, is a "comedy," but it is a "most lamentable" one. This little play, performed by Athenian craftsmen, is a burlesque of *Romeo and Juliet*, which one of the Quartos called "The most excellent and lamentable tragedie." The most cruel death of Romeo and Juliet as well as the most cruel death of Bérenger in *The Killer* and in *Exit the King* have been made comic. Nevertheless these comedies are "most lamentable." "Take a tragedy," Ionesco wrote in his *Notes and Counter Notes*, "accelerate the movement, and you will have a comic play . . . ;" and more emphatically: "A burlesque text, play it dramatic. A dramatic text, play it burlesque."

The first performances of Ionesco's plays in the 1950s aroused simultaneous delight and resistance, admiration and horror at their

---

[1] "This non-Aristotelian theater presents us with a problem which Aristotle had not foreseen: that of pity and fear for which *laughter* is a catharsis" (J. S. Doubrovsky, "Ionesco and the Comic of Absurdity," *Yale French Studies* 23 [1959] : 9).

astounding novelty. And yet, most astounding in Ionesco's tragic farces is their reversion to the most ancient and the most persistent tradition of comic theater and carnival pageantry: the world is set on its head, the beggar is proclaimed king, the ship of fools represents the human condition, clowns conduct laical and religious rites, death struts in a procession of masks through city streets, dying is equated with breeding, and life becomes "more cheerful."

> The darkness has scarcely descended into the narrow, highwalled street before lights are seen moving in the windows and on the stands; in next to no time the fire has circulated far and wide, and the whole street is lit up by burning candles. . . . It becomes everyone's duty to carry a lighted candle in his hand, and the favorite imprecation of the Romans, "Sia ammazzato," is heard repeatedly on all sides.
>
> "Sia ammazzato chi non porta moccolo:" "Death to anyone who is not carrying a candle." This is what you say to others, while at the same time you try to blow out their candles.

In this way, Goethe begins his description in *Italian Journey* of the 1788 Carnival in Rome.

> The louder the cries of *Sia ammazzato*, the more these words lose their sinister meaning and you forget that you are in Rome, where, at any other time but Carnival, and for a trifling reason, the wish expressed by these words might be literally fulfilled.
>
> Just as in other languages curses and obscene words are often used as expressions of joy or admiration, so, on this evening, the true meaning of *Sia ammazzato* is completely forgotten, and it becomes a password, a cry of joy, a refrain added to all jokes and compliments. . . .
>
> All ages and all classes contend furiously with each other. Carriage steps are climbed; no chandelier and scarcely a paper lantern is safe. A boy blows out his father's candle, shouting "Sia ammazzato il Signore Padre!" In vain the old man scolds him for this outrageous behaviour; the boy claims the freedom of the evening and curses his father all the more vehemently.

Ionesco wrote in his *Notes*, ". . . laughter alone respects no taboo . . . ; the comic alone is able to give us the strength to bear the tragedy of existence." His earlier "intuition of the absurd," like his "tragedy of existence," is a debt paid to the philosophy fashionable in the fifties. Ionesco's true "intuition," however, was the return to carnival celebration where, like in the ancient Saturnalia, our modern *angst* was present, but where masks of Death were accompanied by masks adorned with phalluses, and with this inversion of signs, funeral rites were turned into rites of wedding.

"There is nothing unfamiliar," continues Goethe, "about seeing figures in fancy dress or masks out in the streets under the clear sky. They can be seen every day of the year. No corpse is brought out to the grave without being accompanied by hooded religious fraternities. The monks in their many kinds of costumes accustom the eye to peculiar figures. There seems to be the Carnival all the year round. . . ." I once watched in New Orleans an amateur theater troupe which chose a funeral as the subject for a ballet. The rhythmic wailing to blues melodies gradually became more and more ecstatic. Voices rose to an ever higher pitch as a coffin was lifted higher and higher. From beneath long black skirts legs squiggled out as if they had a life of their own. A moment later the coffin swayed in the air, like the dancing hips and bellies.

New Orleans is one of the few places where old carnival traditions, which link together images of sex and death, still retain their compelling symbolism. As Goethe continues in his description of the Roman Carnival, "On the side streets are young fellows dressed up as women, one of whom seems to be far advanced in pregnancy. . . . As if from shock, the pregnant woman is taken ill, a chair is brought and the other women give her aid. She moans like a woman in labour, and the next thing you know, she has brought some misshapen thing into the world, to the great amusement of the onlookers."

According to the oldest traditions of Saturnalia, the woman who gives birth is Death. "In the famous Kerch terracotta collection," writes Mikhail Bakhtin in *Rabelais and His World*, "we find figurines of senile pregnant hags. Moreover, the old hags are laughing. . . . It is pregnant death, a death that gives birth. There is nothing completed, nothing calm and stable in the bodies of these old hags. They combine a senile, decaying and deformed flesh with the flesh of new life, conceived but as yet unformed."

The body, Bakhtin writes, is shown in its twofold contradictory process of decay and growth: a pregnant death. The Saturnalian and carnival signs epitomize the perpetuity and continuity of life and thereby negate completely Samuel Beckett's cruel vision of continuous dying: ". . . one day we were born, one day we shall die, the same day, the same second. . . . they give birth astride of the grave . . . ."

The death that gives birth in a carnival farce is not a young woman, pregnant with a new death, but an old hag pregnant with a new fetus. The body, which is decaying, conceives. Awe occasions laughter: in the symbolism of carnival it is one and the same body. Bakhtin continues:

> One of the fundamental tendencies of the grotesque image of the body is to show two bodies in one: the one giving birth and dying, the other conceived, generated, and born. This is the pregnant and begetting body, or at least a body ready for conception and fertilization. . . . .
>
> In contrast to modern canons, the age of the body is most frequently represented in immediate proximity to birth or death, to infancy or old age, to the womb or the grave, to the bosom that gives life or swallows it up. But at their extreme limit the two bodies unite to form one. The individual is shown at the stage when it is recast into a new mold. It is dying and as yet unfinished; the body stands on the threshold of the grave and the crib. . . .
>
> The unfinished and open body (dying, bringing forth and being born) is not separated from the world by clearly defined boundaries; it is blended with the world, with animals, with objects. It is cosmic, it represents the entire material bodily world in all its elements. It is an incarnation of this world at the absolute lower stratum, as the swallowing up and generating principle, as the bodily grave and bosom, as a field which has been sown and in which new shoots are preparing to sprout.

Carnival imagination and wisdom which Bakhtin discovered in Rabelais are also a surprisingly apt introduction to the world of Ionesco's *Jack, or the Submission* and *The Future Is in Eggs*. In both plays, Ionesco appears to be reusing the old formula for a comedy of manners about two families, a shy young man, an ugly miss, a matchmaker, an engagement, a wedding, and a long wait for progeny. But the "naturalistic comedy" becomes a carnival farce, almost an animal farm. The characters are all "Jacks" or "Robertas" with identical face-masks. Their bodies are unfinished, at once decaying and growing. Herded together, they begin to lose even their human shape. Body parts multiply as with the three noses of Roberta II or the nine fingers on her hand.

> JACK: . . . You're rich, I'll marry you . . .
>
> *[They put their arms around each other very awkwardly. Jack kisses the noses of Roberta II, one after the other, while Father Jack, Mother Jack, Jacqueline, the Grandparents, Father Robert, and Mother Robert enter without saying a word, one after the other, waddling along, in a sort of ridiculous dance, embarrassing, in a vague circle, around Jack and Roberta II who remain at stage center, awkwardly enlaced. Father Robert silently and slowly strikes his hands together. Mother Robert, her hands clasped behind her neck, makes pirouettes, smiling stupidly. Mother Jack, with an expressionless face,*

shakes her shoulders in a grotesque fashion. Father Jack pulls up his pants and walks on his heels. Jacqueline nods her head, then they continue to dance, squatting down, while Jack and Roberta II squat down too, and remain motionless. . . . The darkness increases. On stage, the actors utter vague miaows while turning around, bizarre moans, croakings. The darkness increases. We can still see the Jacks and Roberts crawling on the stage. We hear their animal noises, then we don't see them any more. We hear only their moans, their sighs, then all fades away, all is extinguished. Again, a gray light comes on. All the characters have disappeared, except Roberta, who is lying down, or rather squatting down, buried beneath her gown. We see only her pale face, with its three noses quivering, and her nine fingers moving like snakes.]

In *The Future Is in Eggs*, the barnyard changes into a chicken coop. Roberta II lays eggs, one after the other. She is oviparous. There is no limit to multiplying by way of eggs and the eggs are all the same. The future is in the eggs. Indistinguishable Jacko-Robertas will hatch from them. But even in this carnival chicken coop of boundless fertility, where individuality has been eradicated and life is reduced to the egg, death is present. Even before the young wife begins to lay eggs in a basket, grandfather Jack dies. To "die" means to enter an empty frame. As a matter of fact, he will shock the whole family when he steps out of his frame for a moment to hum to himself.

For Freud laughter is the bribe accepted by the censor of morals for permitting a joke that exposes prurient desires and forbidden wishes. More strictly prohibited, and repressed, is the dread of death, the fear that we will die. All of us. The bribe for revealing this dread and this fear is also laughter. The archaic pregnant Death laughs. Amidst piles of carnival litter, the begetting of a misshapen monster by a man dressed as a woman evokes riotous laughter. Dread of the end spawns a jolly spectacle. According to Bakhtin, "Death and death throes, labor, and childbirth are intimately interwoven. On the other hand, these images are closely linked to laughter. When death and birth are shown in their comic aspect, scatological images in various forms nearly always accompany the gay monsters created by laughter in order to replace the terror that has been defeated."

With characteristic insight, Goethe perceived the same interwoven images of death, sex, and birth in the carnival pantomimes performed on the streets of Rome: "In the course of all these follies our attention is drawn to the most important stages of human life: a vulgar Pulcinella recalls to us the pleasures of love to which we owe our existence; a Baubo profanes in a public place the mysteries of birth and motherhood, and the many lighted candles remind us of the ultimate ceremony."

Pulcinella, as he left the *commedia dell'arte* for the streets, always wore a black leather mask with an enormous hooked nose over his eyes and brow. Harlequin had a similar mask, but his costume was different. Pulcinella wore a large white cylindrical hat, white breeches and jacket, a hump on his back and padding in his belly.

Entertainment for Children,[2] Domenico Tiepolo's ironic title for his series of a hundred wash drawings, is a great "tragic farce." This sad and cheerful, bitter and derisive story covers in a hundred scenes the life of Pulcinella—from his birth out of a turkey's egg to his banishment from eighteenth-century Venice.

The title drawing of Tiepolo's *Entertainment for Children* shows old Pulcinella pensively gazing at a monument inscribed with the title of this series. Perched on his shoulder is a puppet of a beautiful Venetian woman who is smiling flirtatiously. Her head is inclined away from the tomb, in her hand is a fan. She is blithely swinging her legs, having drawn them out from beneath her dress. Possibly, the drawing symbolizes the death of Carnival and the approach of Lent. Or perhaps it is a burlesque parody of a passion play in which Christ arises from his grave.

Pulcinella dies, but not forever. In a Pier Leone Ghezzi drawing from the early eighteenth century, Pulcinella suddenly arises from his bier, terrifying a family of peasants. In one of the drawings from Tiepolo's *Entertainment*, Pulcinella's skeleton, wearing the same large white, cylindrical hat, leaps out of a rococo grave. Death itself wears the clown hat of Pulcinella.

In Tiepolo's drawings, the streets of Venice are peopled with Pulcinellas. They paw young women under the ledges of terraced vineyards; dance at village celebrations, hunt for partridges, ride elephants in the circus, collect rent from peasants, and stare inquisitively at camels, which like Pulcinellas themselves, have humps on their backs. Not all of the Pulcinellas are male; women also wear the hooked-nosed masks. Pulcinellas have Pulcinella wives and Pulcinella children, who enter the world with potbellies, humps, and black noses. But the Pulcinella in Tiepolo's drawings, and perhaps also in some lost story, is not merely the actor and hero in a Venetian comedy

---

[2]See Marcia E. Vetrocq, ed., *Domenico Tiepolo's Punchinello Drawings* (Indiana University Art Museum, 1979).

of manners or a carnival pantomime. Here he is incarcerated; other Pulcinellas visit him in prison. As in the paintings of Callot and Goya where the atrocities of the Napoleonic Wars are depicted, so in Tiepolo's *Entertainment for Children* we find scenes of hangings and executions. A blindfolded Pulcinella, still wearing a black-nosed mask, awaits execution bound to a stake. Another Pulcinella lies on the ground, already shot. The execution squad itself, rifles poised for firing, consists of Pulcinellas in white hats. In another drawing, Pulcinella, bereft of his hat, but still in his black-nosed mask, dangles from a scaffold where a crowd of Pulcinellas has gathered. The hangman is on a horse and wears the white Pulcinella hat; he, too, is Pulcinella. Pulcinella is the hangman and the hanged man; he is the executioner and the executed. Wars and revolutions are also a tragic farce: the actors and victims are Pulcinellas. Pulcinella is a new and timeless Everyman.

All Bérengers in Ionesco's plays are his doubles and at the same time, Everyman. In two small rooms in a basement of the Frick Collection in New York, where in the winter of 1980 *Entertainment for Children* was exhibited for the first time, I suddenly saw Ionesco's great theater. Perhaps the Professor in *The Lesson* who rapes and murders his fourteenth pupil in a row ought to wear the Pulcinella black mask with a hooked nose and the white hat. Perhaps the Pupil, who is able to multiply multi-digit numbers in her head but cannot subtract, and who suffers a sudden toothache, should wear not only the blouse and the short skirt of a schoolgirl, but also a little mask with a black hooked nose.

Perhaps the Old Man and the Old Woman in *Chairs* should also wear Pulcinella masks. Surely, the Orator, who after the suicide of the Elders proclaims his final message to empty chairs, should be masked like Pulcinella and could display a hump as well as a potbelly. Wearing the white blouse of Punch and Pierrot and a huge Pulcinella hat, he would draw letters on the blackboard and gesture with his hands like a deaf man. In *Amédée, or How to Get Rid of It*, gigantic legs of a corpse gradually slide into Amédée's and Magdalena's dining room. This corpse may be a murdered lover or the Past. In any case, it is also Death. But here, Death is present only as the legs of a giant dummy. As in carnival imagery, this Death is "a gay monster created by laughter in order to replace the terror that has been defeated."

We "*do* die," writes Ionesco in *Notes*; "It is horrible and cannot be taken seriously. How can I trust in a world that has no stability, that flits away? One moment I can see Camus, I can see Atlan, and suddenly they are gone. It's ridiculous. It almost makes me laugh.

Anyway, King Solomon has already exhausted this subject." Or, "it is King Solomon who is my master," and yet again, "Yes, the leader I follow is King Solomon; and Job, that contemporary of Beckett." Job and Beckett—the comparison is obvious, but what is Solomon's place in this company? "I am the most foolish of men," says Solomon in Ecclesiastes. Precisely this sentence is the one Folly cites with delight in Erasmus's *The Praise of Folly*.

King Solomon frequently appears in medieval ribaldries as well as in medieval and early Renaissance morality plays. His wisdom is always foolish. Ionesco could have written a tragic farce, "Solomon and Job Discourse on Death." In this "Dialogue of the Dead" we would hear again Lucian's derisive laughter.

The Death which comes to Bérenger in the epilogue to *The Killer* does not utter a word. This is no longer the archaic pregnant Death, nor the gay carnival Death which gives birth to a new creature in order to overcome the terror. The medieval Death calls with a sickle on Everyman: unbribable, irrevocable, and ruthless. When the fifteenth-century Everyman proposes a bribe, Death responds with indignation:

> Everyman, it may not be, by no way.
> I set not by gold, silver, nor riches,
> Ne by pope, emperor, king, duke, ne princes;
> For, and I would receive gifts great,
> All the world I might get;
> But my custom is clean contrary.
> I give thee no respite. Come hence, and not tarry.

In *The Killer*, Death is silent. Bérenger, all alone, must carry on a medieval dialogue with Death:

> You're poor now, aren't you? Do you want some money? I can find you work, a decent job . . . No. You're not poor? Rich then? . . . Aaah, I see, neither rich nor poor! [*Chuckle from the KILLER.*]

According to Ionesco's stage directions Killer-Death is supposed to be ". . . very small and puny, ill-shaven, with a torn hat on his head, and a shabby old gaberdine; he has only one eye, which shines with a steely glitter . . . ." All medieval texts talk about the hideousness of Death. Yet in folk drama, in the Sicilian Opera dei Pupi, and in the Polish folk theater, Skeleton-Death is also quite funny. In the Italian theater of marionettes, Death diligently saws off heads of sinners which then roll off stage to the merriment of the spectators. In Polish folk theater, King Herod's head is a cabbage which Death reaps, like a peasant his crops. Death in Ionesco merely chuckles as it drowns its victims, in a basin in the Radiant City, where Death gathers its harvest to the perpetual accompaniment of *cris de Paris*: the banter of concierges, the mumbling of vagabonds, and the shouts of street vendors. Ionesco's chuckling Death could wear the mask of Harlequin with a hooked nose and have Pierrot's powdered white face. *The Killer* is a tragic farce performed on city streets.

We "do die," Ionesco repeats. "It is horrible and cannot be taken seriously." *Exit the King* is a comedy about dying. It is the only modern comedy about dying and the only *comedy* with a hero and the main actor who begins *dying* in the very first scene before he dies in the last one. If Bérenger were dying in a real bed, if he were mourned by a *real* wife and a *real* mistress, if he were treated and operated on by *real* doctors, if a *real* nurse rearranged *real* pillows for him, this *play* would be insufferable. But Bérenger, who is dying in Ionesco's comedy, is a King.

"The King," wrote Stanisław Jerzy Lec, "is naked . . . but under such splendid robes." Bérenger is dying in splendid robes of royalty. He is King, a fairy-tale King, a King in a palace assembled by children out of cards; he is King of a carnival masquerade.

Bérenger does not die. The King dies in the company of Queen Marguerite, who was his first wife, Queen Marie, his second wife, and the Doctor, who does not take care of him and who is at once, "a surgeon, a hangman, a bacteriologist, and an astrologer." Bérenger is dressed up as King so that he can die only as King.

Among the most enduring of carnival amusements is the crowning and uncrowning of the beggar enacted so that he can later be abused, scourged, and chased. The beggar's coronation in the marketplace shows traces, according to Frazer's *Golden Bough*, of an ancient ritual in which the king's substitute was killed annually in order to "resurrect" the real king. In the carnival travesty, death cannot be taken seriously. The inhabitants of the Isle of Winds in Rabelais's utopia emit gases when they die and their souls, like this unbecoming gas, leave their bodies *via rectum*. In Seneca's satire *Ludus morte Claudii*, Caesar dies in the act of defecation.

In *Exit the King*, the rites of dying are carnivalesque. ". . . We *do* die. It is horrible and cannot be taken seriously." Bérenger is Ionesco's double. King Bérenger dies to enable Ionesco not to die.

I saw *The Bald Soprano* and *The Lesson* for the first time when they opened in Warsaw. I think it was 1956. Subsequently, whenever I was in Paris I would go to the little theater in the rue de la Huchette, where *The Lesson* and *The Bald Soprano* were continually running. When I was there last in 1965, I was not sure whether the same actress was still playing the Pupil. She seemed less childish. After the performance I visited the Ionescos. I recorded my recollections from this evening in my diary, which was later published in *Theatre Notebook*, in Bolesław Taborski's perfect translation:

> "Of course, it's the same actress," said Eugène. "*The Lesson* will go on being performed for another fifty or seventy years. One day the Pupil will die. I mean really die, not just on the stage. She will go to heaven, and St. Peter will sternly ask her: 'What did you do in life, my child?' And she will reply, 'What did I do? I was eighteen when I began to act the Pupil in M. Ionesco's play at the theatre in the rue de la Huchette. Then I got engaged, to be married, and I went on acting the Pupil. Then I got married. I went on acting the Pupil. Then I got pregnant and for three months I stopped acting the Pupil. Then my daughter was born. I went on acting the Pupil. Then I got a divorce. I went on acting the Pupil. Then I got married again. I went on acting the Pupil. Then my son was born. I went on acting the Pupil. Then I got divorced again. I went on acting the Pupil. Then my daughter had twins. I had to leave Paris for two weeks. Then I went on acting the Pupil.' And St. Peter will say, 'M. Ionesco can hardly wait for you; he is attending a rehearsal of *The Lesson*.' "
>
> Ionesco looked at me, became very sad all of a sudden and said in a choked whisper, "It's not true; I shall not die."

I believe him; he is immortal.

NOH,
OR ABOUT
SIGNS

1 It was in Kyoto that I first saw a garden of sand and stones. The fifteenth-century *Ryoan-ji* is the most famous: a rather small rectangle of bright sand, framed by a low wall, like a pond dug in the ground. On its sandy surface is a pattern of fifteen small stones: five, two, three, two, and again, three. Behind the wall, a green screen of maple trees. Boys wearing white shirts, girls in bright, very short skirts, old women wrapped in kimonos, sit along the wall in traditional postures—the lotus, the low squat; all very silent, contemplating the sand and the stones. This rectangle, the cool grays and browns of its gravel, could be a Braque painting. It represents absolute precision and beauty. To move a single stone would be blasphemy, ruining irrecoverably the perfect order.

In Kyoto I also visited *Shugaku-in*, the imperial gardens. In one of the pavilions there are two fish painted on the wall. Every scale glitters separately—they were all painted with the same devotion and mastery, as if the painter had been equally enchanted by each of them. According to the old tale, every night the fish came to life and left the wall to swim in a nearby pond. The Emperor feared that some day they might not come back, and he ordered the artist to add a blue net to the painting in which the fish would be trapped forever. These abstract gardens of sand and stone, and the painted fish from the emperor's palace, seem to me to represent the two contradictory styles, the two different "natures" of Japanese art, and also—perhaps even more—of Japanese theater.

Using European typology, we might describe this opposition as that between Classical and Baroque. The classic Noh, in comparison with the baroque Kabuki, suggests nature still and drained rather than vital, frozen rather than floating; a movement stilled in its final gesture as opposed to the one that overcomes the rules of gravity; an abstract art of ideas as opposed to an equally absolute art of imitation.

2 Iwao Kongo, who comes from one of the four great family-schools which cultivate the art of Noh from generation to generation, allowed me to have a close look at all the masks in his theater. The oldest ones were made four hundred years ago. They are carved in cypress wood and painted, and are so fragile that one can scratch their glossy surfaces by touching them carelessly. They are "chapped," though, with cracks like the network of wrinkles on an aged face. These are masks of gods, demons, old men, young boys, and women. They all smile, even the masks of a lion and a fox. Most astonishing is the smile of *Magojiro*. It is the mask of a young woman, with very long, very narrow, almost horizontal eye sockets. Her forehead is high and uncovered, with two spots where the eyebrows have been painted, as though raised in eternal wonderment. The full lips are slightly open, their corners lifted. It is the same upcurve of the corners of the mouth as on sixth-century Greek sculptures of young men, *kouroi* or Apollos, imitating the Egyptian canon. Ionian *korēs* from the museum on the Acropolis also have that bittersweet smile of full, somehow heavy lips. Historians call it the archaic smile. Leonardo was to repeat it in his portrait of Mona Lisa. The smile makes her a Stranger. It carries her out of her own time. It exists apart from her, as if it grazed her lips for only a moment.

Kongo picked up the mask gently with his two fingers and held it at arm's length. The relation of light to shade changed and the smile disappeared. Now, *Magojiro*'s face looked mortally sad. Kongo lowered the mask again. The lifted lip-corners and the suddenly narrowed eye sockets spoke only of a restrained cry. One more movement of hand and *Magojiro* is now looking at us with her eyes hollow, smiling into her own self. She is absent. I realized for the first time how illusory the psychological interpretation of masks can be, like the anthropomorphization of a fox's smile, an owl's solemnity, a frog's vanity. . . .

"Before I begin to act," says Kongo, "I have to look for many hours at the mask. I do not exist, the mask does. I am not real—the mask is real."

3   The musicians—carrying a flute, two small drums, and a big drum shaped like a huge spool—have taken their places at the rear of the stage, under a screen on which green pine trees have been painted. That is the only set. The stage—an empty shining platform of cypress wood—has a thin roof resting on four pillars. The chorus enters. It sits in two rows, motionless. The flute utters the first sound, like a bird's call. At the end of the *hashigakari*, the long bridge-corridor leading from the stage to a "chamber of mirrors," a little silk curtain has been pulled up on its bamboo rods, like a parasol suddenly swollen by the wind. Slowly, from this unveiled bridge, *Waki* comes to the stage in the garb of a Buddhist monk. He walks but at the same time does not move, as in Zeno's famous paradox of the arrow. All Noh actors walk, or rather glide, like this. They wear buskin sandals with one strap between the toes. In this stiff yet steady walk they never lift their heels off the ground.

Waki has now sat down near the right pillar, his legs crossed, his knees flat on the floor. He and the chorus proceed to converse in song. But all the sounds are muffled as if arrested in the larynx. The drum music becomes more violent, and when we hear the big spool-drum, the curtain goes up for the second time, as if torn by the wind. Now *Shite* appears on the *hashigakari*, wearing the white mask of a young woman. The mask is smaller than the face, and makes the whole body seem longer and at the same time less real. *Shite* approaches and then backs off from *Waki*, as if the Buddhist monk had the magnetic power to attract and repel. In this linear ballet on the rectangular platform, surrounded on two sides by spectators, the directions of movement are dictated by the four pillars. Motionless, *Waki* seems to be attached to his place by one of the pillars, while *Shite* moves along straight lines as if dancing on the invisible threads of a horizontally stretched web.

Nothing happens, at least according to Western notions of dramatic action. Nothing happens, yet the tension grows. Roland Barthes has written about numbness in Racine's theater: numbness of time, action, the whole world. In the Noh theater the numbness is literal; *Waki*'s face and those of the members of the chorus are immobilized, almost flat, devoid of all expression, much less human than the mask.

Shite's movements slow down but never relax, as if his will to move could only be executed by stiffened muscles or legs asleep. The number of movements and gestures is limited. Their patterns are repeated to the refined monotony of the drums. The bodies of the players are stiffened from the waist up. As in Zen meditation, psychic concentration results from somatic arrest. The numbness of the players mesmerizes the audience. Experts maintain that surrender to the art of Noh begins with fatigue.

The choreography is not symbolic, as it is in the Hindu sacred theater. Movements and gestures are either elements of a formal pattern, as in classical ballet, or else represent a gesture real but idealized, free from even a trace of accident, simplified to the point at which they become the essence of gesture. A hand lifted to the level of the eyes, yet never touching them, means crying. In this theatrical writing the movements of the fan are the signs of an alphabet. If open and covering the face, a fan means sleep. Fans folded, open, raised above the head, held horizontally or moved forward, resting on the left or right arm, mean respectively—listening, brooding, looking at the moon, at the water, at the mountains, at flowers.

Of all the kinds of writing, this system of theatrical signs is closest to calligraphy. In calligraphy the relation between the signifier and the signified, between the image and what the image is to transmit, is, as it were, reversed. A sign becomes more important than its meaning, a medium more important than its message. Significance lies in the kind of ink, the choice of brush, the shape of a character; also in the pattern of rows, the size and quality of paper, the proportion between black and white space, like silence and sounds in music. A brush can be pointed or cut square, a line thick, thin, or dotted, angles acute or rounded. All this is a speech full of meaning. In calligraphy the signs "talk" of distinctions, hierarchies, manners; they are stiff and frozen, for their function does not end after reading and they continue to exist, suspended in time. Chinese characters are the simplified image of an object or person, state or concept, purified from chance and idealized, like the choreography of Noh and the positions of the fan.

Noh is a dramatic ceremony whose essential elements have to be rigorously repeated every time it is performed. The stillness of Noh was compared early in the fifteenth century by Zeami, the actor and codifier of the art, to a silver vase filled with frozen snow. The solemn Japanese "tea ceremony" resembles both the art of calligraphy and this theater of rigorous and frozen gestures. A ceremonial bow in which the head almost touches the knees and the hands reach the ground does not merely reflect respect for a welcome guest; respect is the content of the bow itself. In ritual and in ceremony (calligraphy is ceremonious writing) there is respect for the sign itself, a sign that itself is solemn. Ceremony is the semantics of gestures. The Noh actor makes a bow to the mask before the assistants put it on his face offstage. When the Woman Making Tea, dressed in her ceremonial kimono and obi, sitting on her legs, stirs the green brew with a special brush until it turns, contrary to nature, into a thick and fluffy cream, the flow of time seems to be halted. Time that annihilates itself, irreversible time, becomes the time of all ceremonies of steeping and drinking tea, of all holy days and festivals: time that repeats itself, reversible "circular" time.

Dry drumbeats. Rhythms that suddenly break down and then repeat, impatiently accelerated, like a call. For the second time, *Shite* enters. He wears the same mask of a young woman, only the hair is now tied up high with a white band, topped with a kind of cocked helmet. He holds a spear. And again, the same dialogue unwinds between *Waki* and *Shite*, the tight-throated words, the long chants of the chorus. Yet suddenly the actor begins to turn around his own axis like a huge humming top. He lifts up his leg and stamps. Because of the use of resonators under the floor it sounds like a distant thunderbolt. *Shite* moves as if in a trance. The fury and frenzy of *Shite*'s last dance make it seem that the actor has been moved by a power from both within and outside himself. The side sleeves of his kimono rise and fall like cellophane wings; the actor, in his whirring, glittering silks, in reds, yellows, and golds, in his glossy mask with its unchangeable smile, seems to be an enormous flying insect with a long torso, about to take off while slowly transforming itself into another form of being. When *Shite* disappears for the last time, floating along the bridge of *hashigakari* until the silk curtain has finally been drawn behind him, he seems to have been dissolved in the space beyond.

4 Noh is not a literary theater, nor is it an Aristotelian imitation of action. *Waki* happens to be, most often, a wandering Buddhist monk. *Shite* can be a young girl who in the darkness of night comes to fill her ewer with water from a well, or an old woman removing the fallen rocks from the slope of some streamlet, an emperor's jealous wife, an abandoned courtesan, or a woodcutter, a gardener, an old fisherman, or even a young boy who went on a pilgrimage with a monk to a temple on a mountaintop. Yet Noh actors never "play" either a person or a character. An old emperor is played by a child to prevent the slightest deception. In the second part of this two-act drama, after the lonely monk's prayer and meditation, *Shite* enters, transformed now into the ghost of a woman-warrior who cannot rest in peace because she did not die beside her husband in battle; or transformed into the ghost of a brave samurai who suffers agonies because he had died in a duel before he could whisper his name, so that now his poems circulate in the world anonymously. The jealous woman appears, wearing a frightening mask almost like a cow with huge horns. The woman whom the monk had met by the well sees reflected in the water not her own face but that of a poet, an emperor's grandson, who had met his wife by the same well. He left her and wrote his poems for another woman. *Shite* is now the abandoned wife's ghost who has forgiven her husband and wanders around reciting his poems. If Shakespeare were to be adapted for the Noh stage, the girl who wreathes daisies and buttercups and then hangs them up on the willow trees by the riverbank would have been transformed into the ghost of Ophelia wrapped in Hamlet's cloak, and with his rapier in hand; the woman washing her hands in the river would have been the ghost of Lady Macbeth wearing King Duncan's crown and armor; the tormented Banquo's ghost, wandering through the swamps, would have met the witches and after performing his dance of death, would have departed in peace, consoled that his descendants would become the rulers of Scotland.

Dramatic situations, rudimentary plots or events, are only told or sung about on the Noh stage. A real landscape can be represented by the twig of a blooming apple tree, or a bunch of reeds pulled by *Shite*. The narration in Noh, like the herald's or messenger's relation of events in Greek tragedy, is only a voice. According to the liturgical calendar different fragments of the Bible are read and sung during Mass on different Sundays, ornaments and stoles of different colors are used—yet a priest never "acts" the sacred history, or "performs" Christ's passion. The fundamental ritual of the sacrifice is always rigorously repeated, singular and unchanged. In Noh theology, which is also its aesthetic, what is true are the essences, and these are the ghosts of the characters. In a Noh *Hamlet*, everything except the father's ghost would be a transient vision. *Waki* and *Shite* are not the characters or the "roles"—they seem, rather, two persons with different yet strictly defined parts in an unchangeable dramatic ceremonial of transformation. The *Waki* actors never play the *Shite* parts, nor vice versa. The theatrical structure of Noh seems to be the fundamental relation between a caller and the called, the bewitcher and the bewitched, the exorcist and the exorcised. *Shite* and *Waki* are like the shaman or witch doctor and the sick patient.

The language in which Noh is spoken is unintelligible even to educated modern Japanese because of its vocabulary, and even more, its intonation. Spectators carry their own copies of the plays with sketches of the situations and the actors' positions. In an early 1970s production of *Medea* based on combined Greek and Latin texts from Euripides and Seneca, the actors did not know either language, though they obviously understood the general sense of the sentences; they transmitted not only an emotion enclosed in unfamiliar linguistic sounds but also its general semantic structure, which for them was hollow and yet at the same time organized. Peter Brook, in his mytho-dramas performed in Persepolis, about the stealing of fire and the first fratricide, used Orghast, an artificial language composed of Indo-European roots. Jerzy Grotowski demanded that his actors break natural intonations, erasing the pauses between words and blurring the semantic structures. In all these searches and experiments, the signifier has been disconnected from the signified. The streams of voices still have their meaning, but they also mean something else.

Under the influence of Noh, or rather of the first translations of Noh into English, Yeats wrote his cycle of symbolist dramas. Lovers who could never become lovers, friendly ghosts, spirits of lakes, hilltops, and rivers from the Shintoist legends, came to meet their brothers and sisters in the folklore and mysticism of Ireland. Brecht's didactic "school opera," *Der Jasager*, that rigorous morality play on Party discipline, was adapted from a Noh drama about men climbing a holy mountain to the temple on the top, from which there is no way back, and about a boy who lost his strength and let his companions throw him down to the abyss.

There may be many different inspirations from this art of Noh. Modern theater's fascination with Noh—the oldest of all existing theaters, six centuries of almost uninterrupted tradition, frozen but at the same time self-renewing—is concentrated on its dramatic ceremonial and psychomachia, its system of signs, and the psychodrama which is played out between *Waki* and *Shite*. In a moment of rare perspicacity, Grotowski admitted that the only ritual a theater can present and fulfill that would not prove to be fake or apish, is the ritualization of theater as such; the only sacrifice that can save the theater is that of its actors. Their whole bodies—heads, hands, legs, abdominal muscles, midriffs, throats which can modulate or trap the voice—are a medium that transmits signs. Brook kept asking his actors to look for truth in rediscovered gestures, that is, in signs existing as a language independent of a personal idiom. In the poetic experience, rhymes bring meanings; in the experience of acting, the mask is truer and richer in meaning than the face.

The most vital and fruitful humanistic reflection of the last decades seems the understanding of culture as a system of signs, *écriture*, texts which have their letters, grammars, syntax, and rules of transformation. At the very center of interest of this new concept is the persistence of the same signs in civilizations distant in time and space. The human condition is both created and revealed by archetypes of birth, sex, and death. Adapting Lévi-Strauss's famous aphorism—"*les mythes se re-pensent entre eux*," "the myths re-think one another," one could say: "the signs re-signify one another." In this modern scientific hermeneutics, a search for the metastructure of all "signifying structures" seems to revive the alchemist's belief in the ultimate formula: the sign that contains the secret of transubstantiation.

I have seen a dance of bees. The scout fidgets with her legs, then creeps around in circles and small figure eights, moving backward and forward. For a long time this was considered a festive dance. In fact the scout is only informing her sisters about the directions and distances to the flower beds; this "round or tail-wagging dance" of the bee provides information about a particular source of food. When *Shite* in his still mask turns left and right, shakes his hands and legs, and stiff and erect moves slowly on his axis, or creeps like a huge insect on the limited space, when he trembles as if all matter trembled, it seems that in this last dance of Noh some information is also being included, a message unintelligible to us, final and nondiscursive, concerning some earthly and unearthly nourishment.

BUNRAKU AND KABUKI,
OR ABOUT
IMITATION

1   A woman is looking at herself in the looking glass; she puts rouge on her cheeks, smoothes out and blackens her eyebrows, ties up her hair high above her forehead and puts a horn comb in her bun. She is smiling to herself in the mirror. She has three servants: they hold her mirror, put brushes into her tiny hands, help her to put the comb in the bun. Two of them are clad in black cloaks, with hoods covering their heads, like Klansmen in the Southern states; the face of the third is uncovered, but he never looks at his mistress. The lovely lady is a puppet, and her three servants are puppeteers.

A sailor punts from the shore his heavy junk, covered with a canvas roof. He is standing astern, the junk is tilted downwards, when the punt-pole rests against the bottom, the weight of the body slowly passes to the right leg, which is bent and advanced forward; the junk moves, the punt-pole is lifted above the water, the stern is raised upwards, the weight of the body is transferred to the left leg, now straightened. It is hot, the sailor wipes sweat off his face with a big colored handkerchief. He punts again, but he leans out too much, the junk suddenly moves forward, the sailor falls into the water. He is swimming now, he finds it hard, because he has to hold the long and heavy punt-pole in his left hand. He finally catches up with the junk, which has been moved by the current, tilts it, climbs in, grabs the punt-pole. This is not easy, for the junk is high, and he has to get hold of its side with his left hand and left foot.

The sailor is a puppet, operated, like all Bunraku puppets, by three manipulators at the same time. The first of them, the one with uncovered face, carries the puppet on his left hand and with his right hand controls the puppet's right arm and hand; the second puppeteer, "invisible" in his black hood, manipulates the puppet's left arm; the third, also "invisible," handles its legs, or moves the kimono, because female puppets have no legs. The stage has the same width as the auditorium, the manipulators move as if in the orchestra pit, with the balustrade hiding them only up to their knees. They are twice as big as the puppets. On a special rostrum, *yuka*, at the side of the stage, to the right of the audience the samisen player and the singer-narrator are sitting. The samisen is a plucked instrument with three strings. It gives the performance its rhythm and tempo. The three manipulators, who operate one puppet, have to breathe in unison; the samisen in Bunraku conducts breathing. The narrator has in front of him a wooden stand with the text. He is at the same time a chorus and a singular voice; in his *recitativo*, a narration sung-recited in the third person, he introduces the action, interprets the thoughts of the characters and tells about their passions, he is the epic and the lyric poetry of Bunraku; in the first person he lends his voice to all the puppets.

The marionettes, puppets, java dolls—are manipulated from above on strings, from below on bamboo poles, or on three fingers of the hand, of which two move the arms, the third—the head. The technique of manipulating the puppets can be simple—as with the hand-puppets, or highly ingenious, as in the Italian marionette theaters; but the general principle is the invisibility of manipulators. The rule of the game is the illusion. The puppet is to move and speak by itself. Even the puppet manipulated on the hand by one man at least speaks in the ventriloquist's voice. Bunraku is almost the only puppet theater in which the mechanism is completely bared. The aesthetics of this art consists in evoking an absolute illusion, and in its equally absolute destruction. Bunraku is *simultaneously* a theater in which the puppets act human dramas—cry and laugh, love and hate, cheat, sacrifice themselves and kill—and a metatheater, whose protagonists are the manipulators operating the puppets, the narrator and the samisen; metatheater, whose dramatic action consists in revealing the theatrical illusion.

Historical dramas played by the Bunraku puppets, and later introduced to the Kabuki stage, are even bloodier than Shakespeare's royal tragedies of the Wars of the Roses. The action takes place during the civil wars in which, for over a century, great feudal families destroyed one another until, as in England of the Tudors and in

France during the time of Cardinal Richelieu, the Shogunate clamped down with an iron hand on the cruel lords, who had private samurai armies at their disposal, and imposed court ceremonial on the warriors. In English theaters, the most widely used prop since the Elizabethan times has been a cage with the cut-off head. In Bunraku and Kabuki it is the head of a child. In those very complicated dramas—which go on for hours—written down from old chronicles and legends by the dramatists of the Edo period (the Japanese period of enlightened absolutism and military dictatorship), the choice is between the duty of loyalty towards the feudal lord and all his descendants, and towards one's own life and family. In Corneille's *Le Cid*, Rodrigue, in order to avenge his insulted father, has to challenge the father of his beloved to a mortal duel. Chimène, in order to avenge the death of her father, must demand the death of her lover. In Japanese historical drama the price of feudal loyalty is most cruel of all. It is the head of a son.

The box with the cut-off head has been brought in. In a while the head will be raised high so that the persecutors can see with their own eyes that the enemy's son has really been cut down. Two mothers are standing by this box, still closed. They know that the son of one of them has been killed. The samurai Kumagai spared the life of the Emperor's descendant and, when asked to show his head, had to sacrifice his own son. The mother whose son has been saved must hide her joy; the mother who is looking at the cut-off head of her son must hide her suffering. The persecutors are closely watching the faces of both mothers.

This is the classic recognition scene in Japanese theater. But in Bunraku it is played by puppets. What can dolls do? Two mothers, in the same vast gesture, raise their hands hidden in the long, wide kimono sleeves and bite at its hem. In this gesture the despair is concealed. The time for crying shall come later. In another scene of recognition, a samurai, who sacrificed his son, slowly wipes with a towel his bleeding head. After a moment he will be looking at the cut-off head, throwing away the towel. In these two gestures of the puppet there is first tenderness and despair, then brutality as a means of concealing both tenderness and despair. The puppets are best, in being silent. The most difficult task for the living actors is to stand still on stage and be silent. Puppets, left alone by operators, freeze in absolute immobility. They become nothing but silence, nothing but suffering.

In the beautiful album of Bunraku, with the photographs of Kaneko Hiroshi, one can admire the puppets' faces in close-up: the warriors have bristling hair and black erect eyebrows, which can move, and protruding eyes, also movable; the women have white little faces, oval, egg-shaped—which in Japan is a sign of beauty— almond eyes, with moving eyeballs, and small, closed mouths; they bite at the kimono sleeve, or a patterned towel, with the help of a tiny needle in the corner of the lips. In Noh *Shite* only raises a hand to the level of the eyes, and bows the head to signify weeping. The dolls really weep, wipe their eyes with a handkerchief and, as actors in silent films, shake their arms, or huddle themselves up, sobbing.

But in those splendid photographs the puppeteers have been retouched. At the Bunraku performances, next to the face of a puppet one can see—as in a surrealist painting—the face of a manipulator, nearly four times larger. The face of the manipulator seems quite flat; it is the faces of the puppets that are human. But there is also a third face which one can observe at Bunraku performances from the first to the last moment of the action. The singer-narrator, sitting close to the auditorium, gives to the puppets all the voice he can emit from his larynx. He almost cries when the puppets are crying, he bubbles with laughter when they are laughing. He is immobilized, sitting at his stand with crossed legs and flat positioned knees, but all emotions of the puppets are expressed on his face. He is the live Bunraku actor.

In the course of the last half-century, as at one time in the Baroque period, all the arts, like Narcissus, have come more and more frequently to wish to see themselves in water's flat surface. The analysis of art seems to be one of the main themes of twentieth-century art. The theme of painting is painting itself: the analysis of space, perspective, density, shimmer and roughness of matter. Poetry seems more and more a game or *écriture*, a syntactic transformation or an analysis of words close in their phonetics, and of semantic distance between phonemes. The theme of musical compositions is the analysis of phonic series. The novel is often about writing a novel, or at least the destruction of narration, with all tricks laid bare, one by one. Films are about making films, and in more ambitious avant-garde attempts, analyses of space and light, with immobilized camera.

In the theater, the "live" actor is he who *performs*, and the characters of the drama are *performed*, or to put it differently: the actor is he who *signifies*, the characters of the drama are *signified*. In the illusionist theater of the puppets, the puppet is the "live" actor; it acts the despairing mother, the noble samurai, the geisha crossed in love. But in Bunraku one can also see another theater, one of anti-illusion, in which the puppet is only a *thing*, an artificial head, which can roll its eyes, lift its eyebrows, open its mouth; sticks which imitate hands; a wooden cylinder, on which pieces of colored silk are draped, and which is operated by manipulators. The puppet in Bunraku acts, and is acted, signifies and is signified, at the same time; the puppet is an actor who simultaneously takes part in two different shows; in one of them he is the character of the drama, in the other a flexible piece of wood.

As in cubist painting the faces are shown in profile and *en face* all at once, or as drawings of the successive elements of movement; all elements of the theater are shown both separately and together, disconnected and joined. The two theaters in Bunraku: of illusion and anti-illusion; the three faces: of the puppet, the manipulator, and the narrator; the hands of the puppets which with absolute faithfulness repeat the gestures of men, the hand of the manipulators, who operate the puppets, the hand of the musician, plucking the strings of the samisen—are a visible and spectacular analysis of theatricality.

2 In Kabuki, a samurai is returning from the battlefield. In his impressive and heavy warrior's attire, he is like a big dragonfly which has not yet shed its cocoon. He has two swords hanging from his belt. He tells about his recent fight. In a while he will perform it. But he will perform it sitting down, and in this great mime he will not draw his sword. He will act the battle using only his fan. The Noh actor also uses a fan, but there the fan positions are only a figure, metaphor, a shadow of the real gesture. In Kabuki the fan mime is realistic; the fan deals and repels blows, enters the body, slides over the throat. Sergei Obraztsov once said that by means of a box of matches one can demonstrate everything, except a box of matches. One can show a box of matches but then it is only a matchbox. With the help of a fan one can represent everything which is not a fan.

The frailty and delicacy of a fan seem the opposite of the sharpness and strength of a sword. But it is in that fan, which imitates all movements of the sword, that the entire aesthetics of Kabuki is contained: dead matter is to imitate live matter, brightness—darkness, solidity—fluidity, masculinity—femininity; the sign must be set off. Live fishes can be watched through the glass of the aquarium.

But the joy of imitation consists in painting fishes on a roll of silk, which are so alive that one has to paint a net as well, so that they do not escape.

One of the most classic Kabuki scenes is the fight of the hero in darkness with the thugs sent to kill him. They creep, holding out their hands in front of them; they have found his head, but their blow misses him; they creep again, lifting their legs high, so as not to stumble; they walk over his head. The fight in darkness is shown in full light. This mime was taken from Kabuki by Erwin Piscator and Bertolt Brecht. The darkness in full light is the most theatrical darkness of all. It is darkness performed.

Of all the arts, mime seems closest to the manipulated puppet. For a mime, his own body is apart from him, more so than an actor; as if it were outside, it has no voice or soul, it is both dead, like an object, and perfectly mobile; a mime moves his body as a manipulator moves a puppet. He walks on the ground, but at the same time walks on a rope; he cannot show himself, because he walks on the ground; he cannot show him who walks on a rope either, he can only perform him. He has spread his arms wide, is trying to hold his balance, he waddles, in a moment will fall, no, he has caught his balance, has made another step forward. A mime is a body, a puppet manipulated, as in Bunraku, in the sight of the audience. A mime is not an acrobat, he is the sign of a tightrope-walking acrobat. Like the puppet, he is both the performer and the performed, the presenter and the presented, the demonstrator and the demonstrated, the signifier and the signified. He is what he is not, he is not what he is. A mime is split in two, like the Brechtian actor. The traditional mime has his face whitened, to signify that he is only a jester, who will show tricks and perform various characters.

Towards the end of the eighteenth century Kabuki took over the Bunraku's repertory and even today both theaters still perform the same plays; moreover, Kabuki also adopted the acting art of the puppet. The treacherous minister has condemned the innocents to death. The executioner with a drawn sword is standing at the ready; in a moment their heads will fall. But at the last moment the emperor's messenger, with loyal samurais, arrives. The tormentors will now suffer the fate they deserve. Soon their heads are rolling on stage. But the "heads" are only cloth-bound balls, thrown on stage by one of the "dark" assistants, who kneel upstage with flatly crossed knees. In the Sicilian Opera dei Pupi, when a sudden blow will be dealt in a duel of medieval knights, the chopped-off head will fall, and will similarly roll on stage, accompanied by wild metallic percussion.

This *aragoto* style, characterized by naive exaggeration, pathetic gestures, and declamation, makes the theater with live actors similar to puppet theater. Ichikawa Danjuro, one of the greatest actors of the Edo period, used to say that one must act as if one were a six-year-old child. A child who has cut out a human figure of paper proudly displays the scissors. Kabuki is a theater of unashamed illusion. As in the Baroque theater of "open change," the scenery is shifted with the curtain open; the night is coming—from above a huge golden moon on a blue screen comes down, the snow falls; from a big basket thousands of tiny triangles cut out of white paper are falling on stage; the steep roof, down which the pursued lover is running away, is lifted up and the interior of the house is shown. The revolving stage was invented in Japan in the eighteenth century; like a huge quern, it was operated by men harnessed in treadmill, hidden under the stage.

On the left side along the auditorium, on the level of spectators' heads, there is a bridge, *hanamichi*— "the flower way," through which the actors come out on stage. This is the place for actors' "solo" appearances. A messenger runs in, out of breath, the geishas tread their tiny steps, like a flock of white peacocks, a young girl comes to a date, ashamed, hiding behind her open parasol she notices her lover and hides her face with a fan. Sometimes there are two *hanamichi*, on the left and on the right, like two bridges across the auditorium which changes to a river. On those two bridges the lovers, who must part, bid a long farewell, or two brothers begin their journey to different corners of the world.

All theatrical signs in Kabuki are exaggerated. The warriors have thick red lines, like pulsating blood veins, painted on their cheeks, under the eyes and round their eyebrows; traitors have white faces with blue stripes. The ceremonial attire includes trousers so long that the actors walk on them and seem to be polishing the floor. Hence the special walk, with raising the leg, in order to shake the trouser-leg. This historical costume, which looks as if it had been invented by a malicious theatrical tailor, was imposed on the unruly feudal lords by court etiquette. Entangled in the legs of their own trousers, they were as helpless in the emperor's living quarters as marquises in their lacy jabots on the marble floors of Versailles. Male costume from the Edo period with its puffed shoulders, sticking out like roughed-up bird wings, made its wearers look bigger and wider;

kimono and obi with its pillow on the back, high hairdos, and white makeups made the women look like dolls. Both costumes bound the bodies and imposed different gestures for men and women, different ways of moving, of walking. A woman wearing a kimono is in addition to obi bound with twelve belts; her knees rub against each other all the time, and therefore she has that special way of walking, a combination of a bird step and run. A woman's "nature" has to become an artifact.

Ikebana is the great art of flower arranging: the stems are stuck on very thin needles in special stands. Japanese "nature"— dwarfish trees, like coiffured and dainty gardens—is sophisticated and refined, more "artificial," perhaps, than in other civilizations. The aesthetic principle of Kabuki is imitation, but as in the art of Baroque, it is almost always an imitation of artificial nature.

3 When an actress is asked to act a woman, walk like a woman, sit like a woman, sip tea like a woman, she will at first be surprised, then ask: "But *what* woman?" Femininity exists only in the eyes of a man, just as blackness exists only for whites. In the preface to *The Blacks* Genet wrote: "But what does black really mean. And, above all, what is its colour?" Femininity can only be acted by a man.

The origins of Kabuki were in dancing, singing, mime, and short scenes, probably like *commedia dell'arte*, performed by the priestess Okuni and her companions in front of the Izuine Shrine in Kyoto in 1603, that is to say, virtually at the time *Hamlet* was performed in London at the Globe. The dances were wanton and women dressed up as men. It was a gay theater of courtesans. A quarter of a century later, the Shogunate forbade women to perform in the theater. For the same reasons of decency women were excluded from the Imperial opera in Peking. It was the Shogun's ban that, in effect, led to the style of Kabuki, where men perform all female parts and in which the main actor is an *onnagata*—the boy-girl.

According to the eighteenth-century rules, an *onnagata* even in the street and in the dressing room ought to behave like a woman: walk half a step behind his theatrical "husband" and cover his face when eating a melon. I observed those actors while they put on their makeup, polished their nails with a special brush, rouged their cheeks, painted with a small brush a very thin arch of high raised eyebrows. Gradually their voice was changing; it was not a falsetto, but the voice became more and more rippling, like the chatter of birds. More than a woman, an *onnagata* performs femininity itself. It is a femininity closely observed through many generations of actors and, even more so, perhaps, through many generations of Japanese painters. There is in it both enchantment and mockery, adoration and humiliation, idealization and desire; it is a femininity doubly ambiguous, seen through the eyes of a man and performed by a pederast.

An actress who strips on stage performs a woman who strips. But when the striptease is over, she has nothing on. A little while ago she was almost nude, now she is only naked. She can only show. By means of a box of matches—let us once again repeat after Obraztsov—one can represent everything which is not a box of matches, but the matchbox itself can only be shown.

Eroticism in Kabuki is refined and, as it were, under the surface: fingers will search for each other a long time before they are joined, a fleeting embrace, sometimes only a prop—a mat thrown between the lovers. In comedy of manners, whose action takes place in the "gay quarters," the geishas are romantic like la Dame aux camélias, unhappily in love with poor sake porters, postmen, or thieves, who buy them with borrowed or stolen money, and—when discovered—commit suicide together with their beloved. In Kabuki, the fascination with death and with cruelty is more evident than pure eroticism. A beautiful girl comes to a date with her lover. But even before they embrace each other, a skull transfixed with an ax will appear. The young man had once murdered the girl's father. Her face is changing, is covered by red mold, she cannot walk, and limps. The terrified lover will kill the girl with the same ax. He chases her for a long time among the stage trees by the stage river, throws her to her knees, pulls her hair, drives the ax into her body and pulls it out again. The girl's corpse, with the ax driven into her, now rises like a ghost over the bridge on the river. The killer will return to the place of the crime. It is one of the most cruel scenes I have seen in a theater, but the girl is performed in it by an *onnagata*, the torture and cruel deeds are mime and ballet, accompanied by samisens, drums, and wooden sticks, frenetically beating against the floor in the moment of agony.

Sex and cruelty in this theater are signs. Ballet is a system of rigors imposed upon the body. Cruelty changed into rigor becomes a ceremony. On the small stage of the avant-garde theater Byakkosya in Kyoto, I saw a prisoner being tortured in front of a young woman. The torture was a traditional one: a rod was jammed into the mouth of the victim. Two half-naked men turned the heavy rod, which was as long as a wagon shaft, in the wide-open mouth of the prisoner, to the rhythm of drum beats and the pounding of wooden sticks. A naked woman lay motionless on the stage, with her head turned to the spectators, but with her legs spread wide in front of the man being tortured so that he could look at her womanhood throughout his ordeal.

Eroticism as ritual and cruelty as rigor, so disturbingly close to the visions of Artaud and Grotowski, seem to be rooted very deeply not only in the traditions of Japanese theater, but in the whole Japanese ethos. The women sleep on their backs with hard rollers tucked under their necks so that their artful coiffeurs can remain unruffled even in sleep. The classic Japanese novels say that even in the bedroom a man is not allowed to touch his mistress, until he unties her obi, and throws it onto the mat. Since the thirteenth century, geisha schools have been teaching Japanese women obedience, ceremonial behavior, and the strict rigors of eating, serving and drinking sake, and making love.

Theater is the only art whose *medium* and sign are human bodies moving alone or interacting among themselves before the spectator. If sex on stage is to be neither simulation nor performance, a distance must be maintained between the sign of sex and the sex itself. For eroticism in the theater to be fascinating, shocking, or revolting, the signifier must be different from the referent.

In 1968, I was present, for a short time, at rehearsals of *As You Like It*, directed by Clifford Williams in London's National Theatre. Rosalind assumes the name of Ganymede and disguises herself as a boy, who in the Forest of Arden woos her beloved as a boy and as a girl, and acts Rosalind before him. There was an all-male cast and, as in Elizabethan times, a young actor was disguised as a girl, who played a boy, who in turn played a girl. The ambiguity of gender and the ambivalence of desire are one of the most amazing themes in almost all Shakespeare comedies and extremely characteristic for the entire Elizabethan stage. Viola/Cesario is a girl/boy for the Duke and a boy/girl for Olivia. In traditional dramas of Kabuki there is no double disguise as with the Elizabethans, but the theater in which the female impersonator is the main actor seems the most perfect instrument to perform Shakespeare's comedies.

A geisha's lover is in mortal danger. She has to warn him so he can escape in time. But it is the middle of the night, the town is guarded by walls, the gates are locked. There is the alarm bell on the top of the high tower but the death penalty awaits those who would dare ring it. The girl climbs up the tower and rings the bell. The gates open and the lover can escape. But the girl has to die, pierced by arrows. It is possible that Brecht adapted from Kabuki the scene in *Mother Courage* in which the mute Catherine beats the drums on the roof of a farmer's house to warn the whole village against the attack. In Kabuki, this most refined of all theaters, that pathetic scene was played by the living actor in the style of the Bunraku puppets. The disguise device is tripled: a man plays a girl, an *onnagata* plays a puppet, a puppet plays a heroic girl. The hooded operators take the girl-puppet under her arms, fling her up, her little white face is shaking in this frenetic dance of death. The Brechtian alienation—*Verfremdungseffekt*—I found in Kabuki.

Grigori Kozintsev, in his *King Lear*, showed the wanderings of the blinded Gloucester through the Russian steppes to the non-existent cliffs of Dover, and the judgment of the mad old man over his degraded daughters pronounced in a village barn where, apart from the exiled king, his fool, and Edgar—soiled in birch tar and pretending to be mad—scores of other bodies were crowding: beggars and cripples, mothers with babes in arms, village idiots and blind men, driven by war from their mud huts and hovels. Akira Kurosawa, in his *Throne of Blood*, showed Macbeth in the dense, damp, and yellow Japanese fog—clinging to the hands, getting into the eyes and mouth, like sand. Rushing through this fog on black horses were bands of samurais, who slaughtered one another in the civil war. An arrow passed through Macbeth's neck and nailed him to a wooden wall; before rattling his last words, he became like a huge, dying hedgehog. In feudal Japan and the rigors of Noh Kurosawa unexpectedly rediscovered the historic and sensual, dramatic and psychological, relevance of *Macbeth* for our time.

Lear and Shakespeare's fools, kings, usurpers and treacherous lords, Hamlet and Macbeth, Ophelia, Juliet, and Cressida are not only able to speak all languages, they can also find their faces and bodies, gestures and passions, the inner world and landscapes, in all epochs and civilizations. Japanese theaters founded after the Western fashion towards the end of the nineteenth century perform classic and modern European and American plays, of course, repeating and imitating theatrical models, with varying success, often a quarter of a century late. It seems that Japanese traditional theater had a more profound and stronger impact on Meyerhold, Eisenstein, Piscator, Brecht, and the entire European avant-garde, than on the "Western" theater in Japan. Noh and Kyogen, Bunraku and Kabuki are among the purest styles of theater I have seen in my life. But in our era of syncretism the big question is, in what measure can they become an open form? In what measure can Noh, with its *Magojiro* mask— whose bittersweet smile is like the mask of Dionysus—with its immobilized static chorus and the frenzied, insectlike *shite* dance, become an inspiration to rediscover a new theatrical shape for Greek tragedy, and in what measure can Kabuki, the theater of the fan—which could easily imitate a sword—and of the *onnagata* boy-girl, present Shakespeare and Genet?

4 In Osaka I attended *Macbeth* performed "Western" style. The production was mediocre and duplicated certain models of German theater from the early 1930s. But the director borrowed an *onnagata* (who, despite his youth, was already well known for playing geishas) from the Kabuki Theater in Tokyo to play Lady Macbeth. This was the most impressive Lady Macbeth that I have ever seen. I will never forget the final scenes, when she tried to wash the blood from her hands in the invisible washbasin, which she kept carrying in and out. The blood would not come off, even when she tried to scratch it off her palms with her fingernails. She went to get the invisible washbasin once again and kept her hands submerged in its water for a very long time. She tried to shake the blood off along with the invisible drops of water. Then she raised her hands to eye-level, turned her palms in and stared at them as if hypnotized. The washbasin and water were created with gestures, but the blood in this pantomime was a thick layer of red paint.

Afterwards I asked to be introduced to the actor. I had to wait a very long time. The great actors of the Kabuki are treated like princes and have their own court consisting of a "theater mother" and women servants. When the *onnagata* finally entered the large hall, I gave him a deep bow, practically to the floor, in keeping with the custom of respect for great actors. The Japanese Lady Macbeth was a young man in his early twenties. He had very regular features, and striking eyes. The irises were black and flickering, as if on fire. I had to turn away, his look was so piercing. I don't think that there are many men or women who could oppose his will.

He offered me one of the fans that had been specially made for him of silk and tortoiseshell and which bore his stage name in hand-painted calligraphy. Then he called one of his servants and she handed him a brush and ink with which he wrote his best wishes in four signs, each like a picture. I knew that this was the first time that he had played in a theater other than the Kabuki, and so I asked him through the interpreter, if it were that much different playing in a royal Shakespearean tragedy. "No," he replied, "the only difference is that when I play a geisha in my theater I serve the sake on my knees."

THE ICON

OF THE

ABSURD

1 In the casinos of Las Vegas, the blackjack tables do not operate between five and seven in the morning. Only the automatic slot machines are left to gamblers unvanquished by night or fatigue. Besides the tourists, who hate to waste even a single hour, all types of people stop to take a chance at the machines: waiters returning from the night shift; chorus girls and dancers leaving after the last show; and girls who found no takers for a little quick loving and breakfast. Shortly before seven, even a few "normal" inhabitants of this town appear in the casinos: workers on their way to work and old women with large shopping bags who had stepped out to pick up some bread and milk.

The machines do not provide even the illusion that the gambler has some control over the outcome of his play. At best he could stick a sandwich in his mouth and work two machines at the same time. The whole game depends on slipping coins into the slot and pulling the handle. The inevitable is not visible but completely contained in the mechanism. The player can only set the inevitable in motion, which brings either a loss or a win. The slot machines are closed systems: only the gambler and mechanism exist, there is nothing outside of them. "Others" do not exist in this system. There is no one between the gambler and the inevitable. The "God" who sets up and fixes the mechanism, and later removes the money from it, is invisible. He does not exist, at least not for the player.

Las Vegas could be a gigantic setting for the Theater of the Absurd. All the elements of that theater are present in the city: the alienation of the individual is total; man is reduced to a gambler, has the face of a gambler, the reflexes of a gambler, the movements of a gambler; even his money is a mere token, a bet in a game. Man, and we can use the favorite phrase of the existentialists here, is "cast" into a world which does not belong to him and which is stronger than he is. Man is "alien" to the machine and the machine is equally "alien" to man. The processes of reification are realized to the extreme. The machine has power over the gambler, yet the gambler has none over the machine. The machine dictates how the gambler is to act; even more than that, the machine automates the gambler. Of these two automatons, the automaton-player, seemingly possessing free will and intelligence, is, in fact, a much less complicated automaton than the automaton-chance. The automaton-gambler throws a coin into the slot and pulls the lever; the automaton-chance carries out a much more complicated activity. Time alone encompasses them. But as in Theater of the Absurd we have here two different times: the "time" of the gambler—one-way, present, and restricted; and the "time" of the mechanism, which is at once past, present, and future. The "time" of the automaton for the player is eternal; the community of players must lose, since the machines have a limitless amount of time in which to perform.

This spectacle takes place in something like absolute silence. One hears only the sound of the money thrown in and occasionally the unexpected chord of hope, like the trumpets at the Last Judgment, a shrill ringing, a sign that in one of the machines the jackpot has appeared. The gamblers are able to speak to the machines, but are unable to come to an understanding with the machines. Words are useless; they cannot manage to change anything. Here, language does not serve for communication. It is difficult to say what purpose it serves. It is no longer necessary. Sometimes it even seems superfluous.

At five in the morning Las Vegas offers one of the most perfect visions of hell. And it is exactly this vision which was proposed so often by the Theater of the Absurd. The absurdity of human existence is often depicted by the relationship between man and the world-machine. In many plays, the absurd/anti-human was represented as a machine: in Samuel Beckett's *A One-Act Without Words,* in Harold Pinter's *The Dumbwaiter,* and in Sławomir Mrożek's *Strip-Tease.* In Beckett, metaphysics is reduced to a hostile super-machine, in Pinter and Mrożek the mute machine is politics and the social environment.

The absurd in each of these three plays is different, but its theatrical representation is similar.

2   The Theater of the Absurd? Why not a drama of the Absurd? In reflections devoted to the Theater of the Absurd, the emphasis is always on the word "absurd." Martin Esslin, who first introduced this term, was acutely aware of the fact that the texts of the Parisian avant-garde in the 1950s were proposals for an altogether different theater than had existed up to that time and that the "absurd" in those texts was a discovery of a new "theatricality." It was as if the "absurd" had now found itself on the stage and was exhibited via nonverbal means of expression. The "absurd" passed from dialogue to a place beyond words and became a *show*. Linguistic structures in the Theater of the Absurd also underwent a change: a breakdown in communication. Dialogue becomes similar to the children's game called "telephone." The "absurd" in language becomes visual and thus spectacle.

Signs can be divided into literal, mimetic, and symbolic. In a literal sign, the icon and the referent are the same; in the mimetic sign, the icon is an image, an imitation of the referent; in a symbolic sign, "the code" determines the meaning of the icon. In a system of road signs, all three types of signs are used: the barrier lowered before a railroad crossing is a literal sign; a cow or deer on a road sign is a mimetic sign; and a red light or the word "stop" is a symbolic sign. The alphabet is a system of symbolic signs. Chinese ideograms, however, are pictorial signs, and Chinese poetry can be "read" in two ways, either as icons and, therefore, as pictures, or for meaning, as symbolic signs. "Concrete" poetry has similar properties, and the graphic arrangement of lines is both an icon of mimetic and symbolic signs, both image and writing.

A theatrical presentation and the actors' actions, the scene design, and the costumes are a collection of icons, but this collection is ambivalent and inconsistent by its very nature and not homogeneous. A chair in a "normal" theater is a literal sign; it is a chair pure and simple, but trees painted on canvas or on the background are already mimetic. A lighted candle on stage is a literal sign, but the changes in lighting are mimetic signs: bright light indicates day, half-light—evening, and the dimming of lights—night. Flaming torches, however, carried into fully illuminated Chinese theaters (Peter Brook used this device in *King Lear*) are a symbolic sign of night. These three types of signs are mixed up with one another in all elements of the performance. Walking on the stage is a literal sign, but running is already a mimetic sign, because the actor is only pretending to run, he is imitating running. In naturalistic theater, gestures are an imitation of real gestures, but real gestures are also literal, mimetic, or symbolic signs. This semiotics of theatrical signs can be presented in a systematic fashion, and many such attempts have been undertaken, but they have often turned out to be no better than an empty intellectual game. Something else is important here: the analysis of icons and the relationship between icons and their meaning allows one to describe theatrical styles and schools.

A basic icon in the theater is the actor's body. Every art, wrote Eric Bentley, is the baring of the human soul, but it is only in the theater that the baring of the soul takes place through the physical presence of human bodies onstage. When we say that Mme. Z. was an excellent Juliet, but that she has crooked legs, we are judging both the icon and the "signified." We are judging both the mimetic Juliet and the symbolic one. No one has managed to show as radically and as simply as Brecht that basic and perhaps structural paradox of the theater: the actor is a person, that is, the actor, and simultaneously the *persona* which he represents. The time of the performance is measured no differently by the director than it is by the audience, yet the inner time of the spectacle is different: it flows more quickly or slowly, it can flash back or even return to its point of departure, and can be the past or the future. The action takes place in a specific part of the theater building: on the stage, in an arena, on scaffolding made of boards. During rehearsals, the stage has its front and rear sections for the director and actors, and has its left and right wing, yet during the performance the backstage may become a garden, a square, or a street, while the left wing may become a bedroom or prison. Before the beginning of the play, when the curtains are up, the stage and decorations are literal signs, which the dimming of lights and three gongs of the bell can change into mimetic or symbolic signs.

Circus art and the theaters of the East have had an enormous, and as of yet underestimated, influence on the entire European theatrical avant-garde. The Chinese opera, the Japanese Noh and Kabuki are theaters of almost pure icons for the viewer who is unfamiliar with the "codes," that is, the symbolic language of those theaters. Without access to the codes, white is neither a sign of joy nor mourning; it is only the color white; the duel between two actors in red and black makeup who are decked in armor bearing four flags is a show of acrobatic prowess, not a battle between two armies from the North and South. The circus is also an art of sheer action and concrete images. Everything really takes place. The dancer is dancing on a real tightrope strung under the circus top, and animal training represents nothing other than the training of animals. "For real" means that the icon is a literal sign, or a "thing." Brecht and Artaud experienced this dual fascination with the circus and the theaters of the East, but the conclusions that each of these drew for his own vision were different.

The actor's body and costume are an icon, and if the actor represents himself, that is, remains an actor, the icon is a literal sign; if he identifies with the character of the play, the icon is a mimetic or symbolic sign. The *Verfremdungseffekt,* the consciously made leap from the created character to the actor, from theatrical to real time, from the imagined place to the real stage can be described using the same icon once as a literal sign, and then again as a mimetic or symbolic sign.

We watch a performance and, therefore, everything that happens onstage is not "for real"; we are in the theater, we sit in a seat and look at the stage and so everything that happens there, happens "for real": the actors are alive and the props are real. The theater is both the illusion of reality and the reality of illusion.

Brecht, a didactic rationalist raised on Marxism and the cabaret, began to cultivate the play between the icon and its meanings with a great deal of sophistication. An actor in his underpants in *The Life of Galileo* is almost a pure literal sign, a man in underwear, but when he is attired in pontifical robes and a tiara is placed on his head, he is already a Pope and, more than that, he is the Office of the Papacy. Not only are the body and the costume an icon with multiple meanings, but the props are an icon as well. The hanger bearing the robes and tiara is both a literal and symbolic icon: the costume is the Office, the Pope is a mannequin.

Brecht's scenography, his ways of using masks and Eastern makeup exploit the same principle of the icon's ambiguity. An actor in a mask is more theatrical than an actor without a mask; he is more theatrical, which means that he is more of an actor. He is "real" because he is not pretending that the character which he is playing is "real." The mask in Brecht's theater is a literal or symbolic icon but it is never mimetic. Brecht also employed a device which the Russian Formalists in the early twenties called *ostrannenie,* "laying bare the device." A revolving plate, moving in a direction opposite to that of the wagon pulled by the sutler (camp follower) in *Mother Courage,* is a laying bare of the theatrical machinery and utilizing it as a literal sign. Yet because of Brecht's splendid theatrical imagination, the plate, revolving in the opposite direction to that of the wagon, also has two other functions: first, the plate keeps the wagon of Mother Courage and her sons both in motion and in the same place—the middle of the stage, downstage in full sight of the audience; and, second, it fulfills a deeply symbolic function: Mother Courage pushes her wagon and stands in the same place. We could say that she pushes her wagon against forces which are stronger than she is.

In *King Lear,* Brook used an old stage device to produce thunder: the three enormous vibrating sheets of metal that were lowered onto the stage were simultaneously a literal icon and a symbolic sign, a spectacular machine and a storm.

For Artaud this theatricalization of the stage took the form of Theater of Cruelty: "I shall answer," he wrote in *The Theater and Its Double,* "that if we are clearly so incapable today of giving an idea of Aeschylus, Sophocles, Shakespeare that is worthy of them, it is probably because we have lost the sense of their theater's physics. It is because the directly human and active aspect of their way of speaking and moving, their whole scenic rhythm, escapes us. An aspect which ought to have as much if not more importance than the admirable spoken dissection of their heroes' psychology." Artaud's understanding of "cruelty" was interchangeable with the concept of "rigor." "Cruelty is rigor," he wrote. The French word,"*cruauté,*" emphasizes "*cru,*" that is, raw, even more than the English. "*Une viande crue*" is raw meat. This raw meat of the theater was not meanings and "discourse" but "physics," that which happens in the theater: action, the sheer presence of bodies and objects, the material quality of the voice. Artaud had the intuitive understanding of the Balinese theater with its language of symbols, and his Theater of Cruelty was supposed to have been both a theater of icons and of liturgy, a theater of the "raw meat" and of ritual.

How is the modern "metaphysical" sign supposed to look in a theater which was not familiar with this tradition and which had long ago discarded it? Neither Artaud nor Witkiewicz could answer this question. The most mature and still startling answer is the later works of Beckett, from *Krapp's Last Tape* to *Rockaby* and *Footfalls.*

3 In Ionesco's *Amédée,* mushrooms sprout in a room and the feet of a corpse slowly fill the entire stage. What does that expanding corpse and those poisonous mushrooms mean? Perhaps suppressed memories, a hidden betrayal, time that kills love, impending death? The icons of these signs are delineated with unusual precision, their theatrical expressiveness is unquestionable, but their symbolic meaning and their own metaphysical value remain unclear. The icon is richer, more overwhelming than all of its references.

In Beckett's *Endgame,* Ham is blind and cannot get up from his wheelchair, Clov cannot sit down, and Nell and Nagg can only stick their heads out of garbage cans. In the first part of *Happy Days,* Winnie is buried in the ground up to her waist, and in the second part, up to her neck. In Beckett's plays, the stage directions are incredibly detailed and sometimes make up half the text. The dramatic situation is contained almost totally in what is visual. What does it mean? The impossibility of communication? Life understood as aging and decay? Consciousness which for the existentialists is a "hole" in a world of essence? *Vanitas vanitatum?* If Beckett could have or wanted to have *told* us that, he would have used other types of signs. Here the "nonverbal" is more disturbing than any possible dialogue.

Before the war, in the years of my Parisian youth, the favorite pastime of my friends was thinking up so-called surrealistic objects. First prize was once awarded to an iron with a nail pounded into its base. The meaning of the iron as a utilitarian object was completely destroyed in this way. The iron was deprived of its meaning. On another occasion, a prize was won by something called "Paganini's Violin." Today this violin is in the Louvre. This surrealistic object was a small violin securely wound up in bandage. The destruction of things was the destruction of literal iconography. The iron with protruding nail or the bandaged violin were signs of *angst.* The things that make up collages are similar to "surrealistic objects" in that both are stripped of their meaning, their "gestalt," and their inner structure undergoes destruction; they become pure *objets d'art,* icons. Yet from their mutual juxtaposition, from their arrangement arises a new icon which is not only a literal sign, but which has, or can have, symbolic value. It may be a sign of the Absurd, of Horror, or of Meaninglessness.

In Tadeusz Różewicz's, Ionesco's, and especially in Beckett's plays, the dramatic situation as *image* is similar to that of the surrealistic collage. The shoes which Vladimir and Estragon take off and put on, the tree which blossoms, Krapp's tape, the mirror, the revolver, and all the objects which Winnie takes out of her purse, are literal signs. From their juxtaposition and arrangement come symbolic signs. They seem to be the most evocative icons of human existence.

A similar process of "iconization" appeared, to a certain extent, in the linguistic structures of the Theater of the Absurd. What does it mean to understand the statement: "Two times two is blue"? To understand it means to classify it as nonsensical ("Two times two is five" is a false, but comprehensible, statement). Understanding takes place somewhere on a higher plane of linguistic consciousness and has nothing to do with the syntax. The characters from *The Lesson* and *The Bald Soprano* have serious difficulties in understanding one another, but we understand them without problem and we inevitably classify their statements as word clusters, slips of the tongue, clichés, linguistic jokes, or sheer nonsense. We accept them as if in quotation marks, and understand some statements metaphorically when they are meant literally or literally when they are meant metaphorically. These statements could serve as examples for general linguistic or communications theories, including the breakdown of the latter.

Beginning with the later plays of Strindberg, the viewer is often in the position of one who must decode messages. Or in the position of a psychoanalyst who must listen to the ramblings of his patient. For Jacques Lacan, psychoanalysis is a part of structural linguistics. The Freudian id is a linguistic message. Dreams, not only when we are telling them, but even as we are remembering them, already have a linguistic form, and slips of the tongue are an interference with the message. The associations connected with the icon of an ink blot are also linguistic statements. But this is a coded message, in which each icon has two or more meanings: a superficial one and a hidden one, a literal one and a symbolic one. The id speaks in a meta- or infra-language. But no one can translate from non-language into language. The roar of the sea is untranslatable into any human tongue.

4   Genet's theater is called the theater of ceremony, liturgy, and ritual. The ruthless repetition of form is indispensable to the gravity of ritual. Liturgy, to travesty Artaud, is also a rigor. The intention is not important, but the form is. A non-believing priest who repeats the words of the canon transmutes the bread and wine into the Body and Blood of Christ. But if the words are confused, the transmutation will not take place. Ritual is initiation, the passing from one social group into another, a transformation and change: the boy who is introduced into the company of men, the pagan who becomes a Christian, or the layman who is consecrated into the priesthood. I say: "I do!" and raise my two fingers and, behold, I become a President, a Judge, a sworn witness, or a married man. The icon here is the oral formula and certain gestures, the ritual in which both the conductor of the ceremony, and the person subordinating himself to the ritual, take part. Yet he who has submitted to the ritual may be present only symbolically, may be represented by the object or even performed. Traditional magic is based either on the principle of similitude, or on the principle of temporal or spatial proximity or contiguity. In linguistic terminology, as formulated by Roman Jakobson, magic is based on the principle of metaphor or metonymy. The photograph of an unfaithful lover is pierced or burned or the same is done to a doll, an effigy of him. This is magic working on the principle of similitude or metaphor. But the hair of an unfaithful lover may also be used in magic, as can any bit of her clothing or an object which came into contact with her body. This is magic on the principle of proximity or metonymy. In *The Golden Bough,* Frazer called the first of these "imitative" magic and the second "contagious" magic.

In *The Maids,* Genet makes use of both types of magic. Claire plays Madame, and so imagines her. Both Sisters put on the Madame's dresses, look at themselves in her mirror, and wear her perfume. But all the magic rituals are only a game; in reality the Sisters are only aping Madame and can only sleep with and poison each other. The ritual is a repetition of Form. In partaking of the ritual, everyone is an actor and so must repeat the words and gestures, that is, perform the ritual. But what happens if the ritual is played out on the stage? The marriage is not valid, the oath does not bind, the bishop does not receive consecration. The transformation did not really take place. The Mass was merely reflected in a mirror. The ritual repeated onstage was for the sake of appearances. That is, in essence, an unmasking of ritual. The performed ritual is a mirror image of the real ritual, but the real ritual is also mere imitation. In this theater there are only the repeated reflections of gestures in the mirror. This most consistent embodiment of the Theater of Cruelty and Rigor is at the same time its complete contradiction. The "metaphysical" sign repeated in the theater becomes a literal sign. Artaud's rites turned out to be an illusion. That "superior notion of the theater" which will "restore to all of us the natural and magic equivalent of the dogmas in which we no longer believe" does not exist. Grotowski was the last who believed in the possibility of such theater.

5 What does "for real" mean in the theater? The only consistent answer is the *happening*. In a happening, all the signs are literal: the pyramid of chairs is only a pile of chairs arranged one on top of another. The jet of water which sprays the audience is only a jet of water soaking the viewers. Actually, the division between actors and audience does not even exist, and it is in this lack of division that the happening differs from sports events, from the circus, or from athletic contests. Only in the best cases are happenings provocative or themselves provoked. Judith Malina formulated her position quite well: "I don't want to be Antigone," she declared, "I am, and I want to be Judith Malina." The audience cannot go onstage and take the hand of the actress playing Antigone if the stage is a sign of Thebes, and the body of the actress is the icon of Oedipus's daughter. But in the Living Theater, Antigone is only the body of Judith Malina. It is the same concrete sign as the audience. One can touch it and knock it over.

Brecht demanded that the actor represent both the *persona dramatis* and himself at the same time. But in a happening there is no actor; one can only be oneself. And what does it mean to be "oneself?" After Gombrowicz and Genet, after psychoanalysis and contemporary radical criticism of the personality, it is very difficult to accept that one can simply be oneself on the stage. After all, we are on stage all the time. The face is also only a mask, or, in Gombrowicz's terminology, a "mug" which has been affixed to us, or which we ourselves put on. Each outfit we wear is a theatrical costume, a disguise. Only the naked can be "themselves." And even not always. "Are naked women intelligent?" asked Stanisław Jerzy Lec. The effect of nudity, which tempted so many directors, was not just the result of a change in accepted norms of a permissive society. Nudity in theater was also the search for the concrete. Flesh is a nonverbal sign speaking the universal language. But let us repeat another of Lec's aphorisms: "When you get to the very bottom, you will hear a knocking from below." Nudity as flesh also turned out to be an illusion. "Naked as worms" says one of the characters from Sartre's *No Exit*. "Naked as Gods" wrote Nietszche. Perhaps it is simply a matter of being naked as people. A naked and concrete sign turned out, once again, to be a symbolic sign, or perhaps even more, one of those "metaphysical" and universal signs of which Artaud so desperately dreamed. Painting and abstract ballet could have taught us that long ago.

(1969)

WHY SHOULD I
TAKE PART
IN THE
SACRED DANCE?

1 I saw Jerzy Grotowski's Laboratory Theater for the first time in the early 1960s in Opole, a small town in Silesia. The audience was restricted to twenty-five, but that evening only four or perhaps five guests from Warsaw and two young girls from the local school came to the performance of Stanisław Wyspiański's *Acropolis*. I saw Grotowski's theater for the second time three years later. He had already moved to Wrocław, where he was given space in the old town hall. I came then to a festival of contemporary Polish plays and some sort of symposium, for which critics from the entire country had gathered. The forum was boring, the plays mediocre, the productions uninteresting, but all the theaters were filled to capacity. At Grotowski's theater the audience was again restricted to thirty or forty, but at that performance of Calderón's *The Constant Prince*, there were no more than a dozen or so. Grotowski already at that time had his enthusiasts and his enemies, but the number in both camps could be counted on one's fingers. During all those years Grotowski's theater did not enter into Poland's theatrical life; it did not attract even the young. It was in Poland, but really did not exist in Poland.

Grotowski's theater was subsidized by the government from the very beginning. Poland is probably the only country in the world to permit itself the luxury of financing a theater-laboratory and sufficiently poor that this allocation fell short of providing even sustenance for the members of the ensemble. During the first two or even three years, Grotowski and his actors starved—and not by any means in the figurative sense of the word. Poverty was at first a practice of this theater; only later was it raised to the dignity of aesthetics. I don't know whether the members of the group made their triple vows as monks and nuns, but this theater was modeled along the strict lines of a cloister. Grotowski demanded from his followers seclusion, obedience, and physical training almost beyond the limits of human endurance. The renunciation of material goods, given conditions in Poland, was probably the easiest decision. Far more difficult was the renunciation of the theater of politics.

The theater in Poland in the second half of the fifties was perhaps the most political in the world. Even the Western Theater of the Absurd transferred to the Vistula became unequivocally, or one might even say desperately, political. Grotowski's theater developed at a historical moment of prolonged political unrest. After Stalin's death, a short time of thaw ensued culminating in a new defeat. The Prague Spring lasted a month; the Polish Apocalypse of freedom in October 1956 lasted three days. The awakening from an apocalypse is bitter: in Poland the realization of a hopeless situation, and later the resignation to the dread this hopelessness provoked lasted for years. In conditions of arbitrary and unlimited political repression every public activity is a compromise. In the theater a political compromise is always ultimately an artistic compromise. Grotowski made the heroic decision to be uncompromising. But under the conditions of repression, such a decision exacts the price of supplanting politics with metaphysics.

After Grotowski's appearances in England and the United States, a couple of nimble-witted critics noticed with a certain astonishment that the greatest artistic success of a country which considered itself "socialistic" was the mystic theater of obscure religious experiences. Grotowski, especially in his early period, asserted that the task of the actor, the "holy" actor in his terminology, was to experience and incarnate archetypes. I doubt whether the return to "archetypes" is possible in contemporary theater, but I know with complete certainty that "archetypes" are politically harmless; they are, in any case, ambiguous and hard to make out. Julien Sorel in Stendhal's *The Red and the Black* learned very early in his seminary days that gestures are safer than words. The most important question remains: what do these gestures mean? What does the excellence of Grotowski's theater signify?

2 Even a theater that wishes to reach back to archetypes must feed on living ceremony, ritual, and liturgy which stem from its own country. *Acropolis* and *The Constant Prince*, which I saw years ago in Poland, seemed to me contrived and very distant. *Apocalypsis cum figuris*, which I saw in New York, struck me at once with its Polishness.

The pilgrims to the miraculous shrine of Our Lady at Kalwaria Zebrzydowska climb on their hands and knees up steep stairs ornamented with figures of Christ's Passion, bruising their knees on the sharp rocks. Częstochowa, with the holy image of the Black Madonna, the Queen of Poland, is transformed in May, the month of the cult of the Virgin Mary, into a huge campsite. A few streets away from the monastery one finds market stalls, which sell beads and scapulars, all kinds of worthless religious baubles, and rolls with sausages. But the pilgrims generally arrive with their own supplies. The village women unfold large colored kerchiefs right on the marketplace, on which they set great loaves of home-baked bread. The men pull flat bottles of vodka out of their pockets, drink straight from them, and then pass them to the women. The action of *Apocalypsis* begins with this scene. A woman places a loaf of bread on a white kerchief. A man reaches with his hand above his belt and offers the half-closed hand to the woman. He then raises it to his lips. His adam's apple moves up and down—he pours the vodka straight down his throat in the time-honored Polish way.

Along the main street of Częstochowa pass processions led by priests and little boys in white cassocks. The men sing with hoarse voices as in *Apocalypsis:* "Glory to the Highest and Most Just." The women with squeaky and tearful voices wail: "Lamb of God." The religious songs are mixed with drunken hiccups and the squeals of young girls. The men squatting in the square are already drunk. One barely hears the hymn from the monastery: "And I saw the water flowing from the right side of the temple. Alleluia!" Nearby is a figure of the crucified Christ with a pierced side. The artisan did not spare the red paint. In *Apocalypsis* a man with a white coat thrown over his shoulders bares the side of a barefoot beggar in a black jacket which reaches to his knees, and sucks his wounds. Again his adam's apple moves rhythmically up and down; the liquid gurgles in his throat. But others have already pushed him aside. They want to drink too. One after another, like leeches, they suck the blood transformed into vodka.

Częstochowa is full of beggars. It is as though all the country's blind, lame, and crippled, shaking their wooden stumps, had agreed to a vast meeting or mating here. The most numerous are the village idiots. Peasants from Eastern Poland consider them holy. They are afflicted, but no one knows why. They mumble, lisp, gabble; perhaps God wants to say something through them. They look into space with tear-filled eyes; perhaps they have seen something. Ryszard Cieślak, the main actor, "Ciemny" in the play, raises himself from the ground; he has a white stick in his hand and he looks over the heads of the drunken men. Now he runs up to them and looks in their faces and smiles half-wittedly. A man puts his hand into a chunk of bread, crushes it into a hard ball, and throws it, as if it were a lump of earth, into Cieślak's face. The village idiot runs away, skipping across the square in leaps and bounds. But another man catches up with him, jumps on his back, and spurs him on like a horse. Curses and profanities are scattered about. A woman recites the litany. In profanities and litanies the names of God and Mary are repeated. In the American programs, "Ciemny" was translated as "Simpleton." Some critics saw in him the medieval Everyman. However, this village idiot, transformed by the prostitute and drunkards into a figure of Christ, stems rather from Aleksandr Blok's *The Twelve*. But he is not the Christ of any revolution.

At night, Częstochowa is dark. Candles have burned out; street lamps are extinguished. A woman carries out a bucket of water. She soaks her feet, tired from walking. Under the monastery wall the drunkards sleep wrapped up in their coats. Even in their dreams they mumble profanities or prayers. In the darkness someone struggles with a girl. The whores are also pilgrims. The sour smell of equine and human urine is mixed with the sweet smell of incense burners and the odor of vomit. "Go and return no more," says Simon-Peter to the village idiot, tormented beyond human endurance. But if this is beyond human endurance, does this mean it is sacred? If this were Christ, He really had no reason to come. Thus ends Grotowski's *Apocalypsis*, the Polish "Walpurgisnacht."

3 Grotowski brought a Method and metaphysics with him to the West. His Method is precise and verifiable in practice; his metaphysics is obscure and ambiguous. Cieślak was a young man without experience when he surrendered himself to Grotowski's Method. He became one of the greatest actors of the world. Peter Brook told me once that after Stanislavsky, no one knew as much about acting as Cieślak and Grotowski. The corporality of the Laboratory Theater, the ultimate precision of gesture, faces transformed into masks by a simple contraction of muscle, the sounds as language—these can only be compared with the Japanese Noh, in which the actor's art is transmitted from generation to generation. Even Kabuki, in comparison with the Laboratory Theater, seems to be too loose. But recognition of the external perfection of this theater in effect diminishes Grotowski, just as the recognition only of the magnificent ballet of war in Brecht's *Coriolanus* diminishes the Berliner Ensemble.

There remain only two serious questions: what is the final meaning of Grotowski's metaphysics, and is it possible to separate his Method from his murky mysticism and apply it in a theater with other goals and a profane vision? Or to put it bluntly: can one apply his Method in a theater which seeks to replace mysticism with refusal to cooperate with the establishment and its values? Grotowski's teaching, like Brecht's, has the ambition to be a total system: from the theology of initiation to semantics, from the ethics of acting to the technology of lighting. But in practice, these two Scriptures contradict each other. In *Schriften zum Theater* Brecht wrote:

> Give us light on the stage, lighting engineer! How can we,
> Playwrights and actors, present our images of the world
> In semi-darkness? Nebulous twilight
> Lulls to sleep. But we need the spectators'
> Wakefulness, even watchfulness. Let them dream
> In blazing clarity!

The last episodes of Grotowski's *Apocalypsis* are played in darkness on the stone floor of the church. Grotowski returns to the old rite of purification, the only difference being that the catharsis is to be introduced by violent means as by flagellation in some medieval code for monks. The actors offer to the audience a physical humiliation of their bodies. And this to Grotowski represents the holiness and the sacrilege/sacrifice of the actor. For Brecht everything sacred within the system of repression and exploitation was morally suspect. He despised the actor's trance and any aesthetic satisfaction from human suffering. Brecht's famous opposition between the "epic" and "dramatic" theater, when quoted today, could be directed against Grotowski: it implies a rejection of his Method and the metaphysics which goes with it.

> The spectator of the *dramatic* theatre says: "Yes, I have felt the same.—I am just like this.—This is only natural.—It will always be like this.—This human being's suffering moves me, because there is no way out for him.—This is great art: it bears the mark of the inevitable.—I am weeping with those who weep on stage, laughing with those who laugh."
>
> The spectator of the *epic* theatre says: "I should never have thought so.—That is not the way to do it.—This is most

surprising, hardly credible.—This will have to stop.—This human being's suffering moves me, because there would have been a way out for him. This is great art: nothing here seems inevitable.—I am laughing about those who weep on the stage, weeping about those who laugh."

For the theater of the Contestation, which evolved from the school of the Absurd and discovered almost a half-century later the old Dada and surrealism as a new nourishment, Brecht seems old-fashioned with his rationalism, flat and bourgeois with his optimistic didacticism, dry and limited because of his respect for literary tradition and discourse. Grotowski was welcomed by the new theaters as the guru from Poland. He taught the techniques of shock. The languages of *praxis* and imagination, of social and sexual revolution, of Marx and of Freud, of Herbert Marcuse and of Timothy Leary became fatally intermixed. The theater of the counterculture felt that revolution could enter the mind only through the skin, as formulated in the gospel of Artaud.

Marcuse, in his *Essay on Liberation* (1969), the coldest analysis of the impossibility of revolution in sated consumer societies, argues that when a rational revolutionary tactic does not exist, Utopian thought recovers its lost attraction and dignity. If revolution is impossible, rebellion could always be acted out. Rebellion is an instant revolutionary Utopia. But in an objectively nonrevolutionary situation, a revolutionary Utopia which should be realized *instantly* can only be acted out. Sit-in, teach-in, love-in, these are forms of instant liberation. Utopias acted out, and thus theater. The Woodstock Festival was a real Paradise Now. It was also an *Apocalypsis cum figuris,* but the figures in it were not exactly the same. One can accept one of these apocalypses or reject both, but one cannot accept both of them at the same time.

When the village idiot, cast as Christ, has already passed through all the stages of his Passion, when he has been spat upon and ridiculed, and disowned by all, Cieślak's face changes: for a moment he becomes beautiful, as if illumined by an inner light. When the Constant Prince is only a tortured body, the same unearthly smile lights up on Cieślak's face. When in the last scene of *Acropolis* the prisoners go down into the depths of the crematorium, the same light illumines their faces. In Grotowski's theater liberation comes only through death, the torture of the body, and the humiliation of the spirit. I am not sure whether, to accept Grotowski's metaphysics, one must believe that there is a God. But I am certain that one must give up hope and renounce the possibility of revolt.

In Sophocles' *Oedipus the King,* when it seems for a moment that the ominous Oracle of Delphi could have made a mistake and that Oedipus did not kill Laius, the Chorus rebels. Suddenly the tragic world in which the son is predestined to kill his father and sleep with his mother collapses. If man is stronger than the wrath of God, the Chorus shouts, "why should I take part in the sacred dance?"

Why should I take part in the sacred dance?

AFTER GROTOWSKI:
THE END OF THE
IMPOSSIBLE THEATER

1 **P**eter Brook and his interlocutor ascend a steep and winding staircase to the very rooftop of the Théâtre des Bouffes du Nord. The old theater is not tall, and from its roof one can look straight into the windows across the street. Such is the beginning of Peter Brook and Gerard Feil's film on theater. In the window across the street, at roof level, a young woman undressing is seen through a transparent curtain. Is theater nothing but snooping? The window is like the frame of the theater proscenium. Everything outside the window frame, the backstage and other rooms of the apartment, is hidden from the gaze of the voyeur-spectator. The action begins with the raising of the curtain or turning on of the lights. It ends when the lights go off or the curtain is drawn.

In the window, a young woman is undressing, a family sits down at a table, someone enters, someone leaves, a party goes on or a fight takes place, a love scene begins or ends. But whatever has happened *before*—before the lights were turned on, before the blinds were raised—will remain unknown. And when the lights eventually go off, the voyeur-spectator will only be able to guess what happened *after*. Possibly the drapes in the very same window will be pulled apart once more and something will begin to develop again, but we will never learn what took place in between. Even when the window is opened, the spectator remains an eavesdropper, hearing voices and sounds.

Peeping through a window differs from watching a street scene. Some mystery always inheres in the scene viewed through a window. Our information remains fragmentary, because our view is limited and removed. The stage of a theater seen from its wings bears no resemblance to what is observed from the audience. From behind the scenes one sees actors struggling with their roles. Only from the audience are they perceived as characters in the drama. Shadows behind a window curtain, spied upon from another window, rooftop, or street, always enact some drama. For the voyeur, a window scene is a spectacle. Desire is aroused but never satisfied.

The fourth "transparent" wall of Stanislavsky transforms the "window" into the aesthetics of theater. In the first act of *The Ghost Sonata,* Strindberg introduced the facade of a house on stage. The specters appear as shadows in the windows of this house. Modernist drama and theater can be called a window onto "real" life. And post-modernist theater may be described as a persistent decomposition of "window" aesthetics.

A street-scene onlooker is not a voyeur: he's a participant or witness. This distinction has been very clearly shown by Brecht. In the most extreme formulations of *Little Organon,* a street scene, repeated and reenacted by its witness, became a model for the epic theater. For Artaud, also, a street scene constituted a paradigm of theater. But in contrast to Brecht, the voyeur was to be replaced not by an observer or witness, but by a participant. Theater was to become joint participation. The spectators were to enter the window.

The theater can be a window onto "real" life or a wooden floor on which the players present tragic and comic plays. These are two aesthetics, two proposals for the possible theater. "If theater is a double of life," wrote Artaud to Paulhan, "life is the double of the theater." An impossible theater is a mirror into which one can walk.

2 Two of the slogans painted on the walls of the Sorbonne and Odéon during the May revolt in 1968 went down into history. *"Sois réaliste. Faites l'impossible,"* and *"L'imagination au pouvoir!"*—"Be a realist. Ask for the impossible," and "Power to imagination!" They were filled with hope. But, as in Camus, it was hope full of despair. Translated into the cold language of reason, the message was clear: revolution is impossible; it can occur only in the imagination.

The young boys and girls who, during that Parisian May, tore up paving-stones and erected barricades of burning cars represented the last generation of existential revolt. They were also the last generation whose imagination was shaped by surrealism. In the early 1930s, Paul Eluard and his friends were publishing a review, *Le surréalisme au service de la révolution*. Nearly thirty years later, surrealism became for thirty days a manifesto of rebellion. If surrealism is seen as the culmination and the paroxysm of romanticism, then May 1968 in Paris was the last romantic revolution.

When a revolution is impossible it immediately attains theatrical status. An impossible revolution can always be acted out. "Power to imagination! Realize the impossible!" On stage!

I witnessed the first performances of the Living Theater in America, after its return from Europe, which took place in New Haven at the Yale School of Drama a year after the Parisian May. At the beginning of *Paradise Now!* the actors intermingled with the spectators. They recited, as if it were a litany, "We are not allowed to walk around naked—undress, and come onto the stage, and share grass with each other." " We are not allowed to make love in public— come up onto the stage, and make love together." The boys and girls from Yale—slowly, with reluctance, as if deluded by a rat-catcher—went up on the stage and made love. But being aware that, after all, they were in a theater, they performed their mating in a difficult, uncomfortable, and elaborate lotus position.

A year after its performances at Yale, the Living Theater arrived at Berkeley with the same spectacle. The course of the action was by then common knowledge. The spectators were ready. At the moment the actors began their litany, the boys and girls had their jeans already below the knees. When the words "We are not allowed to undress in public" were uttered, in a twinkling of an eye, the entire audience was naked. After the spectacle, Judith Malina said to me with regret: "Very difficult, this Berkeley audience."

Paradise Now! was one of the first attempts at entering the window. But within just a few months "the window" ceased to be the stage and encompassed the entire campus. I still remember from Yale the autumn rituals when immediately after the start of the fall semester the beautiful freshman girls would throw their bras into the fire. At the campuses of prominent universities and in the hippie neighborhoods, *Paradise Now!* was being reenacted.

Instant sex, like instant coffee, can be served up over and over again, but the place for *Apocalypsis cum figuris* is only on stage. And Grotowski well knew why he performed it just for a handful of spectators and, whenever possible, in churches.

The story of the flower children and the Haight Ashbury neighborhood in San Francisco is widely known. I went there during the first weeks of paradise. Very young girls in loose, wide dresses down to the ankles, like gypsies entwined by beads, with bracelets above their bare feet, handed flowers to the passersby. The boys poured herbal brews. In the air, the scent of flowers blended with the sweet-smelling smoke of marijuana—as in Euripides' *The Bacchae,* when during a Dionysiac rite the Maenads breast-fed goatlings and lambs, and thick, golden honey slowly dripped down their thyrsi.

But acting out *Apocalypsis* does not go unpunished. Apocalypses end in rape and murder, and the paradise in Haight Ashbury ended in much the same way as the Euripidean tragedy. Within a few months, Haight Ashbury became San Francisco's most dismal and dangerous neighborhood. Heroin replaced marijuana, and the boys handing out thirst-quenching beverages from natural herbs turned into pimps, while starved girls sold themselves cheaply to whoever passed by. Apocalypse can be performed in a window, but behind the window there always exists a real street where there is no place for either paradise or apocalypse. Even when this window is a green campus and an entire suburb. The Mafia and the narks assumed their control over the lost paradise of the flower children.

There was yet another ending to the "paradise in the window," less spectacular and gloomy but this time final. The window onto paradise was transformed into a huge department store display case. Popularized by the mass media, the counterculture, with all its social and political revolt laundered out, became a merchandise as marketable as any other. The market for "contestation" proved practically unlimited. Within the last two decades successive waves of fashion for rich and poor alike have changed clothing into permanent carnival or *bal masqué;* and among all these disguises, at times as exotic as Danube Cossacks or Eastern odalisques, disguising as youth became most popular.

Teenage fashion belongs already to the past. The blue jeans story, to which, not long ago, the *New York Times* devoted a short editorial, is most instructive. Jeans—inexpensive, sensible, unisex all-weather wear—have been worn around the world for years. For years, and from morning to night. At first they were worn by laborers, later teenagers adopted jeans as their uniform, and finally everyone donned them. Jeans stood for democratization of dress; they obliterated differences between classes and occupations, sexes and generations. They were a nondiscriminative attire.

Then, in the early 1980s the *haute couture* houses dictating the world's fashion began to market jeans elaborately cut—morning, afternoon, and evening-wear jeans for women. These luxury jeans from specially prepared fabrics, practically an *objet d'art* designed by the artists of the craft, have on their seats, as a sign of ennoblement and distinction, not only the trademark but also the name of the creator.

When, after a decade, I once again lectured at the Yale School of Drama, I was not able to explain to the participants of my seminar on contemporary theater the true meaning of the slogans scribbled on the walls of the Sorbonne in May 1968. "Be a realist. Ask for the impossible." *Hopeless hope* was for them but an empty oxymoron. They may have heard of oxymorons in their classes on poetics, but it had never occurred to them that oxymorons do happen in life.

The old theater building in which *Paradise Now!* had been performed stood, as before, two hundred steps away from the place where I lectured. But it was from me that they learned for the first time about the Living Theater happening. They were greatly astonished to find out that their fellow students from ten years before had collectively copulated on stage. "And what for?" they asked. "What are the dormitories for?" They did not believe in paradise, or, at any rate, they had no desire whatsoever publicly to act out paradise and apocalypse. Not even on stage. Before experiencing their short moments of paradise, they carefully drew the curtains in the windows.

3 According to the Gnostic tradition, the language in Paradise was natural. It was spoken by God, the first human couple, and the serpent. According to the orthodox biblical tradition, the confusion of tongues occurred only after the destruction of the Tower of Babel. In the "natural language," names, emotions, and conceptions are embodied both in the sound and the melody of a word as in a baby's babble, a death rattle, a groan or scream of pain and ecstasy. There is no separation between the sign and its referent.

A central myth of the impossible theater is the belief that it is still possible to return to the state of language before the destruction of the Tower of Babel—a language, in the words of Artaud, "halfway between gesture and thought." In the chapter "Metaphysics and the *Mise en Scène*" from *The Theater and Its Double,* Artaud seeks "to make the language express what it does not ordinarily express: . . . to reveal its possibilities for producing physical shock; . . . to deal with intonations in an absolutely concrete manner, restoring their power to shatter as well as really to manifest something; to turn against language and its basely utilitarian, one could say alimentary, sources . . . ."

Grotowski was one of the first to introduce in his "Poor Theater" a form of incantation in accordance with Artaud's prescription—a trans-accentuation foreign to Polish metrics, and the splitting of words into segments in order to restore "metaphysical" shocks by sound alone. Still, in these great spectacles, although the literal meanings were obscured, the purport of the sentences was never totally effaced. In the basement of New York's La Mama theater in the early seventies, André Serban staged Euripides/Seneca's *Medea* partially in Greek, partially in Latin. It was a performance in a foreign language, only remotely understood by the actors and even less so by the spectators. Nevertheless, it was in the languages in which the masterpieces were written, and not in screams and invented tongues.

An invented tongue was "Orghast," used by Brook in his spectacle at Persepolis. There was nothing in this empty version of the myth that could be conveyed by discursive language. At this Asian Acropolis, terrifying and benumbing by its enormity, the story of tyrants is inscribed in stone blocks, smashed temples, and knocked-down walls, in the forest of headless columns, in the lions with two monstrous human heads, and stone tigers tearing at stone horses. From the burning hot, vaporous rocks the air is dense, even late at night. The idiom of stones should have been enough for Brook. *Orghast* in Persepolis was nothing but a chirruping of insects.

Still more fatal for the theater proved the "incantations"— tweeting, whinnying, and yells of the "natural" languages—in the spectacles of imitators of Grotowski and Brook. Artaud, once again, was the evangelist. "No one in Europe knows how to scream any more," he wrote in the chapter "An Affective Athleticism," "and particularly actors in trance no longer know how to cry out. Since they do nothing but talk and have forgotten that they ever had a body in the theater, they have naturally also forgotten the use of their windpipes. Abnormally shrunk, the windpipe is not even an organ but a monstrous abstraction that talks."

Molik, one of the most talented of Grotowski's actors, taught gamboling and screaming to young neophytes of theater in different parts of the globe. The participants of the Berlin Forum in June 1979 had a chance to see two films documenting the exercises which Molik conducted with his students. A fat youngster, unable to utter a deep cry, could neigh like a horse after a few weeks. Two young girls with a waddling gait were "loosened up," and when they jumped, all the muscles of their bodies seemed to dance.

Molik's exercises proved effective. Classes in "corporality" are doubtless essential for all acting aspirants. I have just two reservations. Only those who already know how to speak should be taught how to scream. And it did not seem to me that all of the participants in Molik's class knew how to speak. My second caveat is more serious. The impossible theater's belief in screaming as better than articulate speech for communication is a risky and dangerous delusion. To use Artaud's nomenclature, I prefer "the shrunk windpipe," "the abstraction" reciting *someone else's* text to vocal chords choking with *their own* shrieks.

The participants in the 1979 forum in Berlin also saw Peter Brook's documentary film *Theatre Adventure in Africa,* made in 1973. The film stirred within me very mixed emotions, among others that of embarrassment. Brook with his actors from the International Centre of Theatre Research reached some remote native villages where white people seldom set foot. The arrivals from Paris in blue jeans, colorful shirts, and Mexican ponchos with great mastery performed some tricks with a rope, swung bamboo sticks, twittered like birds, and tried to teach the natives how to play tag, hide-and-seek, and blind man's buff.

One sequence of that movie stuck in my memory. The chieftain of one of the villages, in return for the performance, invited the guests to a ceremonial feast and traditional ritual. Considering Brook the white people's leader, he sat him on a dais, under an umbrella, among his wives and advisers. He smiled at Brook in a friendly and good-natured manner but not without a certain commiseration. He was an old man and might have remembered from his childhood, or might have been told, how once, long ago, other white people had arrived in the same village distributing mirrors and whistles.

After the fete, the ritual dances began—beautiful war, hunting, and wedding dances to the accompaniment of drums and fifes. When they were over, a young member of Brook's party began to beat the drum. He was extremely adept, probably almost as good as the natives themselves. All of Brook's actors went through an excellent "corporality" training: they have a perfect ear for music, acute susceptibility. Instantaneously, they began to reenact the tribal dances. Perfectly.

But at that moment the chieftain's smile waned. The shamans or local dignitaries approached him and for a long while he kept on whispering something into their ears. I could not comprehend what had happened, but a young anthropologist who accompanied me understood immediately. Ritual dances are performed separately by men and women. Brook's actors danced them together. After a while, however, the smile returned to the old chieftain's face. He obviously realized that he was dealing with children who comprehended nothing. Since the arrivals were clapping their hands, he clapped his a few times. And left. So did all the adult members of the tribe. The only ones to stay were children. Till late into the night they played with the seekers for the universal theater who came to this African village from London and Paris.

4 Rehearsals are often fascinating theater. Especially the last ones, a week before the opening, a day or two before the first dress rehearsal. The actors know their parts by heart, but repetition is still creation. They are already in the characters but still alongside them, even if this *alongside* is but hesitation and restlessness. Receptivity is not dulled yet. A butterfly can still be born from the chrysalis.

Observing live the process of hatching has always been for me the most moving experience. I shall never forget the night following the dress rehearsal of *The Tempest* in Milan. In the huge Teatro Lirico, Giorgio Strehler remained alone with the stage technicians. He detained only Miranda and Ferdinand. He sat them on the empty stage in front of a gigantic screen. He began to change the lights. At first he repeated the ones from the last rehearsal, fixed already. But then there were sunrises—misty and pinkish, blood-dripping suns as before a thunderstorm, and silver nights. And then for many hours, until dawn, paradises lost and recaptured, deluges, the birth of worlds in the nebula and their finales in the dark intersections of the cone by which the world was sucked in. Miranda and Ferdinand, naked in the body suits which reflected light on a stage which was the last remaining patch of earth, emerged from darkness and sank into it like the first parents and last lovers.

I know well the fascination of a theater rehearsal. But the impossible theater begins when the aesthetics of a rehearsal become the principle and essence of the theater. During rehearsals, the director is second after God. And if God does not exist, he is God himself. Not only actors, but the lights and stage depend on him.

He also reigns autocratically over the text. He has each line repeated *ad infinitum,* he changes the sequence of scenes, repeats the last act, then the first one, separates the scenes in which the protagonists take part from the group scenes. During a rehearsal, the time sequence of the dramatic structure is necessarily destroyed and replaced by the synchrony of lines repeated over and over again. The director's domination of the author and his text often originates in the very aesthetics of a rehearsal.

The spectators are banned from rehearsals. The actors who are not rehearsing are like rugby players who have left the field; they no longer act but still anticipate, awaiting their re-entrance. The impossible theater, like a theater rehearsal, does not tolerate spectators; it demands co-participants.

Shakespeare presented a theater rehearsal in *A Midsummer Night's Dream,* and he introduced theater within theater at least five times in his plays. Pirandello assigned double roles to his characters: those playing within the stage drama, and those within the "life" drama beyond the stage. Brecht consistently and in full consciousness destroyed the "window," the illusion of reality, by presenting the stage, the reality of illusion.

But identifying theater with a theater rehearsal is a totally different endeavor, derived from different aesthetics. In the theater of rehearsal, the fundamental opposition between the illusion of reality and reality of illusion does not exist, and the Brechtian "alienation effect" cannot be achieved once the division between the stage and the audience, the actors and the spectators, the real crown and the prop has been obliterated.

Rehearsal takes place in a rehearsal room where chalk-marked lines indicate the dimensions of the actual stage. The directors of the impossible theater move the spectacle from the stage into the rehearsal hall. The sum and substance of a rehearsal is trying out: it is a work unfinished, like successive drafts for a painting. Identifying the theater with a rehearsal leads to a public presentation of a rehearsal as a spectacle. Even responsible directors such as Joe Chaikin entitled their spectacles "works in progress."

Videotaping began as a procedure for preserving records of theater. But media create their own aesthetics and dramatic or pseudo-dramatic genres. The documentary tape becomes a movie which is shown. In this process of duplicating media by media, the documentary tape—a record of a rehearsal-sketch, an unfinished work— becomes a model, a paragon of a spectacle. In this *circulum vitiosum* mechanical duplication is being repeated by "live" spectacles of the impossible theater.

In the preface to the English edition of Grotowski's essays, *Towards a Poor Theatre,* Peter Brook wrote: "Grotowski is unique. Why? Because no-one else in the world, to my knowledge, no-one since Stanislavski, has investigated the nature of acting, its phenomenon, its meaning, the nature and science of its mental-physical-emotional processes as deeply and completely as Grotowski. He calls his theatre a laboratory. It is. It is a centre for research."

Brook, who is himself the most daredevil innovator among theater professionals, and the most technical and professional director among the innovators, knows what he is writing. But applied to the theater, the term laboratory is misleading. In a laboratory, research, investigations, and tests are conducted. A laboratory can check its methods, but it does not investigate itself. The theater-laboratory investigates itself. In this metaphysics the search for the essence of the theater *is* the essence of the theater.

Of course, these tendencies are not present solely in the new theater. In all post-modernist arts, in poetry, music, and painting, self-analysis and self-reference seem irresistibly tempting. One of Magritte's paintings represents a room with a window which is a painting representing the very same room with a window. And only from this second window is the landscape beyond visible. But analogies with the theater-laboratory are only illusory. A theater-laboratory, an impossible theater, is a window which watches itself.

The beauty and charm of Italian restaurants consists in a glass wall or a wall-opening through which the kitchen and the cooks are visible. Spectacles by Grotowski's imitators, especially in America, resemble such an Italian restaurant where one can watch the making of a dish. But in that canteen only the kitchen operations are performed. The plates remain forever empty.

5   Grotowski, in his brilliant study of Artaud in which he compares him to the prophet Isaiah predicting the birth of Emmanuel, quotes only two sentences from *The Theatre and Its Double*. The first one reads: "Cruelty is rigour." The second demands that the actors "be like martyrs burnt alive, still signalling to us from their stakes."

Because he chose them, these two sentences must have had a special significance to Grotowski—one of the few gurus of the impossible theater, who was the first to realize that the repetition of exotic rituals is only aping. The only ritual which retained its meaning for him was the Catholic Mass. But Grotowski was well aware that its repetition by actors had to be a profanity. *Apocalypsis cum figuris* in its repetition of sacred drama and Catholic ritual was a blasphemous performance. Foreign audiences did not realize that the "realistic" background for this last, supreme spectacle of Grotowski was a pilgrimage to Jasna Góra in Poland, to the miraculous image of the Black Madonna. The only ritual which can be repeated in the theater without blasphemy is the sacrifice in which the actor is simultaneously the executioner and the martyr.

Grotowski demanded such a sacrifice from his actors. He believed, and so did they, that after months of trials, which were a *trial,* they would, upon wishing it so, ascend into the air. American imitators of Grotowski were certain that they could achieve a theatrical levitation of actors, and even of the spectators, after a one-week session of "body touching."

"Without an element of cruelty at the root of every spectacle, the theater is not possible," wrote Artaud. No other sentence of Artaud has been quoted so often, and the end result of no other has proved as disastrous. The theater was to return to its vanished physicality and corporality. Except that the skin-spanking for Artaud was just a therapy for producing metaphysical shock. The story of the impossible theater is that of another attempt to substitute for theater its delusive doubles: revolt, confrontation, counterculture, the archetypes, rituals, and metaphysical trances of paradise lost.

Artaud wondered, "whether, in this slippery world which is committing suicide without noticing it, there can be found a nucleus of men capable of imposing this superior notion of the theater, men who will restore to all of us the natural and magic equivalent of the dogmas in which we no longer believe." In the system of replacing the theater by its doubles, "the dogmas in which we no longer believe" proved most dangerous. In the United States and, to a certain extent, in Western Europe, theater groups and the weirdest religious and sexual cults began to borrow from and exchange among themselves paratheatrical methods of rigor—cruelty and "metaphysics," which entered ritual orgy, transcendental meditation, brainwashing.

In the prophecies of Artaud, the list of doubles is headed by plague. "If the essential theater is like the plague, it is not because it is contagious, but because like the plague it is the revelation, the bringing forth, the exteriorization of a depth of latent cruelty by means of which all the perverse possibilities of the mind, whether of an individual or a people, are localized." And again: "Like the plague the theater is the time of evil, the triumph of dark powers that are nourished by a power even more profound until extinction. . . . The theater, like the plague, is in the image of this carnage . . . ."

At high noon, in front of the People's Temple, in the heart of the jungle, in a plantation started by white and black arrivals from the towns and ghettos of California, a middle-aged man in dark glasses, already displaying the signs of approaching obesity, ascended a platform as if it were a stage. On huge grounds in front of the Temple, men, women, and children gathered. The sick were brought on stretchers. Religious hymns sounded through the speakers. The man announced that all were to commit collective suicide.

Huge pots of Kool-Aid mixed with cyanide were brought in. One after another, men and women approached the wooden steps of the Temple and drank from the paper cups provided. Afterwards, in tight embrace, they returned to their places where they lay down on the sunburnt earth. Some of the children cried. They were calmed down by white-smocked nurses who gently poured the poison down their throats. The man in the dark glasses committed suicide last.

"In the theater as in the plague there is a kind of strange sun," wrote Artaud, "a light of abnormal intensity by which it seems that the difficult and even the impossible suddenly become our normal element." It took a week to clear away the disintegrating corpses in the hot sun in Jonestown. The count was 918. "We are not free," wrote Artaud. "And the sky can still fall on our heads. And the theater has been created to teach us that first of all." In November 1978, in Guyana's jungle, the sky fell on our heads and the theater of cruelty was consummated.

The impossible took place.

The last two decades in literature and poetry, in painting, music, and theater are more and more generally defined by the term *post-modern*. For me it sounds like *post mortem*.

THE THEATER
OF ESSENCE:
KANTOR AND
BROOK

1 In Tadeusz Kantor's *The Dead Class* the dead return to their old school benches. The benches are placed on stage right in front of those for the audience even before the performance begins. On them sit mannequin boys and girls. When the dead enter, they sit next to their own selves, their old selves, the selves that were. Two different "classes" are summoned from oblivion and examined like pupils by Kantor's memory. The first is a class about to graduate from a Galician small-town gymnasium in the Austro-Hungarian Empire on the eve of World War I. The second "class" in Kantor's hallucinatory spectacle consists of the dead, or rather of the incinerated ethos of that corner of the world where Poles, Ukrainians, and Jews used to live side by side.

I saw *The Dead Class* for the first time at the La Mama theater in New York. When a Jewish lullaby was briefly heard amidst the alternately roaring and whispering cadences of the Viennese waltz *François,* the theme melody of the performance, it suddenly struck me that there probably were at least three or four people in the audience who had been sung to sleep by their mothers or grand-mothers with that same Yiddish lullaby. This small East Village theater is one of the few places in the world where Kantor's dead are still living.

It was also in the East Village at La Mama, off Second Avenue where Polish and Ukrainian luncheonettes serve Russian piroshki, borscht, and zhurek with kielbasa, that I saw *Wielopole Wielopole* for the first time. This too, is a theater of the returning dead, and of mannequins who are doubles of the living. But most disturbing in Kantor's theater is that the living are the doubles of the dead.

The theatrical vision that stubbornly recurs in *The Dead Class* with the physicality and insistence of a nightmare is the procession of the dead returning to their school benches. In *Wielopole* the central image of the spectacle (in Kantor's theater, as in Freudian trauma, image and theme, like a bruise and its chafe, are one and the same) is a faded photograph of seven Austrian World War I conscripts. They stand in battle dress at attention, holding rifles with affixed bayonets.

A photograph is—and this makes photography a unique art—a sign that something *was*. Even when it fades, a photograph is still a reminder, still a trace. For all its fragility, a photographic print, a glossy picture of cardboard, endures longer than the human body. In vast stretches of the world and almost everywhere in Central Europe, this tiny scrap of paper has repeatedly proven itself to be more durable than brick and cement houses and their inhabitants. As Roland Barthes has shown in *Camera lucida*, his last book, a photograph *is* time at once dead and regained. A sign of death, a semblance of what *has been* is immobilized, lives on and endures, subject only to the decomposition of cellulose. Photographs, too, are doubles of the dead. Kantor is both horrified and fascinated by the still life of the dead.

In *Wielopole* the World War I conscripts have faded uniforms and earthy faces. They move like puppets. They are dead, but have been exhumed. In the final scene, after their Last Supper, all the characters are dumped into a single pit. This same mass grave receives their naked doubles, the mannequins.

The characters in *Wielopole* are a family: father, mother, grandmother, four uncles, one of whom is a prelate, aunts and cousins. The father is one of the conscripts. During the wedding ceremony, the prelate uncle binds him to the mother with a stole. Still in her wedding dress, the mother is raped by the other conscripts. With straddled legs her mannequin lies on stage. But earlier, when the wedding photographs are taken, the bride moves like a puppet. The groom/father moves like a skeleton. Then the old-fashioned camera turns into a machine gun. The lens protrudes like a gun barrel. Bullets kill them all.

In Kantor's theater the living are already corpses. The family's history begins with the reconstruction of a room which once existed. "Only, we weren't in this room," says one of the twin uncles. The corpse of the prelate is laid out on the bed. The mattress can be cranked manually so that it turns: the prelate uncle's mannequin is clasped with belts to the other side.

Objects removed from their everyday context and deprived of their regular functions serve as props in Kantor's theater. Kantor admits to kinship with Marcel Duchamp ("Reality can only be represented by means of reality"). His imagination was shaped by late surrealism, as was Topor's—and their obsessions are similar. The annihilated laundry iron and the bandaged violin, which like Duchamp's famous urinal have long since become museum pieces, are props that torment the imagination. But props in Kantor's theater also torment the body. In *Wielopole* macabre jokes are transformed into horror. Horror requires no signature. Words are mere movements of lips. Corpses are resurrected in order to die again to the tune of the war march which, like the waltz *François* in *The Dead Class*, fades only in order to explode a moment later.

Kantor terrifies with images. Their graphic cruelty, like Goya's *Caprichos*, refers to signs which are the *arche* of despair and degradation. The Christian *arche* of horror is the son of God spread-eagled on the cross. A heavy wooden cross is dragged on stage on the shoulders of the prelate uncle who a moment earlier had blessed the parading recruits. The recruits come to resemble tormentors at the Stations of the Cross. The actors of the family drama will be crucified by turns: first the raped bride, and last the prelate. Kantor's theater, which had begun with the degradation of objects, becomes the profanation of *sacrum*. Or perhaps *sacrum* becomes *profanum* at the moment of ultimate degradation. And the ultimate degradation is death.

I call Kantor's stage a theater of essence. In Sartre existence precedes essence. In Kantor's vision essence is the aftermath. Existence is freely created through a series of choices, but essence, as final as the Last Judgment, is what remains of us. Essence is the human drama freed of accident and of the illusion that there are choices. Essence is a trace, like the still undissolved imprint of a crustacean on a stone.

Everyman is a theater of Christian essence. The entire drama is contained in Everyman's last question: "Who will go down to the grave with me?" The Dance of Death also belongs to the theater of essence, although snickering accompanies horror from the beginning. The Dance of Death is the key to Kantor. In each of his spectacles Death is disguised as one of the characters. In *The Dead Class*, the camp follower is Death; in *Wielopole*, one of the aunts. In her hand is a rag. First she washes the corpses, then the blood stains on the floor. Graves are the traces of history. In the twentieth century these are mass graves. "Death transforms life into destiny," wrote Malraux. In Kantor, Death with a wet rag washes away her own traces, and then wrings the rag dry.

In the second scene, Act I, of *Macbeth*, a messenger arrives from the battlefield. Shakespeare does not give him a name.

> What bloody man is that? He can report
> As seemeth by his plight, of the revolt
> The newest state.

Half-naked, drenched in blood, and nameless, the messenger from the front is the Unknown Soldier and so the very essence of history. This is the essence I see in Kantor's theater.

In traditional Japanese theater the stage is still the liturgical site of sacrifice. The brilliant anthropologist Masao Yamaguchi calls it the site of negation, the place of confrontation with death. But in liturgy, in contrast to the theater of essence, death is never individual. It is history that is mortal in the theater of essence. Kantor, present/absent on stage from the first to the last moment of the spectacle, bent over and always in the same black suit and dark shawl, urges his actors on, snapping his finger lightly, almost imperceptibly, as if he were impatient that it all still takes so long. He seems like Charon, who ushers the dead to the other side. But Kantor does not only usher the dead, he also summons them. In this theater of the vanishing trace, Kantor's presence on stage is the memory of lost places and of lost people. This is precisely what is both solemn and exceptional in *The Dead Class* and *Wielopole Wielopole*.

2   I saw the last Parisian performance of Peter Brook's *Carmen* at Bouffes du Nord in March 1982. Bouffes, a nineteenth-century theater with three balcony tiers, resembles a giant bonbonnière. But the building is in ruins and its interior looks as if it had been burnt out. Although more the site of a former theater than a "theater," Bouffes is still a theatrical place. Nothing separates the bare stage with its cracked and stained walls from the wooden benches for the audience, which resemble those used in fire stations. One by one the orchestra members enter the empty stage. There are only fifteen of them. Then they disappear backstage. In Bouffes, there is no orchestra pit.

There is only a pile of rags on the empty stage. Don José crosses the stage. A hand rises from the rag pile and offers the soldier a playing card. The gypsy's cards are messengers of fate. The fate of the soldier and his girl is always the same: love and death—the essence of romantic destiny.

A woman emerges from the pile, scattering the rags behind her. She sings, and her body sings. Carmen sings, Don José sings, Micaëla sings. In the opera, they sing. But *Carmen* both is and is not an "opera." Brook calls his spectacle *La tragédie de Carmen*. It contains Bizet's music, but it is never operatic. Voices are a song in this romantic tragedy of love and death, but song does not exist *apart* from word: song is *natural*, if by nature we mean the opposite of artifice. Like Racine's alexandrines, song in this tragedy of love is transparent and carries all passions within itself. Song articulates passion differently, endowing it with color and grain. Song clarifies. It is contagious confession. The soul erupts into song, as the body into dance. What makes Brook's *Carmen* exquisite is quite simple: dialogue moves when it is sung. No one has ever shown a romantic Carmen who is tragic. Except for Brook.

Artaud wrote that actors, especially in France, have narrow throats and are no longer able to scream. Not too long ago, many theater people thought that the inarticulate scream or groan could express raw passion, "midway between gesture and thought." There was a time when even Brook yielded to such temptations. But "midway between gesture and thought" lies song. Song carries within it the essence of emotions. Those that are elementary and common: love and hate, delight and pain, desire and shame.

When at the end of the sixteenth century opera was being born in Italy out of the *recitativo*, the masquerade, and the pastoral, Florentine eruditi saw in it a renascence of Greek tragedy. The tragic protagonist of these first operas, even before Monteverdi, was Orpheus who summoned Eurydice from the underground with his song. The Baroque had its own vision of total theater, where ballet provided the spectacle, whereas song carried the lyrical theme and tragic tenor.

Wagner's *Der Ring der Niebelungen* represents the last great attempt to reendow the opera with ancient tragedy's function and stature as restorer of archaic myth. Bayreuth became the site of the Wagner cult where the performance of his operas was an annual rite. But the myths Wagner sought to revive were German and they had nothing of the Greek universality. At the beginning of our century, great reformers such as Gordon Craig and Adolphe Appia dreamt of *le théâtre total* where music, ballet, and lighting would accompany poetical drama. But these dreams were never realized. The opera remained the most ossified form of nineteenth-century theater. Not until the last decade did great theater directors become interested in opera. Franco Zeffirelli, Peter Hall, Ingmar Bergman, and recently Jonathan Miller are hoping to find in opera once again a theater rich in devices, *le théâtre total*. Brook's *Carmen* is the first attempt at renewing opera as poor theater, although "poor theater" here means something different from Grotowski. Brook's *Carmen* attempts to rediscover the essence of romantic opera in song and gesture, in the language of passion.

Carmen knows that she must perish. Love and death are not only José's fortune. She has foreseen the same for herself and for all her lovers. Behind the crumbling doors, offstage to the right, is the arena. Her last lover Escamillo will die there. He will return through the same warped doors, carried in from the arena on his friends' shoulders, still in the same splendid attire of a matador. But Carmen cannot return to José. The performance is almost over; only two or maybe three minutes remain. Carmen and Don José go away. They meander through fields out of town. It is almost dark. "Well, here we are." These are her last words. A man and a woman kneel across from each other in silence. Don José stabs Carmen with a knife.

As in *Lord Jim*, a man and woman "mastered their fate." They mastered their fate; that is, they were ready to die. "They were tragic." Brook excised the melodrama from *Carmen*. What remains is "fate" inscribed in cards, the romantic essence so condensed and pure that only Conrad's words could articulate it.

What has remained of the ritual is also only its essence. When the lovers settle down for the night in a gypsy camp, an old woman lights fires on three sides of the world and sprinkles a circle of flour and salt around the sleeping couple. The three fires slowly die out; the white orb melts into darkness. During the last quarter century, rituals stolen from five continents—from Eskimos and the Polynesian islands, from voodoo and from Mongolian shamans—have been reenacted in Western theater. Lost in this arrogant imitation was not only the mystery of ritual but also its elementary meaning. But fires on three sides of the earth, a magical orb, food an old gypsy shares with a man and a woman before they embrace, are signs we are able to understand. They are our common heritage. On this stage, bare as if scorched by fire, Brook briefly restores to the theatrical site its lost *sacrum* and the *arche* we share. Gestures of desire acquire a concreteness that to all appearances had been forever lost to opera.

The gestures in *Carmen* are neither graphic nor inhibited. They are at once acts of passion and metaphors for sex and frenzy. Carmen bends her head backwards. Her lover slices an orange and squeezes its juice into her wide open mouth. To the last drop.

Carmen occurs in Spain. But in which one? In Peter Brook's *Carmen* the corrida takes place behind battered doors, offstage to the right. On stage a rehearsal is taking place: the matador is training for the big encounter. He attempts the sideslip, the dodge, and the thrust. He repeats each step, each turn of his deadly ballet, methodically, solemnly, and sadly. Either he or the bull must die. The corrida takes place under the glaring sun, before the eyes of hundreds of frenzied women. The matador rehearses for the deadly ballet on a bare stage: *pas de deux* with an invisible bull. The dramaturgy is different from Kantor's, but the dance of death is also performed in this other theater of essence.

I have seen nearly all of Brook's productions: *Marat-Sade, King Lear, A Midsummer Night's Dream*, and a year earlier in the same Bouffes du Nord, the vibrant *Cherry Orchard*. These spectacles are more complex and dramatic than *Carmen*, which lasts scarcely more than an hour. But an hour so intense as the theater is able to offer once, maybe twice in a decade. Brook's *Carmen* is perfect. And perfection is almost impossible to describe. Perfection signifies only itself and its own possibility. Like a beautiful nude girl. Like a beautiful nude boy. Perfection signifies nothing other than its own existence.

TADEUSZ BOROWSKI:

A EUROPEAN

EDUCATION

1 Tadeusz Borowski opened a gas valve on 1 July 1951. He was not yet thirty. Borowski's suicide was a shock that one can compare only to the suicide, twenty-one years before, of Vladimir Mayakovski. Borowski was the greatest hope of Polish literature among the generation of his contemporaries decimated by the war. He was also the greatest hope of the Communist party, as well as its apostle and inquisitor; many years had to pass before many of us realized that he was also its martyr. The five-volume posthumous edition of his collected works contains poetry, journalistic writings, news articles, novels, and short stories; among the latter are at least a hundred pages published by a boy of twenty-four one year after his release from the concentration camps at Dachau and Auschwitz, pages that— as was written after Borowski's death—"will very likely last as long as Polish literature exists." Borowski's Auschwitz stories, however, are not only a masterpiece of Polish—and of world—literature. Among the tens of thousands of pages written about the holocaust and the death camps, Borowski's slender book continues to occupy, for almost a half century now, a place apart. The book is one of the cruelest of testimonies to what men did to men, and a pitiless verdict that anything can be done to a human being.

Borowski also left behind the story of his life. There are lives of writers which not only belong to the history of literature but are also literature themselves—that is, human destiny epitomized. These are primarily the biographies of poets who abandoned literature like Arthur Rimbaud, who fell into madness like Friedrich Hölderlin, or who committed suicide like Heinrich von Kleist and Sylvia Plath. The existential experience is contained in those life stories; the boundaries where literature ends and the realm of silence begins are revealed. Borowski's biography is different. It reveals what I would call the historical destiny of man. Romain Gary, a French writer of Polish origin who spent his childhood in Vilna, called his first novel, about the years of the German occupation, *Une éducation Européenne*. There are years and places, sometimes whole decades and entire nations, in which history reveals its menace and destructive force with particular clarity. These are *chosen* nations, in the same sense in which the Bible calls the Jews a *chosen* people. In such places and years history is—as the master of my youth, Jerzy Stempowski, used to say—"let off the leash." It is then that individual human destiny seems as if shaped directly by history, becoming only a chapter in it.

Borowski received a full "European education." One might even say overeducation. He was born in 1922 in Zhitomir, in the Soviet Ukraine, to Polish parents. His father, a bookkeeper, was transported in 1926 to Karelia, above the Arctic Circle, to dig the famous White Sea Canal. That was one of the harshest labor camps. He was exiled for his participation in a Polish military organization during World War I. When Tadeusz was eight, his mother was in turn sent to a settlement a little nearer, on the Yenisei River, in Siberia. Those were the years of collectivization and hunger. The monthly food allowance amounted to two pounds of flour. During this time young Tadeusz was taken care of by his aunt; he went to school and tended cows.

In 1932 the elder Borowski was exchanged for Communists imprisoned in Poland, and Tadeusz was repatriated by the Red Cross. His mother joined the family in Warsaw two years later. The father worked in a warehouse, and the mother made a little money sewing dresses at home; life was difficult. They put their son in a boarding school run by Franciscan monks, where he could study for next to nothing. When the war began, he was not yet seventeen. During the German occupation secondary school and college were forbidden to Poles. Borowski studied in underground classes. In the spring of 1940 the first big roundups began in Warsaw. He was just then taking his final examinations. That day is described in his "Graduation on Market Street": "A long column of automobiles stationed itself at the end of the avenue and waited for streetcars like a tiger tracking antelope. We spilled out of the moving trolley like pears and tore diagonally across a field newly planted with vegetables. The earth smelled of spring. . . . And in the city, on the other side of the river, as in a deep jungle, people were being hunted." This final exam during the roundup was a "European" certificate of maturity.

Borowski obtained a job as a night watchman and stockboy in a firm that sold building materials. At that time, of course, young people worked mainly in order to have a work card, which kept them from being shipped off to the Reich. One made one's actual living through illegal or semilegal trade. Building materials were hard to come by; on the black market they were sold for ten times more than the regulated prices. Borowski tried to make ends meet and studied literature in underground university courses. The lectures took place in private apartments and, for safety, in small groups. Of the group of thirteen to which he belonged, five are not alive today.

He began writing early. In a seminar on English literature he drew attention with his translation of the fool's songs from Shakespeare's *Twelfth Night*. He wrote, of course, his own poems too. He published them in the winter of 1942, in an edition of 165 copies.

With the exception of the official collaborationist daily newspaper and a couple of semipornographic weeklies, not a single Polish periodical appeared legally in German-occupied Poland. Yet in Warsaw alone there appeared each day several dozen underground leaflets and war bulletins transcribed from radio stations in the West. Political periodicals of every orientation came out. "Censorship" did not exist—the printing, distribution, and even possession of such underground literature was punishable by death or, at the very least, the concentration camp. As never before and as never again, Warsaw under Hitler's occupation was a city of the clandestine press. The periodicals were not only from political parties and military groups; a club of mountain climbers published its own underground yearbook, and chess players put out an underground monthly devoted to endgames.

There were also underground editions of poetry. Borowski ran off his first volume of poetry himself on a mimeograph, which— he was to recollect afterward with irony in a postwar story—"while used to run off extremely precious radio bulletins and good advice (along with diagrams) on how to conduct street battles in the larger cities, served also to print up lofty, metaphysical hexameters." His volume, *Wherever the Earth*, predicted in classical cadences the extermination of mankind. Its dominant image was that of a gigantic labor camp. Already in that first volume of poetry, there was no hope, no comfort, no pity. The last poem, "A Song," concluded with a prophecy delivered like a sentence: "We'll leave behind us iron scrap / and the hollow, mocking laugh of generations."

A few weeks later Borowski was arrested. His fiancée, with whom he was living, had not returned for the night. She had fallen into a trap set by the Nazis at the apartment of some mutual friends. The following day Borowski began searching the city for her. He ended up at that very same apartment—and that very same trap. He had with him his poems and Aldous Huxley's *Brave New World*.

He sat in prison a little over two months. The prison was on the border of the Warsaw ghetto. From the cell window he could see soldiers throwing grenades at the tenements and systematically setting fire to one house after another along the opposite side of the street. At the end of April he was sent with a transport of prisoners to Auschwitz. On his arm they tattooed the camp serial number 119 198. His fiancée was brought to the camp in another transport. They were both "lucky." Three weeks earlier "Aryans" had stopped being sent to the gas chambers—except for special cases. From then on only Jews were gassed en masse.

At first he worked carrying telegraph poles. Then he wound up in the camp hospital with pneumonia. "A True Story" is indeed true. In the hospital he was laid on the same straw mattress on which the "boy with a Bible," Borowski's cellmate at the Warsaw prison, had died of typhoid fever. When Borowski was on his feet again, he was kept at the hospital and given the light work of a night watchman. Then he took a class to become an orderly.

In Auschwitz the third chapter of Borowski's "European education" was acted out, and the second chapter in the history of his love. His fiancée was in the F.K.L. (Frauen Konzentration Lager), the women's barracks, at Birkenau, near Auschwitz. In *Escape from the World of Stone*, a book about Borowski written by Tadeusz Drewnowski, his friend and biographer, the chapter on the stay in Auschwitz bears the title "Tristan 1943." The tale "Auschwitz, Our Home" records the letters sent by the mid-twentieth-century Tristan to his Isolde from the men's to the women's barracks in Auschwitz.

Later Borowski was able to see his fiancée. He was sent to the women's camp to pick up infant corpses. Isolde's head was shaven, and her entire body raw with scabies. Tadeusz was reported to have said: "Don't worry; our children won't be bald." Late in the spring of 1944 he was assigned to a brigade of roofers working in the F.K.L. From then on he saw his fiancée every day. At Auschwitz this was the most dreadful time. The Soviet offensive was approaching, and the Germans stepped up the liquidation of the Jews from the occupied lands. In May and June of 1944 more than four hundred thousand Jews from Hungary were gassed and burned.

In the summer of 1944 the inmates of Auschwitz began to be evacuated into the heart of Germany. Borowski found himself first in a camp outside Stuttgart, then in Dachau. On 1 May 1945, that camp was liberated by the U.S. Seventh Army. The prisoners were transferred to a camp for displaced persons in a former barracks of the S.S. on the outskirts of Munich. Once again Borowski was behind barbed wire. He left this camp in September and searched desperately for his fiancée. In December he learned from the Red Cross that she had been moved from Birkenau and was alive and living in Sweden. That first year in Europe after the war, however, "the displaced lovers" could not come together across the borders and cordons.

On the land liberated by the Allies there were more than ten million men and women driven from all the German-occupied countries into camps and forced labor, former prisoners of war, and refugees from bombed-out cities. Never before was there such a thin line between the demand for vengeance and the call for justice, between anarchy and law, between the violent need to begin everything anew and the equally desperate need to return to that which was. In those new "Indies in the middle of Europe," as one Polish writer called postwar Germany, young Americans from every state in the Union, from California to Maine, from Nebraska to Texas, had to fill a fourfold function: judges, gendarmes, missionaries, and food suppliers. It was too difficult a task.

Borowski wrote in his Munich diary at the time: "No doubt the purpose of this whole great war was so that you, friend from Chicago, could cross the salt water, battle your way through all of Germany, and reaching the barbed wire of Allach, share a Camel cigarette with me. . . . And now they've put you on guard duty, to keep an eye on me, and we no longer talk to one another. And I must look like a prisoner to you, for you search me and call me boy. And your slain comrades say nothing."

Europe was divided, right down the middle, into the spheres of influence of the non-Communist Allies and of Russia. Confronting millions of former prisoners of war and refugees was this choice: to remain in exile or to return to the countries in which the Communists had seized power. From Munich Borowski went for a short while to Murnau, in Bavaria, the headquarters of those Polish soldiers and officers who had decided not to go back. From there he wrote in a letter: "They would give us American pineapples and products of the white man's civilization not seen in Europe for ages: tooth-brushes, razor blades, and even chewing gum and powdered eggs, with which we sprinkled our beds, since they were great for keeping off the fleas. . . . All the same I ran from Murnau. I wasn't soldier material—I avoided the meetings, I was no flag-waver, I took to the fields with a stack of books and wandered—the lake in that region is very pretty too."

He went for a short while to Paris, from where he wrote in a letter: "A visitor from a dead, detested country, I plunged into hypocrisy as into the current of a mountain stream. . . . I drank wine with hired women and was even in the Allied Troops Theater, since I am wearing a threadbare uniform, once an English soldier's. I came, I saw—and am sad. . . . A visitor from a dead, detested country, in this place where among shattered homes the girls go walking with Negroes into the eternally reborn vegetation, a poet without listeners and without friends—I don't feel well in Paris." Borowski returned to his country in a repatriation transport on the last day of May 1946. He did not want, as he wrote in one of his last letters from Munich, "to live with corpses."

For a long time his fiancée did not want to leave Sweden to go to Communist Poland. She returned only in November, after Tadeusz's desperate letters. Borowski rode out to meet her at the border point. "Their first night together, no longer in war but in the liberated homeland," writes Borowski's biographer, "took place behind barbed wire, in the quarantine of a repatriation camp." They were married in December.

Two stories by Borowski, "This Way for the Gas, Ladies and Gentlemen" and "A Day at Harmenz," written back at Munich as soon as he had been freed, were published in Poland before his arrival. They produced a shock. The public was expecting martyr-ologies; the Communist party called for works that were ideological, that divided the world into the righteous and the unrighteous, heroes and traitors, Communists and Fascists. Borowski was accused of amorality, decadence, and nihilism. Yet at the same time it was clear to everyone that Polish literature had gained a dazzling new talent. All the publications and all the possibilities the party offered young writers were opened up to Borowski. He was as distrustful as he was ambitious, but he could not resist that most diabolical of temp-tations—to participate in history, a history for which both stones and people are only the material used to build the "brave new world."

At the beginning of 1948 he became a member of the Communist party.

Farewell to Maria, a volume containing his Auschwitz stories, was published around this time, and then the short-story cycle *World of Stone*, about the D.P. camps in Germany and the return to his hometown, where people carry their food and bedding wrapped in bundles from place to place among the ruins like ants. These were the last of Borowski's great stories. After this he wrote stories each week for the Sunday edition of a Warsaw daily which are nothing more than the impassioned journalism of hate. For this, the weakest of his work, he received a government prize. In the summer of 1949 he was sent to Germany to work in the Press Section at the Polish Military Mission in Berlin. The Polish Bureau of Information was located in the Soviet sector of Berlin, the Military Mission in the American sector. These were already the years of the cold war. Borowski found himself at the juncture of two worlds, in a Europe divided down the middle after Yalta.

At that time a few dozen young writers and college graduates in the party traveled from Poland to the East and the West, either to study or to carry out special missions. From Moscow they returned with an incurable ache, depressed and frightened; from the West they returned with smiles and much contempt for decaying capitalism. When Borowski returned to Warsaw after a year in Berlin, it seemed that he no longer had any doubts. In the party they were saying he had "grown into an activist." Literature was supposed to help the party build socialism. Borowski took upon himself the role of taskmaster.

"Literature is not as hard as you think," he wrote. For him literature had become only agitation. "I don't care if they lament my wasting myself on journalism. I don't consider myself a vestal virgin consecrated to prose." It was only to his closest friends that he confided in nightly conversations that—like Mayakovski—he had "stepped on the throat of his own song." I think he was fully aware of the meaning of those words; he had, after all, described many times how the guards in the camps would place a shovel across the neck of a prisoner and jump on it with their boots until he expired. Less than fifteen months after his return from Berlin Borowski committed suicide.

The reasons for suicide are always complex, and Borowski took the mystery of his death with him to the grave. Two attempts at suicide had preceded that final turning on of the gas valve, but at the conclusion of this life history, which is an emblem and a model of the "fate" of Europe, the plot thickens, the threads all tangle, as though spun by the Greek Moirae—the relentless daughters of Inevitability. After his return from Berlin Borowski entered into a liaison with a young girl. Three days before the suicide his wife bore him a daughter. He saw his wife for the last time at the hospital, on the afternoon before the night he killed himself. Thus ended the tale of Tristan and Isolde.

And there is a second thread. A couple of weeks before the suicide an old friend was arrested, the same friend in whose apartment eight years earlier, in occupied Warsaw, Borowski had fallen into the trap set by the Germans while looking for his fiancée. At that time the friend was tortured by the Gestapo; now he was tortured in turn by Polish Security. Borowski interceded with the highest party officials and was told that the people's justice was never mistaken. This was after the denunciation of Tito by Stalin, and the Communists were then hunting down "traitors" with "rightist-nationalistic deviations." Borowski never lived to see his friend's trial.

And there is a third thread. When Borowski left for Berlin, he was entrusted with a special mission—"the kind you don't even tell your wife about," wrote Borowski's closest friend a few years after his death in a thinly veiled short story. In the years of the cold war, on both sides of the iron curtain, in the name of two different ideologies—yet each considering itself to stand above morality—such missions were accepted more than once by writers and professors, experts on human conscience. The only difference was that in the West "special" missions usually ended with one's returning home. "He was successful," continues Borowski's friend in that story à clef, which was clear to everyone, "so when he came home, they gave him a new mission." The title of the story is "Cruel Star." Borowski completed the full course in his "European education." The Moirae, who spin men's fates, have grown mocking in the twentieth century.

2 Borowski's Auschwitz stories are written in the first person. The narrator of three of the stories is a deputy Kapo, Vorarbeiter Tadeusz. The identification of the author with the narrator was the moral decision of a prisoner who had lived through Auschwitz—an acceptance of mutual responsibility, mutual participation, and mutual guilt for the concentration camp. "It is impossible to write about Auschwitz impersonally," Borowski wrote in a review of one of the hagiographic books about the camp. "The first duty of Auschwitzers is to make clear just what a camp is. . . . But let them not forget that the reader will unfailingly ask: But how did it happen that *you* survived? . . . Tell, then, how you bought places in the hospital, easy posts, how you shoved the 'Moslems' [prisoners who had lost the will to live] into the oven, how you bought women, men, what you did in the barracks, unloading the transports, at the gypsy camp; tell about the daily life of the camp, about the hierarchy of fear, about the loneliness of every man. But write that you, you were the ones who did this. That a portion of the sad fame of Auschwitz belongs to you as well."

The four million gassed, led straight from the ramp to the crematoriums, had no choice to make, nor did the prisoners selected for the ovens. In Auschwitz there were individual acts of heroism and a clandestine international military network. Auschwitz has its saint, a Catholic priest who went to an underground cell and a slow death by starvation in order to save the life of an unknown fellow prisoner, but the Auschwitz "of the living," like all the other German camps—and Soviet camps too—was based on the cooperation of the prisoners in the "administering" of terror and death. From the Kapos, who almost without exception were German criminals, to the lowliest functionaries like Vorarbeiter Tadeusz, everyone was assigned a double part: executioner and victim. In *No Exit*, Sartre's postwar play, the dead in hell are surprised not to see torturers. Hell is organized like a self-service cafeteria. ". . . an economy of man-power or devil-power. The customers serve themselves."

Literature, from the very beginning, recognized this dread identity of executioner and victim. Aeschylus's Agamemnon, who sacrificed his own daughter on the altar so that the Greek ships could sail to Troy, was murdered by his wife after his victorious return to Greece. Shakespeare's usurpers, in climbing the great staircase of history, murder everyone who stands in their way; at the top of the steps, when they have finally seized the crown, they themselves are murdered by the sons of their victims. In Borowski's Auschwitz stories the difference between executioner and victim is stripped of all greatness and pathos; it is brutally reduced to a second bowl of soup, an extra blanket, or the luxury of a silk shirt and shoes with thick soles, about which Vorarbeiter Tadeusz is so proud.

Auschwitz was not only, as Borowski writes, "the bloodiest battle of the war," but also a gigantic transshipping station, where the plunder from the murdered victims was diverted to the Reich. Scraps of this plunder fell to the privileged prisoners. "Work is not unpleasant," says Vorarbeiter Tadeusz, "when one has eaten a break-fast of smoked bacon with bread and garlic and washed it down with a tin of evaporated milk."

When life is cheap, food and clothing are worth their weight in gold. I was never in a concentration camp myself, but I spent two days and two nights between the German and Soviet cordons on a narrow strip of land no more than a third of a mile across when, toward the end of November 1939, I went illegally from one oc-cupation to another within Poland. The Germans were letting every-one through in both directions, although they beat the Jews and robbed them of everything; the Soviets let no one through in either direction. On that patch of earth were camped nearly four thousand refugees—men, women, and children. During the day the first snow fell; by night we had a biting frost. The first night a loaf of bread cost a gold ring, the following day—two. On the second night on that no-man's-land, which was a great field of stubble without a single tree or bush, sheds made out of boards sprang up. In them were sold hot soup and piroshki with kasha for gold and dollars. In the last shed, at the very end of the stubble, they were selling women.

"All of us walk around naked." "This Way for the Gas, Ladies and Gentlemen" begins with an image that may seem similar to Dante's Inferno. "Twenty-eight thousand women have been stripped naked and driven out of the barracks. Now they swarm around the large yard between the blockhouses. The heat rises, the hours are endless." They are naked as worms. Only later, when the scene draws nearer, as in a camera close-up, is it possible to distinguish in that wriggling mass of vermin different specimens of the same species: a few in pressed uniforms, with riding whips and high boots like glittering scales, and the common variety, with abdomens in stripes of blue and yellow. They differ also in weight: A few are well-nourished, fat, and sleek; the common types move their shriveled extremities with difficulty. Only their jaws are in constant motion. "Around us sit the Greeks, their jaws working greedily, like huge human insects. They munch on stale lumps of bread."

Borowski describes Auschwitz like an entomologist. The im-age of ants recurs many times, with their incessant march, day and night, night and day, from the ramp to the crematorium and from the barracks to the baths. The most terrifying thing in Borowski's stories is the icy detachment of the author. "You can get accustomed to the camp," says Vorarbeiter Tadeusz. Auschwitz is presented from a natural perspective—a day like any other. Everything is common-place, routine, *normal*. ". . . First just one ordinary barn, brightly whitewashed—and here they proceed to asphyxiate people. Later, four large buildings, accommodating twenty thousand at a time without any trouble. No hocus-pocus, no poison, no hypnosis. Only several men directing traffic to keep operations running smoothly, and the thousands flow along like water from an open tap."

Auschwitz—with its black smoke from the crematoriums and its ditches clogged with corpses, there being no room for them in the ovens—is nothing out of the ordinary. "The camps, aren't they for people?" Auschwitz—with its whorehouse and its museum containing exhibits made of human skin, with its sports field where soccer is played and its concert hall where Beethoven is played—is merely an inevitable part of the world of stone. "Between two throw-ins in a soccer game, right behind my back, three thousand people had been put to death." Albert Camus wrote of the "logic of crime" and of the "crime of logic." For Borowski, the son of Soviet prisoners and the posthumous child of Auschwitz, the whole world is a concentration camp—was and will be. "What will the world know of us if the Germans win?"

Borowski called his book about Auschwitz "a voyage to the limit of a particular experience." At the limit of that experience Auschwitz is no exception but the rule. History is a sequence of Auschwitzes, one following the other. On his typhus-ridden straw mattress in the Auschwitz hospital he wrote, in a letter to his bald fiancée in the women's barracks: "You know how much I used to like Plato. Today I realize he lied. For the things of this world are not a reflection of the ideal, but a product of human sweat, blood and hard labor. It is we who built the pyramids, hewed the marble for the temples and the rocks for the imperial roads. . . . We were filthy and died real deaths. . . . What does ancient history say about us? . . . We rave over the extermination of the Etruscans, the destruction of Carthage, over treason, deceit, plunder. Roman law! Yes, today too there is a law!"

The Polish biographer entitled his book on Borowski *Escape from the World of Stone*. Borowski did not escape the world of stone. "The living," he wrote, "are always right, the dead are always wrong"—an optimistic statement. If the dead are wrong and the living are always right, everything is finally justified; but the story of Borowski's life and that which he wrote about Auschwitz show that the dead are right, and not the living.

A CAGE IN
SEARCH OF
A BIRD

For Stefan Zółkiewski

1 In his admirable study, *On the Kabbalah and Its Symbolism*, Gershom Scholem cites a parable from *Patrologia Graeca* which Origen had taken from an anonymous rabbi of the Talmudic Academy in Caesarea and repeated in his commentary on the Psalms. The Scripture is likened to a castle with thousands and thousands of chambers. At the foot of each chamber door lies a key, but a key to *another* door.

It is entirely possible that Kafka knew this parable. But I am not concerned here with direct influence, as philologists understand it, of the Kabala on Kafka. I am more interested in the *reading* of this parable. What is a wrong key? A wrong key is the right key to another door. This distinction between right and wrong keys may be moral, or valid only with respect to one door. Another distinction may be more to the point: doors only are either right or wrong. There are no wrong keys; each fits just one lock. The key that opens every door is the lockpicker's key—the false key. No key is false in the kabalistic parable: every key opens one door only, but all keys have been interchanged.

But by whom? And why? Was it chance or an unforeseeable intervention of cosmic forces? A practical joke, mismanagement, or a doorkeeper's revenge? Perhaps it was a test administered for unknown reasons by the castle's warden, or a trial by the Lord. Who has the answer?

The key is an object, but it could also be a prop. "The spirit becomes free," writes Kafka in his *Reflections on Sin, Pain, Hope and the True Way*, "only when it ceases to be a prop." The *key*, of course, is not only an object or a prop. It is also a sign. A change of key is always a change in interpretation.

The parable about keys is based on a common, almost universal, experience. As a short story, it is at once plausible, lifelike, and theatrical. Let us imagine the annual convention of the Modern Language Association. Three thousand participants meet at one of the huge Hiltons. The keys have been interchanged and each of the three thousand eminent scholars stands before the door to his hotel room with a key to another room. Translated into a realistic theatrical situation the parable is ludicrous and insane. We are already in the world of Kafka's *Trial*.

"You have studied the story more exactly and for a longer time than I have," said Joseph K. toward the end of his encounter with the prison chaplain in the cathedral. "They were both silent for a little while. Then K. said, 'So you think the man was not deluded?' 'Don't misunderstand me,' said the priest, 'I am only showing you the various opinions concerning that point. You must not pay too much attention to them. The scriptures are unalterable and the comments often enough merely express the commentators' despair.' "

A commentary is a key, but to another door in a castle with thousands of chambers. The way to hell—the chaplain might have added—is paved with good commentaries. Hence the despair of commentators.

2 Zen Buddhism, like the Kabala, is a symbolic interpretation of eternal Truth and the essence of Being. Truth is nondiscursive and may be grasped or summoned with a symbolic gesture rather than articulated in language. Chü Chich of the ninth century is regarded as one of the greatest masters of Zen Buddhism. A parable about him has survived and has been retold many times.

> This Master, whenever and whatever he was asked about Zen, used to stick up one finger . . . "What is the supreme and absolute Truth?"—answer: the silent raising of one finger. "What is the essence of buddhism?"—answer: again the selfsame silent raising of one finger.[1]

---

[1] Toshihiko Izutzu, "Sense and Nonsense in Zen Buddhism," *Eranos 1970* (Leiden: Brill, 1973), pp. 184–86.

The master's favorite was a young boy who had been put under his tutelage and who served him at home. The boy carefully observed his master and, as pupils usually do, began to imitate him. Whenever he was asked about Zen or Buddha, he, like his teacher, raised his index finger. When the master found out what the boy had been doing behind his back, he became furious. One morning he hid a sharp knife in the sleeve of his kimono, summoned the boy, and asked him:

> "What is Buddha?" The boy stuck up one finger. Master Chü Chich suddenly took hold of the boy and cut off with the knife the finger which the boy had just raised. As the poor boy was running out of the room screaming with pain, the Master called to him. At that very moment quick as lightning came the Master's question: "What is Buddha?" Almost by conditioned reflex, we might say, the boy held up his hand to raise his finger. There was no finger there. The boy on the spot attained enlightenment.

He now knows who Buddha is. The sign of Being is non-Being, and the sign of presence is absence.

Modern masters of linguistics and semantics, Roland Barthes and Roman Jakobson, call this type of sign the "zero sign." The lack or absence of a sign, when we are expecting one, is also a sign. Non-presence also presents itself. The telephone's silence when we cannot bear the waiting is more potent than the voice in the receiver. Silence is not voiceless.

"What is laid upon us," writes Kafka in *Reflections*, "is to accomplish the negative; *the positive* is already given" (italics mine). In the metaphysic of "negative theology," nonpresence is the sole sign of God's presence. And exactly this term, "negative theology," the God who is hidden in his own self, has been invoked repeatedly by Kafka's critics.

The parable about the Buddhist monk and his disciple has all the ambiguity of Kafka's short stories. And it is not necessary to read this parable in the light of negative theology. Pointing the finger upwards and raising the hand with its finger amputated are gestures in the Brechtian sense of *gestus*, which, as Walter Benjamin showed for the first time, becomes an important device in Kafka's stories.

The ninth-century Buddhist parable of the amputated finger is a sign of non-Being and could be both performed and drawn. The parable would then become graphic; but as soon as a parable is visualized, it takes on a different meaning. Drawn, it becomes a comic strip, with the dialogue coming out of the mouths of characters in bubbles; performed, it is a burlesque, as in a Renaissance interlude or a *kyogen* mime in the tradition of Japanese theater. The parable becomes a cruel farce, eliciting raucous laughter from the spectators.

The absent finger is no longer the Buddha, nor a Platonic form inaccessible to the senses: it is the finger of a pupil cut off by the knife of a cruel and jealous guru. As in Kafka, *gestus*, the gesture in this parable, is polysemic; when read as a *graph*, it belongs to another system of signs. The raised finger and the amputated finger become obscene signs, as in the carnival tradition, in Rabelais, and in Gombrowicz's theater. The sense of signs has been reversed. Metaphysics has become physics, that is to say, carnal.

3   "A cage went seeking a bird," the shortest aphorism in Kafka's *Reflections*, is even more graphic than the Zen parable. The cage walks on the ground seeking a sitting bird. I visualize this aphorism as a drawing or a short sequence in an animated cartoon. Jan Lenica, the brilliant Polish animator, would have made it into a little masterpiece.

Translated into a picture, this aphorism is an emblem. It could belong to the great tradition of emblematic art which flourished in Italy, and even more in Germany, during the late Renaissance and the Baroque period. An emblem is a picture of a paradox or a gnome. One of the best-known emblems represents "the serpent eating its own tail."

Emblems can be given an almost unlimited number of symbolic or paradigmatic readings. "The cage" that goes "in search" of a bird, the cage in motion, the active cage, may signify within symbolic codes the devil's snare for catching souls, a spiritual trap, Calvinistic predetermination of the saved and the damned. In political terms, the cage is the state and the state is a prison. For Freud, the searching cage is an image of the superego. Similarly, the Grand Warden who exchanged the keys is either the hidden God, *deus absconditus*, the kabalistic *En Sof*, or mere chance, and man is alone in the world he has created. The parable about keys changes into a Hegelian or Marxist discourse on alienation: theology in a different key. But keys, whether they fit or not, are material, and meta-keys for unlocking gates do not exist.

In *The Trial*, the cage comes one morning to Joseph K. as Death does to the sinner in the great masterpiece of medieval drama, *Everyman*. *The Trial* is a story nearly as theatrical as *Everyman*. With its gestures, interiors, and movements, *The Trial* can be watched. Kafka's *Trial*, however, is not waiting for its adaptation to theater and film—those have been done already—but for its graphic transcription.

A graphic transcription is a de-symbolization, a de-allegorization. *Graph* and the graphic reading are sudden and violent visualizations of unexpected and unsuspected linguistic relations. The discovery of the unknown, *l'insolite*, as in Max Ernst's paintings and even more in Magritte's, produces shock.

Two readings of Kafka's aphorism—metaphorical and metonymic—are possible. "A cage" is of course a metaphor; "went in search" is a metaphor; "bird" is a metaphor. But the genius of Kafka's searching cage is its unexpected metonymy. The metaphorical reading of this aphorism and its conventional symbolism are trivial. Kafka despised literary metaphors. "Metaphors are one among many things which make me despair of writing," he wrote in his diary on 6 December 1921.

Metaphor is the transference of meaning based on similarity or the illusion of similarity between objects or ideas. Metonymy depends on relations of contiguity and succession. Moreover, as Frazer had described long before the structuralists, metonymy is marked by the relation of contagion and contamination. Dread of *miasma* is born of the metonymic imagination. Kafka knew this fear and this dread.

The relation between the predator and its prey, between the hunter and the hunted, is also metonymic. The relation between the cage and the bird is metonymic. The hunting cage is metonymy in motion. We are the prey.

The metonymy which destroys allegory is even more evident in Kafka's "Four Legends Concerning Prometheus." According to the first legend, Prometheus "was clamped to a rock in the Caucasus for betraying the secrets of the gods to men, and the gods sent eagles to feed on his liver, which was perpetually renewed." According to the second, "Prometheus, goaded by the pain of the tearing beaks, pressed himself deeper and deeper into the rock until he became one with it."

The end of Prometheus is the end of mythology. "There remained the inexplicable mass of rock." In Michelangelo's unfinished statues of the Slaves, their bodies, as if in the pangs of birth, struggle to break out of the blocks of stone. Kafka's vision is different: Prometheus is one with the rock. The end of Prometheus and the end of the myth is stasis. The metonymy of the end is the undifferentiated mountain of stone.

The mountain under the empty sky remains the last imprint of myth. Kafka's metonymy found its final dramatic fulfillment in Beckett's stasis. In *Happy Days* a woman sinks into a mound of sand under an empty sky.

Kafka's Poseidon has also been stripped of his mythological attire. "Poseidon sat at his desk, doing figures. The administration of all the waters gave him endless work." What irritates Kafka's Poseidon most is that he is invariably presented "riding about through the tides with his trident." In fact, "he had hardly seen the sea." His office is located deep in the earth, beneath all the oceans. He sits there day and night doing involved calculations and drawing diagrams. He has no time for travel. What possible use could he have for the trident?

Kafka's Poseidon resides in a fusty, stifling room like the court chambers in *The Trial*. In his hand he is holding a rusty compass; on the table lies an abacus. This version of the Poseidon myth also ends with stasis. Poseidon has become bored with his job; he can endure it no longer. "Silently he sat on the rocky coast and a gull, dazed by his presence, described wavering circles around his head."

Kafka's dead-tired Poseidon sitting on a rock by the sea can be found in Camus's image of Sisyphus, who, having descended from the mountain, sits at its foot, as the same boulder he has pushed up to the top an infinite number of times rolls down to the bottom, once more. Sisyphus understands his fate. In the universe suddenly restored to its silence, "His fate belongs to him." Camus concludes, "One must imagine Sisyphus happy."

Camus's Sisyphus will once again roll the rock to the mountain top. Poseidon's and Sisyphus's work is never done. Kafka's Poseidon heads the global enterprise, Oceans and Storms, Ltd. Deadly bored with his job, he is waiting for the end of the world. Only then will he be able to imagine himself happy.

All Kafka's mythical heroes have been deprived of classical decorum and are of this world, from Prometheus to Abraham. Two different Abrahams appear in Kafka's parables. The first Abraham "could not get away . . . without having his house ready," but "the house was never ready." It is possible that Abraham and Sarah "did not even have a son, yet already had to sacrifice him. These are impossibilities, and Sarah was right to laugh."

Kafka's second Abraham "wanted to perform the sacrifice altogether in the right way . . . but could not believe that he was the one meant, he, an ugly old man, and the dirty youngster that was his child." He was

> afraid that the world would laugh itself to death at the sight of
> him. . . . this ridiculousness will make him even older and uglier,
> his son even dirtier, even more unworthy of being really
> called. . . . It is as if, at the end of the year, when the best student
> was solemnly about to receive a prize, the worst student
> rose . . . from his dirty desk in the last row because he had made a
> mistake of hearing, and the whole class burst out laughing.

This is how Kafka concludes his parable about Abraham:

> And perhaps he had made no mistake at all, his name really was
> called, it having been the teacher's intention to make the
> rewarding of the best student at the same time a punishment for
> the worst one.

Kafka surely knew Kierkegaard's "Panegyric upon Abraham" in *Fear and Trembling*. For Kierkegaard, the patriarch is not a tragic hero; he "is either a murderer or a believer." Abraham knows no doubt. Like Tertullian's *credo quia absurdum*, Abraham has faith "by virtue of the absurd," as Kierkegaard puts it. But what is faith for Kafka? "Faith like a guillotine," writes Kafka in *Reflections*, "as heavy, as light."

"Faith like a guillotine . . . " is the most Kierkegaardian line Kafka wrote. Once again, this aphorism, translated into a picture, made concrete, loses its metaphysical meaning. Faith like a guillotine is a trial that ends in execution.

> . . . but one of the partners was already at K.'s throat, while the
> other thrust the knife deep into his heart and turned it there
> twice. With failing eyes K. could still see the two of them
> immediately before him, cheek leaning against cheek, watching
> the final act.

"Faith like a guillotine, as heavy, as light."

4 Mircea Eliade and many historians of religion use the term *tremendum* to designate mystical experience. *Tremendum* is the sudden apprehension of God's presence and of the approach of death. *Tremendum* is enlightenment full of dread and exhilaration. In Kafka's world, of this mystical *tremendum* only the *horrendum* remains. Faith like a guillotine. The sacred and the impure are closely related; they belong to the same prohibited zone and are marked by the same taboo, even though their signs are reversed or, at any rate, reversible. Both the sacred and the impure are dreadful. But in Kafka's world the sacred does not exist, only dread is left.

Kafka's life, and especially the last ten years, might be given the Kierkegaardian title *Sickness unto Death*. Fear and trembling can be found on almost every page of his diaries, letters, and stories. But Kafka's fear and trembling is different than Kierkegaard's.

As his diaries show, Kafka was scared to death of mice. When he heard them squealing and scratching, he would tremble and become nauseous. The example is vulgar. Nevertheless, in Kafka's life, in almost everything he wrote, horror is always physical, always of the flesh. Dread, *horrendum, angst*—and this is one of the singularities of Kafka's writing—always mean humiliation and shame, and are often ridiculous. As Max Brod attests, Kafka roared with laughter when he read his work to his friends. The same has been said of Gogol. But in Kafka, this Gogolian "horrible laughter" is even more glacial.

When the artist in "A Hunger Artist" is carried out of his cage after many weeks of fasting, he whispers dimly into the ear of the circus overseer, "I have to fast, I can't help it . . . . I couldn't find the food I liked. If I had found it, believe me, I should have made no fuss and stuffed myself like you or anyone else."

The canine narrator of "Investigations of a Dog" is upset and astonished that food sometimes is found on the ground, and sometimes falls from above into his mouth. He decides to retire to a secluded spot and wait for food from above. But no food falls from the sky.

In Kafka's world, the hungry await nourishment from heaven. The image of this metaphysical starvation is a hunger artist in a circus cage, a dog squatting on his hind legs with his mouth agape. In Kafka's world there is no God and no biblical Abraham. All that remains of Abraham is the shadow of the vindictive Father. There is no Sinai and no mount of Moriah; instead of the chosen, there are only the sacrificed. From the biblical *arche* there remains only Isaac, but an Isaac without God and without Abraham. Isaac is murdered with a knife thrust into his heart and turned there twice. Kafka is often read as foreshadowing the Holocaust.

"Someone must have been telling lies about Joseph K., for without having done anything wrong he was arrested one fine morning." He waited in vain for the landlady's cook to bring him breakfast as usual. Two strangers had eaten it and entered his bedroom. Gregor Samsa also waited in vain for his breakfast; he "awoke one morning from uneasy dreams," and "found himself transformed in his bed into a gigantic insect."

The initial shock is different in *The Trial* than in "The Metamorphosis." But in both stories, as always in Kafka, there is no escaping the *horrendum* which swells gradually within a tightly sealed world. In *The Trial*, the whole town is transformed into stuffy, dirty rooms in attics and cellars all owned by the court and into dusty dark staircases, which K. indefatigably ascends and descends answering summonses or seeking counsel. Connected with the court, professionally or intimately, are all of K.'s acquaintances and everyone he encounters; it is as if the whole town were made up only of judges, guards, bailiffs, lawyers, and legal secretaries. Even the clerks at the bank where K. works, even his own uncle, even Fraulein Burstner, who is renting a room from K.'s landlady, are associated with the court. Even the washerwomen all wash the judges' linen, even the painters paint only their portraits.

In "The Metamorphosis," the whole world is reduced to a small apartment on the second or third floor of an old tenement. Behind the closed doors to the family dining room, Gregor Samsa, who has been transformed into a giant bug, walks along the walls or naps clinging to the ceiling in his room, which has been emptied of all furniture. On the other side of the wall, mother, father, and sister speak in hushed tones and eat human food. Gregor Samsa cannot make a human sound; rotting remnants of human food are brought by his sister into his room, and this not even every day.

Both stories end with death. "Like a dog"—those are K.'s last words. Dogs are not put to death by stabbing them in the heart. Joseph K., Everyman, is not killed like a dog, but he dies "like a dog." Death—the last horror—is senseless. " 'Like a dog!' he said; it was as if the shame of it must outlive him." Gregor Samsa dies like a dog, on the stairs, in darkness, turned out of his apartment, alone. The door slams. The living remain on the other side.

Our own *horrendum* bears Kafka's signature. One morning we will not have our breakfast. Two strangers will walk into our room. One morning we will wake up transformed in our bed into a monstrous worm. We are under arrest. We have cancer.

The cage always finds a bird. Kafka's *l'imaginaire* is our reality. The telephone is still ringing, but there is no longer anyone at the other end.

THE SERPENT'S
STING

Adam Ważyk (1905–1983)
In Memoriam
We were expelled from Paradise, but Paradise was not destroyed. In a
sense our expulsion from Paradise was a stroke of luck, for had we not
been expelled, Paradise would have had to be destroyed.
—Kafka,"Paradise"

1 It is perhaps best to begin with etymology. The "sting" (*piqûre* in French), is present in "instinct," "in-stinct." It is derived from the Latin *stingere* (to sting), whose root is *stig*, as in *instigare* (to urge, to instigate). *Stigare* means to arouse, to instigate, to bite like a snake, to sting like a wasp, and to prick. A "prick" is a spear, a phallus, a sting. Contained in *in-stigare* and *instiguere* is the "sting," the Indo-European *steig*, and the Greek *stigma*. The "stigmatized" are stung and bitten. The German *stechen* means to pierce, to sting, and, colloquially, to deflower a girl. Young women still untouched are said to be *stichreif: stich*—sting, *reif*—ripe, ready. But "to sting" etymologically is not only to pierce, but also to arouse, to prod, and to urge with animal passion: "For thou thyself hast been a libertine, / As sensual as the brutish sting itself" (*As You Like It* II.vii.65–66). Instinct incites "our carnal stings, our unbitted lusts" (*Othello* I.iii.329).

The French *piqûre* has connotations similar to the "sting"; *pique* also means phallus, and *piquer* means to screw ("*C'est parce qu'il piquait les pages au lieu de piquer les chevaux,*" wrote Agrippa d'Aubigné in the sixteenth century); *piquage* means intercourse. The contemporary "pick up" is close to the old meaning of *piquer*. But *piquer* is not only to pierce, to perforate, and to prick, with all its

189   THE SERPENT'S STING

derivative synonyms, but also, as in *piquer des deux,* it means to spur a horse.

Piqûre and *piquer* are semantically related to the Latin *excitare,*[1] which means to train, to arouse, to spur a horse to rear. The sexual symbolism is apparent. The body is aroused, the soul tempted. The Latin *incitare* means to prod, to arouse to action and to the act itself. The "sting," in both its *arche* and semantics, always produces a physical action first: the horse is spurred, the apple is bitten; only later, as its second effect, does it master the mind and intoxicate the senses.

Eros is an in-stinct, a bite. In its beginning is the sting. *"Ce n'est plus une ardeur dans mes veines cachée: / C'est Vénus tout entière à sa proie attachée* [It is no longer an ardor hidden in my veins; / It is Venus clutching her prey]"—in Racine's *Phaedra* (I.iii).

And now, the first and fundamental paradigm of the sting.

2 The serpent's tongue is forked; there is venom in its sting. But there are different kinds of venom. The first sting marks the end of the state of nature, the revelation of nudity, and the expulsion from paradise. Animals are either not nude or unaware of their nudity. Born in the steppes, Enkidu of the Babylonian epic *Gilgamesh* has never met a human being. The first woman he sleeps with is a harlot sent by King Uruk to restore Enkidu to human form. She might have been a priestess. In the morning Enkidu covers his naked body with her robes and, as usual, goes to the stream to drink water. The animals flee as he approaches; henceforth the gazelle refuses to lie beside him. But Enkidu "now had wisdom and broader understanding" (I.iv.20). The priestess-harlot says to him: "You are wise, Enkidu, you are like a God" (I.iv.34).

Sex is knowledge, but its price is death. "And the Lord God commanded the man, saying, Of every tree of the garden thou mayest freely eat: But of the tree of the knowledge of good and evil, thou shalt not eat of it: for in the day that thou eatest thereof thou shalt surely die" (Genesis 2:16–17). The tempter-serpent offers the knowledge that is the end of innocence: "then your eyes shall be opened, and ye shall be as gods, knowing good and evil" (Gen. 3:5). Knowledge leads to procreation, procreation to death. The biblical sequence is here reduced to an essence. "And Adam knew Eve his wife; and

---

[1] Pierre Guiraud, *Sémiologie de la sexualité* (Paris: Payot, 1978).

she conceived, and bare Cain" (Gen. 4:1). This is the beginning of human history. Then Cain kills Abel. It is the first death.

The biblical "apple," the fruit from the tree of knowledge, was a fig or a pomegranate. According to oldest Jewish tradition, the fig tree, in penance for bearing the forbidden fruit, offers its leaves to Adam and Eve to cover their nudity. The pomegranate is an archaic symbol and an astounding image of cosmos and the womb. Dissect the pomegranate: in its grains immersed in redness and arranged into spheres you will see the one in the many and the open sex of the woman.

In the *Mystère d'Adam,* the Christmas intermedium from the end of the twelfth century, Eve says: "No man ever tasted the like. Now my eyes are so clear-sighted, I seem like God the Almighty. All that was, all that will be, I know entirely and am master of it. Eat, Adam, do not hesitate." An illumination from an early fifteenth-century French manuscript of Saint Augustine's *De civitate dei* shows a young woman leaning forward beneath the abundant foliage of a tree laden with apples. Her breast is exposed and she is naked down to her belly. Wound around the tree trunk is her long serpent tail. On a miniature from Jean Duc de Berry's *Les très riches heures,* which Jung so admired for its paradise scenes set up on the circular island in the form of a mandala, is again a young woman beneath a small apple tree, offering the fruit to Eve. Her breasts are exposed and her golden tail is wound around the tree trunk. Her face resembles Eve's as if she were her sister. The long golden braid that falls down her back is exactly like Eve's.[2]

The tradition of representing the biblical serpent with a woman's head dates back to the Middle Ages. Bede (d. 755) writes that Lucifer endowed the serpent with the head of a woman better to tempt Eve, because "like are attracted to like." In medieval theater, the serpent "played" with a female head. In painting, the tradition of representing the infernal serpent with the head of a woman, which began with the images in the catacombs, was already well established at the beginning of the fifteenth century. The well-known Masolino fresco (ca. 1424) at the Brancacci Chapel in Florence shows the serpent suspended from the tree above Eve. It has a tiny female head

---

[2] According to the old Rabbinic tradition Lilith has long hair. In the Talmud " . . . a fetus winged as Lilith" (*Nidd.* 24b) and " . . . she left her hair growing up like Lilith" (*Emb.* 100b). Goethe should have known well this tradition, as he wrote in *Faust:* "Lilith, with her dangerous lovely tresses, / Of this her sole adornment, best beware . . . ."

and fair locks which grow directly out of its golden-green skin. On a painting by Van der Goes from the second half of the fifteenth century, the serpent stands under the apple tree on short hind legs with devil's claws. Its pawlike hands embrace the trunk. And growing out of this half-serpent half-woman body is a woman's head with golden hair flowing down her back. The serpent is staring derisively at Eve as she herself plucks the forbidden fruit from the tree.

The serpent/midget is a she-devil. The tradition perhaps derives from the Kabala and the Apocrypha about Lilith, the *mater malorum*, whom God had supposedly sent to Adam even before He created Eve. But God did not create Lilith out of Adam's rib, nor from pure dust, but from the mud that settles after the water recedes, and from dirt. Lilith was a demon from the beginning. She is related to the Greek Lamias, who copulate with sleeping men and suck their blood. She returns in the Middle Ages as a succuba. In Ashkenazi folklore, the image of demonic Lilith merged with the popular figure of Helen of Troy. In the post-Gnostic Christian tradition, Lilith transformed herself into a serpent to bring doom upon Eve.

On Michelangelo's Sistine Chapel fresco, the serpent again has a human head which could belong to either a woman or a man. "Now the serpent was more subtle than any beast of the field which the Lord God had made" (Gen. 3:1). In all Eastern mythologies the serpent is bisexual. Mircea Eliade has shown that in the Mediterranean Basin the serpent has been related to goddesses and the feminine element ever since the Cretans. In Michelangelo's fresco, the serpent is wrapped around the tree, which is a common female archetype. But perhaps for just that reason, the serpent/dragon is an equally common phallic sign.

> and toward Eve
> Address'd his way, not with indented wave,
> Prone on the ground, as
> since, but on his rear,
> Circular base of rising folds, that tow'r'd
> Fold above fold a surging Maze, his Head
> Crested aloft, and Carbuncle his Eyes;
> With burnisht Neck of verdant Gold, erect
> Amidst his circling Spires, that on the grass
> Floated redundant: pleasing was his shape,
> And lovely, never since of Serpent kind
> Lovelier
>
> [*Paradise Lost* IX.495–505]

This image of the erect serpent-as-seducer stems from the Kabala. Milton knew by heart not only the *Aeneid,* but also *De civitate dei* as well as the writings of the Manicheans and Gnostics whose arguments Saint Augustine refutes. According to the apocryphal Gospel of Philip, one of the Coptic Gnostic texts discovered at Nag Hammadi, Cain was born of Eve's union with the serpent, which was the guise assumed by the fallen archangel Samaël: "What nobility. First adultery came into being, afterward murder. And he was begotten in adultery, for he was the child of the serpent. So he became a murderer" (II,3;61.5–10). But the Gnostic Ophite sect worshiped the serpent as a spiritual element, an incarnation, not of the fall, but of liberation.

On the *Très riches heures* miniature I have mentioned, above the baptistry and from the center of the island of paradise rises a Gothic tower, lofty and azure like the copestone of the Sainte-Chapelle in Paris. A red cherub with enormous wings chases Adam and Eve out of paradise through magnificent Gothic gates adorned with little spired towers, onto a rocky beach. Adam and Eve cover their sex with fig leaves, but they do not seem in the least repentent.

The Gothic portico through which Adam and Eve are cast out is on the east side of paradise island. From the illuminations in Saint Kalkist's mid-ninth-century Bible to Michelangelo's Sistine Chapel fresco and to the great canvases of Baroque masters, Adam and Eve are expelled from paradise always by a cherub with a glowing sword and always *toward the east.* The single exception I know is Cranach's *Paradise,* where a tiny Adam and Eve in the upper left-hand corner scurry out of paradise hand in hand, toward the west. According to an ancient rabbinical tradition, Adam and Eve were expelled from paradise through the eastern gate. Cain killed Abel "east of Eden" (Gen. 4:16).

According to Jung and in the archetypal school, the "right" direction leads to the real world, to experience and consciousness. It is where the sun rises. The "left" is the side of the approaching night and of falling into darkness and unawareness. It is on account of the serpent that we were cast out, eastward, toward the right, into the terrifying brightness of day. The penance for picking the forbidden fruit is consciousness. It is an unhappy consciousness or the consciousness of unhappiness.

"But Paradise is locked and bolted and the Cherub is behind us. We must make a journey around the world, to see if a back door has perhaps been left open." So wrote Kleist in his perpetually astonishing essay "On the Puppet Theater." Adrian, in Thomas Mann's *Doctor Faustus,* cites the last words from Kleist's dialogue: " . . . we would have to eat of the tree of knowledge a second time to fall back into the state of innocence." In the apocryphal Gospel of Philip, we find the curious line, "This is the place where I will eat all things, since the tree of knowledge is there. That one killed Adam, but here the tree of knowledge made men alive. The law was the tree" (II,3; 74.1–5). Kafka was certainly familiar with this Gnostic reading of the Scriptures. And as certainly, Borges is as well.

When Adam and Eve tasted the forbidden fruit, they clenched their teeth for the first time, and were ashamed of their nudity. God dressed them, according to Genesis, "in coats of skins" (3:21). Yet God could not have killed any of the animals, for they too, were immortal in paradise. According to rabbinical commentaries, these skins are serpent skins. The serpent sheds its skin. It slides along the earth and disappears—as if swallowed up by it. The serpent appears from underground and disappears into the underground. With the Freudian sting, the serpent offers its own darkness as absolution and salvation. It offers darkness as brightness. *"Flectere si nequeo superos, Acheronta movebo* [If I cannot change the will of Heaven, I shall release Hell]" (*Aeneid* VII.312). Freud gave his *Interpretation of Dreams* this motto from the *Aeneid*. And in his *Three Essays on Sexuality,* he wrote, "The highest and lowest in sexuality are everywhere most intimately connected" ("From Heaven to the world to Hell").

The serpent sheds its old skin and appears once more before Adam and Eve. "Sin itself is not the misfortune," he tells them, "guilt is the misfortune. The sting is not the misfortune, the trace of the sting is the misfortune. Evil is a sign." The serpent, "more subtile than any beast of the field," has mastered not only psychoanalysis, but also semantics. "The dissected pomegranate," he continues, "is the sign of the woman's open sex. Is that perhaps why eating the pomegranate is an evil deed? Shame is merely the sign clothes leave on the flesh. Undress, and you will return to paradise, where once more you will be naked like the gods. And like animals."

Adam and Eve go to look for paradise. But they do not find it. They walk naked to the beach and lie down in the sand.

3   When Hades abducted Persephone from a green meadow in broad daylight and took her to the underworld, her mother Demeter raised a great cry. She threatened that unless her daughter was returned, the seeds in the field would not sprout, the trees in the orchard would not bear fruit, and the people would starve to death. Zeus ordered Hades to release Persephone from Tartarus. But in the last moment before her departure, Hades "secretly put in [her] mouth sweet food, a pomegranate seed, and forced [her] to taste against

[her] will." So the seventh century B.C. *Hymn to Demeter* has it (II.411–13). The living could not touch the food of the dead if they were ever to leave the underworld. Persephone was restored to her mother, but she had tasted the food of death.[3] Therefore she would have to return every year to the land of the dead. According to still another tradition, Persephone ate not one but seven pomegranate seeds. Seven is a magical number, the union of a triangle with a square, signifying fullness and the completion of the cycle. When at the end of the third winter month Persephone leaves the underworld, it is spring and the seeds sprout in the fields.

"In a certain sense, myths re-think one another," wrote Lévi-Strauss in the "Ouverture" to *Le cru et le cuit*. On the famous Rossetti painting at the Tate Gallery, Proserpina holds a half-eaten pomegranate to her bosom with her left hand. In a dress draped like a Grecian tunic, this modernist and Pre-Raphaelite Proserpina, demonic and fallen, is deliberately depicted as a second Eve. With slightly parted lips, she gazes into nowhere. Everything is already over and she already knows everything. This daughter of Demeter has also eaten of the biblical tree of knowledge.

> Afar the flowers of Enna from this drear,
> Dire fruit, which, tasted once, must thrall me here.
> Afar those skies from this Tartarean grey
> That chills me: and afar, how far away,
> The nights that shall be from the days that were.
> [Dante Gabriel Rossetti, *Proserpina: For a Picture*]

The tasting of a forbidden fruit is central to both myths. The plot is similar: forbidden food is linked to sex, and knowledge is linked to death. Sex and food are the mediation between life and death. Lévi-Strauss's students would add that food and sex together constitute the primeval mediation between nature and culture. While natural, and thus essential and unchanging, they are at the same time cultural, subject to commandments and prohibitions, to changing rules, and to the sphere of the taboo. Both orders are contained in the symbolism of the pomegranate.

---

[3] "A primitive taboo rested on red-coloured food, which might be offered to the dead only; and the pomegranate was supposed to have sprung—like the eight-petalled scarlet anemone—from the blood of Adonis, or Tammuz. The seven pomegranate seeds represent, perhaps, the seven phases of the moon during which farmers wait for the green corn-shoots to appear. . . . Hera, as former Death-goddess, also held a pomegranate" (Robert Graves, *The Greek Myths,* I, 24, 11).

The red, juicy pomegranate grew out of the spilled blood of Dionysus, as the anemone grew from the blood of Adonis and the lily from that of Attis. In other variants, the pomegranate grew from the blood of Adonis or Attis. The Syrian Adonis seems to be the same deity as the Phrygian Attis. Dionysus, Adonis, and Attis, like Persephone, are vegetation deities presiding over the yearly cycle of death and renewal. But unlike Demeter's daughter, who awakens every spring from her winter sleep, they die the violent death of humans and animals. The pomegranate tree springs from their spilled blood.

The sweetly bland pomegranate seeds put into Persephone's mouth are an infernal food, taboo for the living. Eating them meant eternal death, and thus infertility. The initiated were forbidden to eat the pomegranate seed although they adorned their heads with its leaves for Thesmophory, the autumn mysteries in worship of Demeter. The pomegranate is endowed with two values which oppose each other like plus and minus signs. In this binary system, infertility corresponds to fertility. Attis's mother, Nana, was a virgin who bore him after swallowing a pomegranate seed or, as other sources have it, a ripe almond. In another version, she conceived by placing the pomegranate seed or the almond between her breasts.

The pomegranate is a multivalent and polysemic symbol. Victor Turner uses this term in his fascinating *Forest of Symbols*, a collection of anthropological studies about the Ndembu people in northwestern Zambia. In the symbolic system of the Ndembu, trees play a central role, and among them, two in particular: *mudyi* and *mukula*. From the *mudyi* tree, which Turner calls the *milk tree*, a white fluid can be obtained by squeezing the thin sheets of the tree's bark. One set of successive symbolic meanings of *mudyi* are "breast" and "breast feeding," as well as "womb" or "bosom," two terms which at the same time denote kinship on the maternal side. Another symbolic set of the *milk tree* runs from "women," "womanhood," and "married woman" all the way to abstract notions of the woman's "knowledge/experience" and her "pain/experience." Because the *milk tree* is the site of the girls' initiation rite, the necessary step to the woman's maturation, it is also "the place of death" and "the place of suffering." But the symbolic order contains at the same time its own series of negations: the "not-milk tree" or the "absence of milkness" may mean a still uninitiated girl, a menstruating woman, or an uncircumcised boy.

Mukula is a kind of gum tree. It secretes a red resin that dries like blood, and both menstrual and birth blood belong to its order of symbols. But in the "male" order, the *mukula* may mean warrior's wound, the blood of the hunted animal, and the hunter's courage. *Mudyi* and *mukula,* the "milk tree" and "the tree of the coagulating fluid," belong to a rich symbolic system in which the colors "white" and "red" harbor, even within themselves, opposing values. "White-milk" is a sign for the relationship of the mother to the child, the "white-seed," for copulation. "Red female blood," on the other hand, stands for the relationship of the child to his mother, and "red male blood" for the hunt, for war, the man's work, and for the tribal kinship of successive generations.

Turner contrasts the symbol's denotative function, in which the compared terms are linked analogically on the basis of proximity, continuity, and contiguity, to the instrumental function of symbols where the relation of terms is founded on abstract thought alone. In archaic civilizations, symbolic thought serves, as Lévi-Strauss might have said, the purposes of classification. Or, to put it most succinctly, primordial thought is the logic of symbols. "Thy lips are like a thread of scarlet, and thy speech is comely: thy temples are like a piece of a pomegranate within thy locks" (Song of Solomon 4:3). In the lexicon of symbols, the pomegranate, both flower and fruit, is the sex and bosom of a woman. "Let us get up early to the vineyards; let us see if the vine flourish, whether the tender grapes appear, and the pomegranates bud forth: there will I give thee my loves"(Song 7:12). Sensual affinity means color and shape, texture and odor. "I would cause thee to drink of spiced wine of the juice of my pome-granate. His left hand should be under my head, and his right hand should embrace me" (Song 8:2–3). And perhaps the most beautiful verse from the Song of Songs: "A garden inclosed is my sister, my spouse; a spring shut up, a fountain sealed. Thy plants are an orchard of pomegranates . . . "(4:12–13).

In the East, the pomegranate is a common figure in the vo-cabulary and poetry of love. As in Firdausi's poetry: "Pomegranate apples have blossomed from your bosom." In Turkey the yet un-touched bride is "an unknown rose, an unopened pomegranate." "Her cheeks," writes Robert Greene in *Menaphon* (1589), "like . . . faire pomegranate kernels washt in milke." At the end of Juliet's first and last night with Romeo, the nightingale "sings on yond pomegranate tree" in her garden (*Romeo and Juliet* III.v.4).

The pomegranate is a "natural" symbol of eros and of the woman. But the Song of Songs can also be read as a mystical tes-timony where the bride and the bridegroom, the man and the wife represent God/Christ and synagogue/church. "And then we shall go forth / To the lofty caverns of the rock which are well hidden, / And there we shall enter / And taste the new wine of the pomegranates." So runs the Spiritual Canticle by Saint John of the Cross, his paraphrase of the biblical versette from the Song of Songs, to which he appends a commentary:

> The pomegranates signify the divine mysteries of Christ, and the lofty judgments of God . . . For, as the pomegranate has many small seeds, all of which have been born and are nourished in that one round orb . . . so mystery and judgment of God contains within itself a great multitude of seeds . . . .
>
> The new wine of these pomegranates, which the Bride says that they will taste, is the fruition which, in so far as may be in this estate, the soul receives in the knowledge and understanding of them, and the delight of the love of God which she tastes in them.

> [XXXVI.6]

The concrete, the corporeal, and the sensual are symbolically transformed into abstractions, or, in Turner's terminology, symbolic naming assumes instrumental function. The pomegranate is perfectly suited to both functions, and for a moment it seems that the pomegranate is the universal fruit of all myths. Since myths, as Lévi-Strauss wrote, answer questions that have no answers, they necessarily contradict each other. A myth that says A is always a reply to another which says not-A. The most astounding feature of the pomegranate fruit is its semantics which permits the creation of symbolic series containing opposite values. Everything the pomegranate symbolizes has two values. And each at once signifies and contradicts what it signifies.

In André Gide's recitativo *Persephone,* written for Stravinsky's melodrama, Mercury brings the pomegranate fruit to the underworld.

> He plucks a pomegranate ripe,
> Doth make sure
> It hath the sun's faint-glowing stripe,
> Persephone to lure.
> She marvels at the sight,
> To find again, within her night,
> This memento of the light
> And of the earth,
> Pleasure's forgotten hue, desire; . . .

> [*Persephone* I]

Gide reverses the sign of the Greek myth. The pomegranate seeds, no longer the food of the dead, are communion for the living. In the course of Balanchine's astonishingly beautiful *Persephone,* produced for Stravinsky's centennial, Greek symbols turn Christian, and in the last tableau, a children's choir in surplice greets Demeter's returning daughter. The fruit of death has become the fruit of resurrection.

The pomegranate signifies fertility and infertility, sensual ecstasy and mystical ascesis, the one in the many and the many in the one, the commandment and the prohibition, heaven and the underworld. Because it is a sign of guilt, it has become a sign of forgiveness; because it was a sign of despair, it has become the sign of hope. In paradise, the pomegranate tree was the tree of knowledge, or of life, or perhaps even of both. According to Robert Graves's *The White Goddess,* the pomegranate is the tree of the seventh day of creation, the sabbath tree of Saturn and Jehovah. In Deuteronomy Israel is called a "land of wheat, and barley, and vines, and fig trees, and pomegranates; a land of olive oil, and honey" (8:8).[4]

In Christian symbolism, the fruit of damnation is also the fruit of mercy. Early in the Renaissance, the pomegranate begins to appear in paintings of the Madonna with Child. In Botticelli's *Virgin and Child,* Christ holds a dissected pomegranate in his left hand and red beads in his right. Giovanni Bellini's infant Jesus (*The Virgin and Child,* National Gallery, London) too, holds a pomegranate in his hand. Occasionally, as in Joos van Cleve's *The Virgin and Child* (1513), a half-eaten pomegranate is placed on a platter of grapes, pears, and apples.[5]

---

[4]The pomegranate is the sacred fruit of the Old Testament. At Chanukah, Moroccan Jews adorn the Chanukiah with a small pomegranate, and at other times pomegranates are kept on the sticks around which the Torah scrolls are wound. The sticks are called "the tree of life." The Torah contains 613 commandments, and according to legend, the human body contains 613 nerves and the pomegranate 613 seeds. One of the earliest Kabalistic treatises, written by a Spanish Jew, Moses Cordovero, who settled in the small town of Safad on the Galilean lake, bears the title *Pardes Rimmonim ("The Garden of Pomegranates")* and was published in Cracow in 1592.

"Saul dwellide . . . under a pomgranate tree" (1 Sam.14:2). It is here, in Wycliff's translation of the Bible from the Vulgate in 1382, that the "pomegranate tree" makes its first appearance in English. "Litil bellys of moost puyr gold, the whiche thei puttiden bitwix the powmbe garnettis [1388, pum garnadis] in the nether more party of the coote bi enuyronn"(Exod. 39:34; cited in the *Oxford English Dictionary).*

[5]"The pomegranate which sprouted from Dionysus's blood was also the tree of Tammuz-Adonis-Rimmon; its ripe fruit splits open like a wound and shows the red seeds inside. It symbolizes death and the promise of resurrection when held in the hand of the goddess Hera or Persephone" (Graves, *The Greek Myths,* I, 27, 10). The pomegranate held by the divine Christ Child repeats the same old symbolism.

The fruit of death becomes the fruit of rebirth. The lethal sting, the stinger, and the phallus become the vaccine against death: "O death, where is thy sting? O grave, where is thy victory? The sting of death is sin; and the strength of sin is the law" (1 Cor. 15:55–56). The fundamental symbolic meaning of the pomegranate is the opposition between life and death.

"The principle of restoration is found in thought, and thought only," wrote Hegel in his *Logic*, "the hand that inflicts the wound is also the hand that heals it."

4

> And the devil, taking him up into a high mountain, showed unto him all the kingdoms of the world in a moment of time. And the devil said unto him, All this power will I give thee, and the glory of them: for that is delivered unto me; and to whomsoever I will, I give it. If thou therefore wilt worship me, all shall be thine.
>
> [Luke 4:5–7]

The biblical apple is also the gilded one which, along with the crown and the scepter, belongs to the insignia of Christian rulers. In Trevelyan's well-known 1603 portrait of Elizabeth I, the queen is holding a scepter in her right hand and an apple bearing a crucifix in her left. The golden apple, *orbis mundi*, is the icon of the reign over the world by God's deputy.

To Faustus, the devil offers not only power but, perhaps for the first time since the temptation of Eve, also knowledge. The first Faustus, the man of flesh and blood, or rather of body and soul, who rashly sold the latter to the devil, was a doctor of theology, a provincial magician, a conjurer, a pyromancer, and a globetrotter. He was banned from one German university after another for sodomy, drunkenness, fraud, and insolvency. He died suffering terribly in 1540 or 1541 when the mysterious substances with which he was experimenting exploded. The first Faustus, like all his literary successors, was a victim of an unrestrained intellectual curiosity. Believers in archetypes who do not believe in accidents would have Faustus die consumed by a heavenly fire, as did Prometheus, the first, and Don Juan, the third, of the heroes of transgression.

The first Faustus had Leonardo and Agrippa as his contemporaries. The brilliance of both illuminates him, although quite differently. Leonardo da Vinci drew models of wings, flawlessly calculating their aerodynamic properties; but the materials at his disposal were too heavy and muscle power did not suffice to propel man into flight on them. Twardowski, the Polish Faustus (Faustus did in fact wander as far as Cracow, where he studied the secret arts), who conjured for King Zygmunt August his deceased young wife Barbara Radziwill, was carried off to the moon tucked under the devil's arm. (Poles have never had much faith in technology.) The means of transportation available to the Renaissance Mephistopheles were also limited, and he had to harness dragons to his chariot in order to carry Faustus beyond the moon and the planets, all the way to the *primum mobile.* Mephistopheles had hardly glanced at Copernicus's *De revolutionibus orbium coelestium,* and to Faustus's disappointment, his knowledge of recent astronomical achievements was quite meager. From the heights to which Faustus had been carried, the earth appeared no larger than a fist. This was the only discovery Faustus made during the journey.

Mephistopheles was ready to deliver to Faustus all women who are and all women who were. Faustus, who had conjured Alexander's ghost for the German emperor, chose Helen. Alexander and Helen—the fascination of grandeur—these are the Renaissance choices. In the recent exhibition "In Search of Alexander" there was a marble head with a chipped nose: at once the head of god, lion, and man. Reflected in the gaze of the widely open bright eyes were both heaven and earth.

The choice of Alexander and Helen is also the spell of immortality. "Sweet Helen, make me immortal with a kiss." Helen sinks her teeth into lips, as a medieval succuba, to suck the soul; yet the kiss of Helen/Lilith imparts immortality—the immortality of destruction. As she had been by the Kabalists, Helen is once again associated with Lilith, the arch female demon.

"Was this the face that launched a thousand ships / And burnt the topless towers of Ilium?" (V.i.99–100). Helen, whom Faustus chose among all women, is the Helen of destruction and death, the Euripidean Helen from *The Trojan Women* and *Hecuba,* the reason why timeless Troy burns. Even for this Helen, who is simply nothing, he is prepared to burn Wittenberg down. "And all is dross that is not Helena" (V.i.103).

In Shakespeare, too, timeless Troy "burns so long" (*The Rape of Lucrece,* 1468) and Alexander is nothing but dross. "Alexander died. Alexander was buried, Alexander returneth into dust; the dust is earth; of earth we make loam . . . "(*Hamlet* V.i.194–96).

The Faustian sting, just like the serpent's, incites to knowledge, the infernal temptation. The terms of this infernal pact signed by the Renaissance magus prohibit Mephistopheles from lying. In the *Faustbuch,* too, this is the chief provision of the contract. Science always tells the truth. Like the devil. For Goethe, science was still a source of optimism. Thomas Mann was perhaps the first to comprehend fully the horror of the devil/science which is unable to lie and must tell the truth, the truth of the possible total extermination of life.

Despair, *desperatio, désespoir,* literally means "no hope." The devil speaks the truth: ". . . where we are is hell, / And where hell is, there must we ever be" (*Doctor Faustus* II.i.120–21). Hell is in us—that is not Sartre's invention. The Faustian sting annihilates hope, in salvation as well as in history. God does not forgive. Troys burn eternally, and all that remains of Alexanders and Helens is skulls collecting dirt in the mass grave.

In Christian theology, Satan is the teacher of despair. To doubt God's mercy is among the gravest sins against the Holy Spirit. "Damned art thou, Faustus, damned; despair and die!"(*Doctor Faustus* V.i.56). After the Faustian sting comes the fall. The first and perhaps the greatest university drama begins and ends in a study. "And this the man that in his study sits" (*Doctor Faustus,* Prologue, 28). In the last scene, in the same Wittenberg study, his colleagues discover Faustus's body: bones smashed, neck twisted, face downward.

5 Loss of hope is the symptom of the Faustian sting. But the old serpent/seducer sheds its skin again and appears as the harbinger of hope. All stings are historical, even in the Garden, but in the Hegelian sting, history itself becomes poison. The French Revolution and the Napoleonic period provide the two models that no historical reflection can escape. History has been present ever since, observed always in the process of becoming, forever in flux. History begins with the Revolution. Therefore, the Revolution is the beginning of time. The Revolutionary calendar marks the First Year of the Revolution, and all the Revolutionary Years to follow—until the advent of Paradise. Even the names of the months were changed under Jacobin rule; in accordance with the principle of equality, they were each to have thirty days.

From the tribunes to the Caesars, from the Revolution to the Empire, Napoleon is the personification of history. But in this model, too, history is malleable, kneaded by hand like dough; it can be molded and it can be raped. Everyone is beckoned to take part in history, or enticed, or forced. To the twenty-five-year-olds who, like Stendhal, quartermaster in the Great Army, watched Moscow burn from the hills, everything else until the end of their lives seemed bland. The nausea of history which has come to a halt can be sensed in Musset's *Confession d'un enfant du siècle* and in Stendhal's *The Red and the Black*. It is not easy to be twenty-five and nobody, when the generation of one's father became marshals of France at twenty. If history is permanent revolution, then revolution is indeed, as Marx claimed, the midwife of history. But who then is the obstetrician? "The time is out of joint. O cursed spite / That ever I was born to set it right!" (*Hamlet* I.v.189–90).

For Hegel history is the unfolding of Mind; its incarnation in time. If history is rational, it is possible for reason to shape it as the blacksmith shapes the iron. History molten in the crucible is a Hegelian idea, or perhaps it is Marx's reading of Hegel. If history is rational, reason can hasten it so that it becomes rational sooner, or at least a bit more rational. If history is rational, whatever endows it with more reason, whatever accelerates it, is permitted and justified. From the top and in advance. At this point the Hegelian sting takes effect.

The *in blanco* justification of history has proven to be most sinister. That was the pitfall we fell into when we were still twenty, during the first Moscow Trials and the Spanish Civil War. But solidarity with the *"No pasaran!"* of the International Brigades in Spain and silent acquiescence to the Moscow Trials were not the the same choice. My political biography and that of my generation begins in those years.

If I had to choose again, once more in the thirties, then I would once more choose *"No pasaran!"* and death to the fascists. For this was the choice against terror, and not for a history "rational and necessary," the choice to be alive, not deaf, to the signs of human distress. The Moscow Trials began before the Spanish Civil War. The very same people who had chosen freedom from violence and oppression now covered their eyes and plugged their ears. The best went to Spain to join the International Brigades, and so gave their answer to the Moscow Trials. Others among us said that whatever is necessary is also rational. Years had to pass before painstakingly, bloodying our hands, we climbed out of this abyss. To avoid it, Nicola Chiaromonte's and George Orwell's clarity of vision and conscience would have been necessary. Intellectuals of my generation rarely possessed such lucidity in those years.

Everything that is necessary, taught Hegel, is rational, and thus justified. But do "the rational and the necessary" contain what *was*, what *is*, as well as what *will be*? History can be transformed into *logos*, or even into an *ethos*, but after the fact; retrospectively it can be neatly arranged into a chain of causes and effects. To justify the past means at the very least to understand it. But what does it mean, even in Hegel, to justify the future? *In blanco.* "Freedom," wrote Marx, "is the consciousness of necessity." Thus slavery, when it is "conscious," is also "freedom." To understand the present—so the serpent's most perfidious whisper—means to justify slavery. But for those who have been cured of stings, to understand the present means not to absolve it. To understand slavery is to repudiate it.

The serpent-procurer offers Faustus all the women of the past. That is the allure of the Faustian sting. The Hegelian sting offers you Universal Mind. You are part of the Mind. You are part of history. You belong to history, and history belongs to you. Who can resist this temptation?

Under the sway of the Hegelian sting, mankind is envisioned as the most magnificent creation, worthy of the highest esteem, while each man and woman is but dung, worthy only of contempt. Shakespeare knew it too:

> What a piece of work is man! how noble in reason! how infinite in faculties! in form and moving how express and admirable! in action how like an angel! in apprehension how like a god! the beauty of the world, the paragon of animals! And yet to me what is this quintessence of dust? Man delights not me—nor woman neither . . .

Read today, Hamlet's monologue sounds disturbingly contemporary. It could be the monologue of a terrorist. Lord of creation and dung of history: I do not know of a more violent formulation of the opposition between deification and contempt of man. When read today, Hamlet's monologue sounds modern, but it is merely reiterating the ancient whisper of the serpent: "Your eyes shall be opened, and ye shall be as gods" (Gen. 3:5). Serpent eyes are cool and beady. The serpent hypnotizes with his stare and then he stings. The victim is trapped inside the charmed circle where only false oppositions hold: you are either equal to gods, or a mere handful of dust. But after all, we are neither equal to gods nor are we a mere handful of dust.

The serpent's sting overpowers the mind. Czesław Miłosz entitled his book about the sting of the Communist serpent *The Captive Mind.* Within the charmed circle, the mind moves in a fictitious universe, unable to distinguish reality from illusion. The history of the schism of Communist intellectuals has yet to be written to the very end. Two of its chapters, two moments, deserve to be described in detail: joining the Communist movement and leaving it, enchantment and recovery. The moment of recovery is perhaps more important. Its most bitter account in Polish literature appears in Adam Ważyk's "Poem for Adults":

> I will never believe, my dear, that a lion is a little lamb,
> I will never believe, my dear, that a little lamb is a lion!
> I will never believe, my dear, in a magic spell;
> I will never believe in minds kept under glass;
> But I believe that a table has only four legs,
> But I believe that the fifth leg is a chimera,
> And when the chimeras rally, my dear,
> Then one dies slowly of a worn out heart.

This essay is merely an introduction to stings, those of my generation and my own. They require a description of another order, however, the order of experience and sober assessment. But without pointing the finger at others, or even at oneself. This essay is in a certain way an introduction to my autobiography.

THE SERIOUSNESS
OF THEATER

1 **A** few months ago, a friend of mine, who happens to be a young director, invited me to his college not far from New York for a *Hamlet* rehearsal. The auditorium was small, the benches were arranged like seats in an amphitheater, and the stage was like a very white, empty plate. The sole audience was the friends of the young actors and myself, the only guest. The play was to open in two or three weeks, but my friend had told me that the rehearsals were more important than the premiere. He warned me that this would be a *reading* rehearsal, and it was, but it turned out to be a reading rehearsal unlike any I had ever attended. The actors were holding their texts before them, and since the rehearsals had been going on for over a month, I thought that either the director had little confidence that the young actors had learned their roles, or that it had been his intention that they should have copies of *Hamlet* in front of them. And that they should *read* the play.

At first, the tall, light-haired boy who played the role of the Danish Prince just rattled off his lines. It was obvious that he knew them inside-out. But about halfway through the first act, he began to flounder through the text. He would pause and look at the words. "Let us go in together; And still your fingers on your lips, I pray." He said these lines from memory and even shifted the text of the play to his left hand so that he could put the finger of his right to his lips. Someone in the auditorium laughed. The boy became disconcerted and recited his next line, "The time is out of joint," very tentatively. He looked at the audience, at his friends, as if he sought confirmation or even negation. And then he read from the book: "O cursed spite." He paused again, as if in amazement, as if this were something new and he were reading these lines for the first time. No, I am mistaken, as if he were *hearing* them for the first time. And then, after what seemed like a very long pause, and, looking at the text as if he did not believe it, as if he had to read it twice before he could say it, and as if this were a statement which he was making for the first time, he said: "That ever I was born to set it right!" Then he put the book aside and calmly now, almost cheerfully, said to his friends: "Nay, come, let's go together." We all sighed with relief.

In *S/Z*, Roland Barthes calls a classic text a "galaxy of signifiers," because it contains a multiplicity of meanings. *The Pleasure of the Text*, or rather the delight (as *plaisir* in French has a sexual connotation), is the gradual discovery of new meanings in the same text, just as one constantly discovers new women in one woman with whom one shares an intimate relationship. A classic text must be reread, and the other classic texts contained in it must be reread: those that came before and those that came afterward, those the author knew and those he did not know and could not have anticipated. The *Odyssey* is in *Ulysses,* and now *Ulysses* is in the *Odyssey.* The *Book of Job* contains Beckett and now Beckett is contained in the *Book of Job.* The *Aeneid,* which Shakespeare knew, is in *The Tempest,* but so is *The Divine Comedy,* which Shakespeare did not know. Masterpieces live in many different time dimensions all at once; the time in which each arose is but one of many such dimensions.

But what happens when a *written* text is spoken? That evening in the small college theater, I took part not just in a rehearsal of *Hamlet,* but in a *testing* of the text. The text in this intriguing, though perhaps not entirely conscious synchronization of rehearsal and performance, was present, all at once, in the written word, in the reading of it, and in the actor's voice. The text was unchanged, yet it bristled with a thousand subtexts and a myriad of meanings as Stanislavsky and Barthes taught. The text, which is always, as the deconstructionists believe, self-contradictory, became, or rather was in the process of becoming, the unequivocal illocution of a young man speaking to the others on the blank plate of the stage and to the few dozen male and female friends that were sitting in semidarkness in the rows of rising benches.

When a passage is uttered on the stage, and a sudden murmur rushes through the auditorium like a wind that raises a wave on a placid lake, old actors say that the play has "caught hold" or that there is a "good house." But what does a "good" house mean? The living voice is always here and now, *hic et nunc*. Theatrical time is but one time: the one, two, or three hours of a play's duration. Who imposes upon a classic text, who articulates, that one meaning which hits the mark? The director? The actor? Perhaps it really is the spectators. And that is what is meant by a "good house."

Waiting for Godot made its debut in Warsaw just a little less than a year after its premiere in Paris, and I was at its first showing in the Polish capital. The audience was a rather select group, as was usual for a premiere in the capital, but the play was received coldly: even though the acting was excellent, there was little applause. Almost half the audience left after the intermission, but even those who remained had a difficult time understanding what the play was about. *Waiting for Godot* was my first taste of Beckett. I didn't really know how one should go about eating him. He stuck in my throat. I was a theater critic then and called my review "Nearly Brilliant Boredom."

For the first week and a half, there were nothing but vacant seats in the theater. At the beginning of the third, the tickets were sold out in advance. The premiere had taken place on 2 January 1957. It was about then that news of Khrushchev's "secret" speech (on the subject of Stalin's crimes) at the XXth Communist Party Congress reached Warsaw. "Top-level" Communist party officials soon received a summary and excerpts from Khrushchev's speech. These texts were numbered and had to be returned after being read. In a week, however, they began to circulate in hundreds of *samizdat* copies. *Waiting for Godot* was now greeted with a burst of applause after each performance. Everyone now knew what Godot was: socialism.

At more or less the same time, *Macbeth* was playing in Moscow. When Lady Macbeth returned from the bedroom of the murdered Duncan, stood on the proscenium facing the spectators, and raised her bloodstained hands, the house went silent. I was told that, at first, no one clapped, but that on the second and third evenings, the entire audience rose to its feet. The blood-spattered hands were Stalin's.

Three months before the Warsaw premiere of *Godot,* I was in Cracow for a new production of *Hamlet*. When the line "something is rotten in the state of Denmark" was uttered onstage, a murmur rippled through the audience from the gallery right under the ceiling to the first row in the orchestra. When, later, the line "Denmark's a prison" was repeated three times, I felt the house go silent, like the sudden lull before a storm. Then applause broke somewhere in the center of the auditorium, and then somewhere in the gallery: individual, quiet applause that seemed frightened at its own audacity. In another moment the entire auditorium had broken into a fierce applause that lasted until hands went numb.

That same murmur stirred the auditorium when the Clown in Act V said "the gallows is built stronger than the church." I realized then, for the first time, that the audience viewing *Hamlet* can be either in "Wittenberg" or "Elsinore." At this Polish *Hamlet,* not only the cast, but the entire audience was in "Elsinore," where both the people and the walls have ears. This Polish Elsinore in *Hamlet* was not determined by directorial decision or choice. The *Hamlet* premiere in Cracow took place in late September 1956, and my review of it was entitled "Hamlet after the XXth Congress." It was this Polish Elsinore that inspired my book, *Shakespeare Our Contemporary.* The first Polish edition appeared in 1961, and it will soon be twenty-five years since it was first published. Shakespeare, my "contemporary," has belonged to history for quite a while.

2   François Sarcey was considered the most illustrious French theater critic of his time. He published a weekly *feuilleton* on the theater without interruption for thirty-three years, from 1867 to almost the end of the nineteenth century. In his last years as a critic, he attended the theater more and more rarely, until he stopped going altogether. His well-known theater reviews, however, kept appearing. Someone once asked him how this was possible. Sarcey looked down his nose at the brash fellow and replied: *"Je ne veux pas me laisser impressionné"* (I do not wish to submit to my impressions). I, on the other hand, always did. It seemed to me that that is why I was a critic. I am sent to the theater so that I can tell others what is going on there.

Enjoyment of a text is a solitary pleasure. Someone writes a book in solitude and then someone else reads it, also in solitude. One can go to the movies alone, but it is more difficult to go to the theater that way. The theater has never been the delight of those who like solitude. It is a public place, where there is always a meeting of the text and the actor, the actors and the spectators, and the theater and the street and the marketplace. These theatrical meetings also include conversation about the theater. Writing about the theater is one of these loud conversations. That is why even when I had stopped being a theater critic, I still liked to write about the theater more than about anything else. Yesterday there were five hundred or a thousand people in the audience, tomorrow there will be an equal number give or take a few, as there will be the day after tomorrow, in a month or even a year from now. When I write I mix with their opinions, with something that has its own time and place.

"Time-space," *chronotope*, is a basic term in Mikhail Bakhtin's *The Dialogic Imagination*. He uses the term to illustrate the changes that take place in the novel. Theater, however, is even more of a *chronotope* than the novel. Theater is a place where time is always present. It is enough for the actor to open his mouth in an auditorium where there are even three people, and a three-thousand-year-old text is immediately contemporary. Theater is subordinated to politics and custom more than any other art form. One always walks into the theater off the street, from a café, or a bar. Not only spectators come in, but actors and mechanics, too, and sometimes even the author.

The classic paradigm of the theater is the mirror. Hamlet tells his actors to pull up the mirror so that they may view themselves. But if the theater is a mirror, then the right is left in it and the left, right. In the mirror our heart is on the right side. We cross with our left hand; and our reflection in the mirror offers us its left hand. This helps explain why falling into naturalistic literalness or naive didacticism can be wrong, if not dangerous. Even the great Ibsen occasionally fell victim to this form of moralizing. In his greatest dramas, however, he was rescued from this danger by his misanthropy and revulsion for bourgeois morality. The potential shallowness of realism and the inherent ambiguity in moralizing from the stage were very clear to Brecht in our own time. He made the nonevident in the evident, and the evident in the nonevident, the basis of his theater aesthetics and morality. And not just in the theater, but in his own life as well. This allowed him to avoid the calamities of socialist realism. For Brecht, theater was a game with the devil. Especially his own theater, the Berliner Ensemble, in East Berlin when Ulbricht was in power. The moral and artistic problems of realism are transcended in two of Brecht's plays: *Mother Courage* and *Galileo*.

3 What is "for real" in the theater? Or rather, what in the theater is real? The simplest answer would be: the chairs. Yet these chairs, when taken from the auditorium and set on the stage, are no longer just chairs, but the imagining of chairs, a sign, as semanticists would say, a sign in the theater like the empty chairs waiting for the viewers invited to the Celebration in Ionesco's *The Chairs*.

Northrop Frye has written about the play between the illusion of reality and the reality of illusion in the theater. Shakespeare and Calderón cultivated this play quite consciously. It is enough to recall *A Midsummer Night's Dream* or *Life Is a Dream*. The play between reality and illusion is also present in Renaissance and Baroque painting: Quentin Massys incorporates the face of a peeping Tom, reflected in a round mirror, into his portrait of the moneychanger and his wife, and Velázquez includes himself as the artist in his painting of the court scene in the Escorial. Michel Foucault wrote about this in one of his most penetrating essays in his book *Les mots et les choses*.

Opposing illusion to reality is helpful when thinking about theater, but it is also deceptive. In theater there is always reality in the illusion and illusion in the reality. Jacek Woszczerowicz, who died ten years ago, was one of the greatest actors of the postwar Polish stage. He made as excellent a Richard III as he did an Arnolf, and had the custom of playing tragedy almost like a comedy and a comedy, almost like a tragedy. He was a "cold" actor, to use Diderot's term, that is, an actor who could simulate anything. Once we were in the hospital together for a couple of weeks. Woszczerowicz came to see me: he was in hospital pajamas, a robe, and a nightcap, which made him look like a clown. He sat down on my bed. I asked him how he managed to cry on the stage. Woszczerowicz laughed aloud and stared for a while at the empty wall over my bed. Suddenly huge tears began to roll down his cheeks and then and there, in that hospital bed, I realized that real tears and feigned emotions are the very nature of acting.

The "merchant of masks," Marcel Marceau, is not just an enthralling mime, but also an engaging allegory of theater. Marceau takes invisible masks out of a basket and puts them on his powdered clown face. One follows another: tragic and comic masks, dignified and grotesque masks, and scary and tearful masks. The last of these is the powdered face of a clown with a red nose and gaping mouth. He cannot tear this last mask from his face. It has stuck and refuses to come off. Finally Marceau does tear it off and, under this last mask, finds his own face of a clown with white cheeks and a red nose. The mask is just one of his faces and his face is just one of his masks. This is why in that other Renaissance paradigm of theater (which we find in Shakespeare), the theater is not an image of the world, it is the world that is an image of the theater.

Acting is putting on other faces and embodying someone else's soul. And that is why, in the Christian tradition, in which souls and bodies cannot be exchanged, acting was condemned as a mortal sin. Only Satan embodies other souls. And that is why great actors and actresses are so fascinating. All their roles are contained within them. There is a certain falseness, however, in the word *em-body*. Embodiment is not the taking of someone else's body, but of someone else's soul.

One of the most splendid descriptions of acting is the passage devoted to Berma's *Phèdre* in Proust. But whose melodies and cadences, whose steps and handwringing, whose wide-eyed look is Proust describing? Phèdre's or Sarah Bernhardt's? They have two souls but just one body. My fascination with the theater dates from my fascination with the corporeality of acting.

As a five-year-old boy, I often played on Ida Kamińska's lap. Her mother, Esther Rachel, was the greatest actress to come out of the Jewish theater. Esther and her husband, Abraham, were the founders of the Jewish theater both in Russia and in Poland before World War I. During the last years of that war and right afterward, they lived in Warsaw in the same building and on the same floor as my parents. Whenever my parents went out for the evening, they left me in Ida's care. She was twelve years older than I, and was already acting in the theater from time to time.

I don't remember much from that time: some sort of rustling dresses all covered with lace and ruffles, which Ida put on when her mother was not at home, and long, white chamois gloves in which Ida acted out vague tirades, which I couldn't understand, but which enchanted me, nevertheless. I still remember the stifling scent of musk that came from the gloves. I also remember that Ida told me that only the theater was real.

Ida became the greatest actress in the Jewish theater, as her mother had been before her. She directed that theater even when only a few members of the audience could understand the language spoken on its stage. Ida acted in Yiddish for the last time in Peter Weiss's *The Investigation,* a semi-amateur production put on in a synagogue on Manhattan's Upper West Side. She played an old woman who had survived Auschwitz.

Ida herself died practically on stage, just after the third or fourth performance.

In the United States, Ida Kamińska was known for her role as the old woman in *The Shop on Main Street,* for which she received an Oscar. But I will always remember her as Mother Courage when she finds her murdered daughter in an empty field. She does not cry out. She does not even cry. In a hollow, lifeless voice, she sings a child's lullaby that is drawn somewhere out of the dark recesses of memory. She knows that she cannot stay behind to bury this last of her children. She pulls out a few coins and gives them to strangers to bury her child. She must leave to continue pulling her wagon. Here she was a Jewish mother from the time of the holocaust. She was all Jewish mothers from the time of the holocaust. If there is a theater of essence, then this is it.

Aristophanes. *The Birds*. Trans. William Arrowsmith. Ann Arbor: Univ. of Michigan Press, 1961.

Artaud, Antonin. *Lettres d'Antonin Artaud à Jean-Louis Barrault*. Paris: Bordas, 1952.

———. *Ouevres completes*. Paris: Gallimard, 1961.

———. *The Theater and Its Double*. Trans. M. C. Richards. New York: Grove Press, 1958.

Bakhtin, Mikhail. *The Dialogic Imagination*. Ed. Michael Holquist. Trans. Caryl Emerson and Michael Holquist. Austin and London: Univ. of Texas Press, 1981.

———. *Rabelais and His World*. Trans. Helene Iswolsky. Cambridge: M. I. T. Press, 1968.

Barthes, Roland. *Camera lucida [Reflections on Photography]*. Trans. Richard Howard. New York: Hill and Wang, 1981.

———. *Critical Essays*. Trans. Richard Howard. Evanston: Northwestern Univ. Press, 1972.

Beckett, Samuel. *Waiting for Godot*. New York: Grove Press, 1954.

Brandwajn, Rachmiel. *Twarz i maska: rzecz o "Świętoszku" Moliera*. Warsaw: Wiedza Powszechna, 1965.

Borowski, Tadeusz. *This Way for the Gas, Ladies and Gentlemen*. Trans. Barbara Vedder. New York: Penguin, 1976.

———. *Utwory zebrane*. Warsaw: Państwowy Instytut Wydawniczy, 1954.

Brecht, Bertolt. *Schriften zum Theater*. Quoted in Martin Esslin, *Brecht: The Man and His Work*. Garden City, N. Y.: Doubleday, 1968.

Chekhov, Anton. *Chekhov: The Major Plays*. Trans. Ann Dunnigan. New York: New American Library, 1964.

Drewnowski, Tadeusz. *Ucieczka z kamiennego świata (o Tadeuszu Borowskim) [Escape from the World of Stone]*. Warsaw: Państwowy Instytut Wydawniczy, 1972.

Eichenbaum, Boris. "Kak sdelana 'Shinel'' Gogolia." *Poetika* 1 (1919): 151–65.

Erasmus. "The Praise of Folly." In *The Essential Erasmus*. Trans. John P. Dolan. New York: New American Library, 1964.

Everyman and Medieval Miracle Plays. Ed. A. C. Cawley. New York: Dutton, 1967.

Foucault, Michel. *The Order of Things: An Archeology of the Human Sciences*. New York: Random House, 1971.

Frazer, Sir James George. *The Golden Bough*. New York: Macmillan, 1950.

Freud, Sigmund. *Character and Culture*. Ed. Philip Rieff. New York: Collier, 1963.

———. *Three Essays on the Theory of Sexuality*. Trans. James Strachey. London: Hogarth Press, 1962.

Frye, Northrop. *A Natural Perspective: The Development of Shakespearean Comedy and Romance*. New York: Columbia Univ. Press, 1965.

Genet, Jean. *The Blacks: A Clown Show*. Trans. Bernard Frechtman. New York: Grove Press, 1960.

Gide, André. *Persephone*. Trans. Samuel Putnam. New York: Gotham, 1949.

The Gilgamesh Epic and Old Testament Parallels. Trans. Alexander Heidel. Chicago: University of Chicago Press, 1946.

Goethe, J. W. *Faust*. Trans. Philip Wayne. Baltimore: Penguin, 1955.

———. *Italian Journey*. Trans. W. H. Auden and E. Mayer. New York: Pantheon, 1962.

Gogol, Nikolai. *The Government Inspector*. Trans. E. O. Marsh and J. Brooks. London: Methuen, 1968.

———. *The Inspector General*. Trans. B. G. Guerney. In *Great Russian Plays*. New York: Dell, 1960.

———. *The Inspector General*. Trans. G. R. Noyes and J. B. Seymour. In *Masterpieces of the Russian Drama*. New York: Dover, 1961.

———. *Letters of Nikolai Gogol*. Ed. and trans. C. R. Proffer. Ann Arbor: Univ. of Michigan Press, 1967.

———. *Selected Passages from a Correspondence with Friends*. Trans. Jesse Zeldin. Nashville: Vanderbilt Univ. Press, 1969.

Gombrowicz, Witold. *Dziennik, 1957–1961 [Journal]*. Paris: Instytut Literacki, 1982.

———. *Ferdydurke*. Trans. E. Mosbacher. New York: Grove Press, 1968.

———. *The Marriage*. Trans. Louis Iribarne. New York: Grove Press, 1969.

———. *Operetta*. Trans. Louis Iribarne. London: Calder & Boyars, 1971.

"Gospel of Philip." Nag Hammadi Codex, II. In *The Nag Hammadi Library in English*. New York: Harper & Row, 1977.

Graves, Robert. *The Greek Myths*. 2 vols. Baltimore: Penguin, 1955.

———. *The White Goddess*. New York: Farrar, Straus & Giroux, 1969.

Grotowski, Jerzy. *Towards a Poor Theatre*. New York: Simon & Schuster, 1968.

Guiraud, Pierre. *Sémiologie de la sexualité*. Paris: Payot, 1978.

Hegel, G. W. F. *Logic*. Quoted by Geoffrey H. Hartman, "Romanticism and 'Anti-Self-Consciousness.' " In *Romanticism and Consciousness: Essays in Criticism*. Ed. Harold Bloom. New York: Norton, 1970.

———. *Philosophy of Right*. Trans. T. M. Knox. Oxford: Clarendon, 1942.

Hollander, Anne. *Seeing through Clothes*. New York: Viking, 1978.

Hymn to Demeter in *Hesiod*. Trans. Hugh G. Evelyn-White. Cambridge, Mass.: Loeb Classical Library, 1967.

Ibsen, Henrik. *The Complete Major Prose Plays*. Trans. Rolf Fjelde. New York: Farrar, Straus & Giroux, 1978.

Ionesco, Eugène. *Exit the King*. Trans. Donald Watson. New York: Grove Press, 1963.

———. *Fragments of a Journal*. Trans. Jean Stewart. New York: Grove Press, 1968.

———. *Jack, or the Submission*. In *Four Plays*. Trans. Donald M. Allen. New York: Grove Press, 1958.

———. *The Killer and Other Plays*. Trans. Donald Watson. New York: Grove Press, 1960.

———. *Notes and Counter Notes: Writings on the Theatre*. Trans. Donald Watson. New York: Grove Press, 1964.

———. *Victims of Duty*. In *Plays II*. Trans. Donald Watson. London: John Calder, 1958.

Jacobsen, Thorkild. *The Treasures of Darkness: A History of Mesopotamian Religion*. New Haven: Yale Univ. Press, 1976.

John of the Cross, Saint. *Spiritual Canticle*. Trans. Allison Peers. New York: Doubleday, 1975.

Joyce, James. "Epilogue to Ibsen's *Ghosts*" and "Ibsen's New Drama." In *The Critical Writings of James Joyce*. Ed. Ellsworth Mason and Richard Ellman. New York: Viking Press, 1959.

Kafka, Franz. *Diaries of Franz Kafka, 1914–1923*. Ed. Max Brod. Trans. Martin Greenberg. New York: Schocken, 1949.

———. *Selected Short Stories of Franz Kafka*. Trans. Willa and Edwin Muir. New York: Modern Library, 1952.

———. *Parables and Paradoxes*. New York: Schocken, 1961.

———. "Reflections on Sin, Pain, Hope and the True Way." In *The Great Wall of China: Stories and Reflections*. Trans. Willa and Edwin Muir. New York: Schocken, 1960.

———. *The Trial*. Trans. Willa and Edwin Muir. New York: Schocken, 1964.

Kleist, Heinrich von. "On the Puppet Theater." In *An Abyss Deep Enough*. Trans. Philip B. Miller. New York: Dutton, 1982.

Kott, Jan. *Theatre Notebook: 1947–1967*. Trans. Bolesław Taborski. Garden City, N. Y.: Doubleday, 1968.

Leach, Edmund. *Claude Lévi-Strauss*. New York: Viking Press, 1974.

Lec, Stanisław Jerzy. *Myśli nieuczesane*. Cracow: Wydawnictwo Literackie, 1959.

———. *Unkempt Thoughts*. Trans. Jacek Galazka. New York: St. Martins Press, 1962.

Lévi-Strauss, Claude. *Le cru et le cuit. Mythologiques. 1*. Paris: Plon, 1964.

———. *The Elementary Structures of Kinship*. Trans. J. Harle Bell, J. R. von Sturmer, and R. Needham. Boston: Beacon Press, 1969.

Lucian of Samosata. *The Syrian Goddess*. In *The Works of Lucian of Samosata*. Trans. H. W. Fowler and F. G. Fowler. Oxford: Clarendon Press, 1905.

McCarthy, Mary. "The Will and Testament of Ibsen." In *Sights and Spectacles*. Farrar, Straus & Cudahy, 1956.

Mann, Thomas. *Doctor Faustus*. Trans. H. T. Lowe-Porter. New York: Knopf, 1946.

Marcuse, Herbert. *An Essay on Liberation*. Boston: Beacon Press, 1969.

Marx, Karl. *The Eighteenth Brumaire of Louis Bonaparte*. New York: International Publishers, 1977.

Meyer, Michael. *Ibsen: A Biography*. Garden City, N. Y.: Doubleday, 1971.

Miłosz, Czesław. *Traktat poetycki* [*Treatise on Poetry*]. Paris: Instytut Literacki, 1957.

Molière. *The Misanthrope and Tartuffe*. Trans. Richard Wilbur. New York: Harcourt, Brace & World, 1965.

"Mystère d'Adam." Quoted in Eric Auerbach, *Mimesis*. Trans. Willard Trask. Princeton: Princeton Univ. Press, 1953.

Nabokov, Vladimir. *Nikolai Gogol*. New York: New Directions, 1944.

Nicoll, Allardyce. *The World of Harlequin: A Critical Study of the Commedia Dell'Arte*. Cambridge: Cambridge Univ. Press, 1963.

Rabelais, François. *The Portable Rabelais*. Ed. and trans. Samuel Putnam. New York: Penguin, 1977.

Racine, Jean. *Phaedra*. Trans. Wesley Goddard. New York: Chandler, 1961.

Rossetti, Dante Gabriel. "Proserpina: For a Picture." In *Poems with Illus-*

trations from His Own Designs, Vol. II. Ed. Elizabeth Luther Cary. New York and London: Knickerbocker Press, 1903.

Sartre, Jean-Paul. Introduction to Jean Genet's *The Maids* and *Deathwatch*. Trans. Bernard Frechtman. New York: Grove Press, 1954.

Todorov, Tzvetan. *Littérature et signification*. Paris: Larousse, 1967.

Turner, Victor. *The Forest of Symbols: Aspects of Ndembu Ritual*. Ithaca: Cornell Univ. Press, 1967.

Virgil. *Aeneid*. Trans. W. F. J. Knight. Harmondsworth: Penguin, 1969.

Ważyk, Adam. "Poem for Adults." Trans. Lucjan Blit. *The Twentieth Century* 158 (December 1955): 504–11.

Witkiewicz, Stanisław Ignacy. *Insatiability*. Trans. Louis Iribarne. Urbana: Univ. of Illinois Press, 1977.

———. *The Madman and the Nun and Other Plays*. Trans. D. C. Gerould and C. S. Durer. Seattle: Univ. of Washington Press, 1968.

———. "On a New Type of Play." Trans. C. S. Durer and D. C. Gerould. *Drama Survey* 6 (Fall 1967): 173–80.

———. *622 upadki Bunga* [*622 Downfalls of Bungo*]. Warsaw: Państwowy Instytut Wydawniczy, 1972.

———. "Wstep do teorii czystej formy w teatrze" ["Introduction to the Theory of Pure Form in the Theater"]. In *Nowe formy w Malarstwie. Szkice Estetyczne Teatr*. Warsaw: Państwowy Wydawnictwo Naukowe, 1974. (First ed. 1923)